THE SCANLON WAY
TO IMPROVED PRODUCTIVITY

THE SCANLON WAY TO IMPROVED PRODUCTIVITY:
A Practical Guide

Brian E. Moore
University of Texas at Austin
Austin, Texas

Timothy L. Ross
Bowling Green State University
Bowling Green, Ohio

A Wiley-Interscience Publication
John Wiley & Sons
New York   Chichester   Brisbane   Toronto

Library of Congress Cataloging in Publication Data:

Moore, Brian E 1935–
    The Scanlon way to improved productivity.

    "A Wiley-Interscience publication."
    Bibliography: p.
    Includes index.
    1. Incentives in industry. 2. Profit-sharing.
3. Industrial productivity. 4. Organizational change.
I. Ross, Timothy L., 1938–   joint author.
II. Title. III. Title: Scanlon principles for
organizational development.

HF5549.5.I5M64   658.31'42   77-14396
ISBN 0-471-03269-7

Printed in the United States of America
10 9 8 7 6 5 4 3 2

To Carl F. Frost and Fred G. Lesieur

FOREWORD

Picture a plant where the workers do not stay idle during delays in getting parts, materials, or service. Instead they get on the loudspeaker and ask support people to expedite what they need, or, as an alternative, they go to a vacant machine and work until their parts or materials arrive or their own machine is repaired. Picture a plant in which the union steward says, "Everyone's more cheerful and open here. We don't really have production quotas anymore; we just get out as much as we can."

Picture a plant where grievances, absenteeism, and turnover have been greatly reduced, where the adversary relationship has disappeared, and where the workers, union, and management all are pulling together for everyone's benefit.

No, the above is not a description of a Japanese plant; rather, it is an accurate account of just a few of the remarkable changes that have taken place at one of Midland-Ross Corporation's Electrical Products plant following implementation of a scanlon plan.

Behavioral scientists and knowledgeable personnel executives for years have been telling managements that there is a better way, that the traditional authoritarian management style belongs to another era, indeed if ever there really was any place for it.

Chris Argyris attributed the "illness" in most organizations to authoritarian methods, a denial of the workers' needs to use their own ideas and knowledge, and a lack of understanding of the compatibility of the goals of the organization with the goals of the individual.

Frederick Herzberg broke the list down into "dissatisfiers" and "satisfiers," emphasizing the worker's need for achievement, responsibility, accomplishment, and challenging work. He advocated ". . . restructuring of jobs to increase to the maximum the ability of workers to achieve goals meaningfully related to the doing of the job."

Douglas McGregor aimed his attack at the traditional authoritarian and counterproductive management style and zeroes in on ". . . the need to create a situation in which a subordinate can achieve his own goals best by directing his efforts toward the objectives of the enterprise."

But this country's past industrial success has been geared to two basic ingredients: an abundance of natural resources and great technological innovations. We have been systematically wasting our natural and human resources while relying on our technology to carry us. Today, we find our natural resources dwindling, our human resources mostly unresponsive, and our foreign competitors at least our equals and in some cases even achieving technological superiority. Concerned executives and serious students of the free-enterprise system recognize that something must be done and done quickly to meet the needs of both the enterprise and of the individual. Fortunately, for a great many organizations, the answer already is available to those with the courage and the vision to take the necessary steps. The one frontier left to industry, the one untapped resource, so to speak, is the knowledge that lies within our own employees.

In the pages of this book, Professors Tim Ross and Brian Moore have compiled the most thorough and informative document available on a management concept that can help unlock the vast treasure house of knowledge that lies within our own employees.

The scanlon plan is for those organizations where management recognizes the dignity and worth of every individual regardless of what his job may be. It is a way to fulfill those requirements identified to the workers themselves while at the same time meeting the needs of the organization in the critical areas of productivity and quality.

In reality, the scanlon plan is not a plan at all. Rather, it is a concept, a philosophy, and a management style rather than a formal plan. Its greatest strength is its simplicity, a simplicity which is deceptive in description but which when put into practice can produce truly remarkable results.

At the beginning of this foreword, I described several highlights of employee attitudes in our Midland-Ross plant in Tennessee, attitudes which I believe it is fair to say certainly are not typical of most industrial situations. These, however, are only the frosting on the cake. The total impact of the plan has been richly rewarding for the company and for the employees.

In addition to opening up numerous lines of meaningful communications, the program has resulted in a high level of employee participation, greatly improved morale accompanied by greater productivity, greater concern for quality, and a steady flow of cost-saving ideas and suggestions. Over and above the psychological rewards, the employees have earned monthly bonuses averaging between 12 and 15 percent. At times their efforts have earned them as much as 20 percent more in a single month's paycheck.

From the company standpoint, the results have been equally dramatic. Direct-labor efficiency has improved 10 percent in one major area of the plant and 8½ percent in the other, and there has been a substantial increase in the use of indirect labor, or resource worker, as the authors prefer. Using the same equipment, there has been a 16 percent increase in productivity. An immediate direct result of this has been a savings of $250,000 that had been set aside to expand the plant by adding another line to obtain more productive capacity.

This means savings of not just the quarter of a million dollars for expansion but also elimination of the need to hire additional people to work a new product line. We can document savings of at least 30 additional people, which in this case would be 10 percent of the work force, and there is reason to believe that in actuality we will have saved 60 additional hires.

Grievances have been cut in half, absenteeism has dropped considerably below the former level and well below the national averages, and the quit rate, which at one time was annualized at over 30 percent, has been running less than 5 percent annually.

Previously (before scanlon), one of the Fortune 100 plants in the area was considered the choice place to work. That honor now goes to our Midland-Ross plant, which enables the operation to have a better selection from which to pick new employees.

The plant personnel manager summed it up this way, ". . . As far as people, attitude, and interest are concerned, it's plain to see that everyone is becoming involved in the scanlon plan. The hourly and salaried employees alike feel that the program has helped tremendously in breaking down communication barriers between management and union employees. The 'us' and 'them' attitudes have disappeared and it's now 'we.' The scanlon committee meetings and screening meetings clearly demonstrate the concern on everyone's part for improvements in the quantity and quality of production."

Our experience is no different from hundreds of manufacturing operations across the country. The results achieved in Tennessee are available to any management willing to make the commitment and willing to scrap the traditional authoritarian approach to running an industrial shop.

The real success of the American free-enterprise system lies in extending our democratic principles to the shop floor. Only in this way can we provide a channel for workers to express themselves and to earn a "piece of the action" when their efforts contribute directly to the success of the enterprise.

Professors Brian Moore and Tim Ross have collaborated in this book to produce a treatise which could not be more timely. Their effort fills a serious need in the scanlon plan literature, because it is complete, comprehensive, and easy to grasp and provides an objective analysis which should become "must" reading for any executive who is considering a scanlon or other alternative in an effort to improve a business operation.

Even those executives who are unwilling or unable to implement a full scanlon plan program should acquaint themselves and ultimately their key managers with the principles which are fundamental to this document. The management approach which is vital to a successful scanlon plan program should be the basis of supervisory and management training programs for every organization regardless of whether a scanlon program is the ultimate goal. Those of us who believe in participative management and who have seen hard evidence that it works are constantly encountering the argument that traditional authoritative management methods are more efficient.

In today's highly competitive business world, where other countries are competing with us at every level, we cannot tolerate just a pacified work force. There may have been a time when industrial-relations and management people believed that a pacified work force was the epitome of labor-relations success. I do not agree that this ever was truly the case, but it is apparent that it cannot be the case any longer.

One of the former members of management in Sony, Shigeru Kobayashi, expressed it this way, ". . . Despotic exercise of authority denies a worker an independent personality, turns him into a 'cogwheel' or 'pebble,' makes him *actively* unhappy as a human being. It inhibits productivity, results in the misuse of authority, and leads naturally to the self-destruction of the company itself."

I believe that if we treat a man as he is, he will remain as he is, but if we are willing to treat him as he can be and ought to be, he will become what he can be and ought to be.

The concept of participative management, particularly when channeled through a proven program such as the scanlon approach, is a way to release the power of the individuals in your plants. No, the scanlon plan is not an easy way to manage and certainly not for the weak at heart, but business executives who fail at least to investigate what the scanlon concepts have to offer may one day very soon find that the parade has passed them by.

GEORGE SHERMAN
Vice-President,
Industrial Relations and
   Personnel Administration
Midland-Ross Corporation
Cleveland, Ohio

ACKNOWLEDGMENTS

We wish to acknowledge the cooperation and support of the scanlon companies and their employees who have shared their experiences with us. Without their dedication to scanlonism and their willingness to share information this book would not have been possible. In addition, the Scanlon Plan Associates, under the long-term leadership of Dr. Carl Frost, Michigan State University, and the National Center for Productivity and Work Quality are two organizations that have contributed significantly to the development of scanlon principles throughout the world. We are deeply indebted to them.

SPECIAL COMMENT

If you have a profit-sharing plan and are completely satisfied with it, you probably will not benefit by reading these comments. But if you are one of the 175,000 to 200,000 firms with profit sharing but feel that it is not motivating your people as you expected it to, you may benefit by reading on.

For one thing, I have normally found profit-sharing plans to be more susceptible to neglect than scanlon plans, perhaps because their strategy for employee involvement is not integrally "built in," as in most scanlon plans. The structure of the scanlon plan gives involvement a good start.

Professors Moore and Ross also maintain that the two types of plans are compatible and further that the scanlon plan would bolster the profit-sharing plan and make it more useful. I concur and believe that the synergy can work both ways: profit sharing can make a scanlon plan more successful than if the scanlon plan was adopted alone. A profit-sharing plan can be especially relevant when engineering, research, advertising, and styling loom very important.

The two plans do not necessarily compete for the same dollars. The scanlon payoffs are derived from improvements in performance over which the work force has substantial or close control, and many of the factors which determine profit-sharing rewards are only loosely under most employee's control.

There are a number of other reasons why the two kinds of plans work well together in many organizations. The frequent, generally monthly, payoffs in the scanlon program provide the fast feedback between current performance and rewards presumed prerequisite to realization of strong incentive motivation, and the more deferred rewards—the "money earned in June and paid in January," to use our authors' description—usually extending even till separation or retirement under profit sharing, exert holding power on short-term workers and a deeper sense of belonging in career employees.

WILLIAM J. HOWELL
Howell & Sisler of Chicago

CONTENTS

Chapter 1 Philosophy, Goals, and Productivity   1

  1.1   The Philosophy and Practice of Cooperation   2
  1.2   How is This Philosophy to be Achieved?   5
  1.3   The Involvement System—How the Philosophy is Achieved   6
  1.4   The Formula   7
  1.5   Is This Formula Different from Profit Sharing?   8
  1.6   What the Scanlon Plan is Not   8
  1.7   Why Productivity is Important to Scanlon Plan Companies 9
  1.8   What is Productivity?   9
  1.9   Performance versus Financial Models of Productivity   9
 1.10   What to Pay For   11
 1.11   Summing Up   12

Chapter 2 Program Guide   14

  2.1   How Do You Know if You Will Benefit?—Phase I   16
  2.2   Checklist of Conditions   17
  2.3   Staff Meetings—Phase II   20
  2.4   Analysis of Experience Data on Labor—Phase III   22
  2.5   Explaining the Formula   24
  2.6   Presentation of the Plan—Phase IV   25
  2.7   The Involvement System   25
  2.8   Yearly Evaluation and Survey—Phase V   27
  2.9   Comprehensive Chronology of Installation Steps   27
 2.10   Comprehensive Chronology of Formula-Installation Steps 30
 2.11   Summing Up   31

Chapter 3   Management and Staff Preparation   32

    3.1   Reading Assignments and Discussion   32
    3.2   Molding Proper Attitudes   34
    3.3   Planning for Installation   35
    3.4   The Election and Record Keeping   37
    3.5   Committee Structure   37
    3.6   Memo of Understanding—Principles   40
    3.7   Procedure for Handling Suggestions—The Involvement
         System   40
    3.8   Some Thoughts on Involvement-System Process   42
    3.9   Summing Up   44

Chapter 4   Equitable Sharing of Benefits—Formula Calculation   45

    4.1   Diagnostic Analysis   46
    4.2   Ingredients of a Productivity-Sharing Calculation   47
    4.3   Beginning the Diagnostic Analysis   51
    4.4   Diagnostic Analysis for the Ratio Method of Calculation   51
    4.5   Items to Include and Exclude—Rationale   59
    4.6   Determining Sales Value of Production   63
    4.7   The Single-Ratio Calculation—A Way to Get Started   64
    4.8   The Base Ratio   65
    4.9   Normalizing the Ratio and When to Install   65
  4.10   A Typical Month's Calculation   66
  4.11   Bonus Reserve   69
  4.12   Distribution to Employees   70
  4.13   Single-Ratio Summary   72
  4.14   Single Ratio-Critique and Expansion   73
  4.15   Product-Mix Problems and a Solution   74
  4.16   Problems of Base Ratio Adjustments and Other Problems   76
  4.17   More Comprehensive Calculations   78
  4.18   Multicost Ratio and Profit-Sharing Methods   78
  4.19   Value-Added Methods   80
  4.20   Allowed-Labor Calculation   81
  4.21   Other Calculations   87
  4.22   Newly Formed Organizations   88
  4.23   Overall Evaluation and Quality Considerations   88

4.24   Calculations for Service, Retail, and Other
        NonManufacturing Organizations   90
4.25   Hospitals—A Sample Calculation for Service Organizations   91
4.26   Summing Up   96

Chapter 5   Policy   98

5.1   Participating Payroll—Who Should Participate   98
5.2   Bonus and Good Compensation Practices   100
5.3   Profit Sharing   101
5.4   Financial Policy   102
5.5   Role of Management   103
5.6   Industrial Relations and Scanlonism *and* Unionism   104
5.7   Terms of Office for Committees with Implications for
        Training   105
5.8   Your Policy Considerations   106
5.9   Summing Up   106

Chapter 6   Operating the Plan Over Time—Feeding the System   108

6.1   Management Support—The Catalysts   108
6.2   Involving Resource Workers   112
6.3   Organizational and Departmental Goal Setting   113
6.4   Maintenance of Suggestions   116
6.5   Feedback of Information—Some Experience   120
6.6   Vigilence of the Formula—Analysis and Adjustment
        Procedures   124
6.7   Calculation Education   130
6.8   Managerial Succession   131
6.9   Year-End-Meeting Preparation   132
6.10   Summing Up   133

Chapter 7   Evaluation Strategies   134

7.1   Plan for Evaluation at Various Intervals   134
7.2   The Survey—Before and After   136
7.3   Data Assessment—Management and Committee Involvement   137
7.4   Financial Evaluation   140
7.5   Outside Evaluation   141
7.6   Summing Up   142

Chapter 8   Summing Up, Experience of Others, and the Future   143

  8.1   The Philosophy, The Formula, and The Involvement System   143
  8.2   Other Corporate Experience   144
  8.3   Scanlonism, Organizational Development, and The Future   148
  8.4   Scanlon Working Principles   153

Appendixes   157

  A   Questionnaires   157
  A.1   Before and After and Annual Survey   157
  A.2   Plan-Evaluation Questionnaire   165
  A.3   Coding and Scoring Your Questionnaire   178
  B   Memo of Understanding   182
  C   Sample Forms   190
  C.1   Employee's Suggestion   190
  C.2   Example of Screening-Committee Minutes   192
  C.3   Example of Production-Committee Minutes   195
  D   Evaluating Your Company's Economic Facts of Life and
         Sophistication of Accounting Systems   198
  E   General Steps for Converting Bonus Calculation from Single-
         Ratio-of-Production Method to Allowed-Labor Method   212
  F   Feedback Strategies   214

Bibliography   219
Index   227

THE SCANLON WAY
TO IMPROVED PRODUCTIVITY

PHILOSOPHY, GOALS, AND PRODUCTIVITY 1

The scanlon plan is a total, organization-wide, productivity-improvement plan. It focuses the attention of workers and management on productivity, with everyone sharing in the benefits of improved productivity. This sharing is achieved by increased levels of true involvement, cooperation, communication, and bonus earnings.

The scanlon plan can be thought of as an organization-wide, productivity-improvement system made up of three basic elements. The first is the philosophy and practice of cooperation. In some firms cooperation is replaced by antagonism. In others, teamwork exists at a bare minimum. In scanlon firms high levels of teamwork are a way of life. Everyone cooperates because he understands that economic rewards are contingent on honest cooperation.

The second element of the plan is the involvement system. The involvement system is designed to increase efficiency and reduce costs. Since practically all management systems purport to increase efficiency and reduce costs, the plan needs to be understood as to why it is different and yet compatible with other management systems. The vehicle of involvement looks like a suggestion system. It is! But it is not just a suggestion system, since it gathers in suggesters and nonsuggesters alike. Also, it produces many more demands on the entire organization than just a suggestion system. Everyone is challenged to take a fresh look at work with an aim toward increasing efficiency and reducing costs. And, unlike most management systems, this involvement system is like work itself in constantly evolving and adapting to the requirements of technology, people, and the marketplace. Also, the involvement system increases accountability, since without accountability involvement is hollow.

The third element of the plan is the productivity-measurement sharing-of-benefits formula. This formula is simple in principle, and it is essential that it

1

be understood. Its implications for the firm are profound. Good ideas are often simple; yet acceptance of the implications of the formula is the key to productivity. This key is the belief that each person contributes to the measurable productivity of the firm. Thus the plan formula is the measurement. The simplicity of this measurement leads to its understanding and its ultimate acceptance.

Although productivity measurement is the third element of the plan, one additional point is in order—the quality of management. You must be willing to make decisions, be fair, be open, and accept criticism. These, we believe, are qualities of good managers and essential to the success of the plan.

Let us review these three elements separately, but with the understanding that they are all interrelated; that is, the philosophy and practice of cooperation, the involvement system, and the productivity-measurement formula mutually reinforce one another. If only one element of the plan is adopted, failure of the total plan is the likely result.

1.1 THE PHILOSOPHY AND PRACTICE OF COOPERATION

The heart of the scanlon plan centers on worker-management cooperation. In fact the plan's founder, Joseph Scanlon, always insisted that ". . . participation and partnership are prerequisites."[1]

Cooperation under the plan is no different from the objectives of organizational development (OD). For example, a normal sequence of the OD process is diagramed in Figure 1.1.

The typical OD activities that support this model are:

1. Attitude and opinion measurement.
2. Interviewing for diagnostic purposes.
3. Problem identification and problem solving.

---

[1] A brief historical note is in order. The plan owes a debt to Joseph Scanlon, a former cost accountant, steelworker, United Steel Workers Union official, and, finally, a lecturer at the Massachusetts Institute of Technology. During the mid-thirties Scanlon was instrumental in saving Empire Steel and Tin Plate Company, of Mansfield, Ohio. In 1947 Studebaker Corporation acquired Empire Steel and Tin Plate Company. This small steel company was saved from bankruptcy by increasing union-management cooperation. Scanlon's approach was to devise a formula for sharing the profits of the firm with all employees. At the same time cooperation, aimed at reducing costs and increasing quantity, was stressed. The wholehearted cooperation that ensued was considered to be instrumental in turning the financial corner. From this experience, Scanlon's career blossomed into assisting management and labor with the principles of cooperation and participation. Although never claiming authorship, the three elements of the plan became identified with Scanlon and his work. Since then, the plan has been accepted as a generic term for a whole range of production-sharing plans.

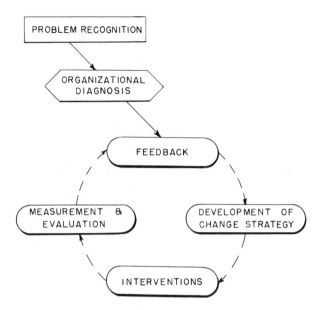

Figure 1.1   A model of the organizational development process.

4. Goal setting and methods of achievement.
5. Communication improvement.
6. Conflict identification and resolution.
7. Task forces and temporary systems.
8. Job design for motivation and productivity.
9. Measurement and evaluation.[2]

The OD model in Figure 1.1 and the nine activities that support it are often part of the natural process of a scanlon plan. Sometimes they are made unnecessary by the acceptance of the plan's philosophy. Why?

As we said, the heart of the plan centers on worker-management cooperation. Indeed, the earliest characterizations of the plan described the plan as a vehicle in which every man became a capitalist. The worker and manager are to accomplish capitalism together by the shared belief in teamwork. Belief by the team that every worker, direct or indirect, and staff person has valuable information that he will share with management. Management, in turn, has information which will be exchanged with the worker. Shared knowledge includes areas vital to enhanced productivity. Examples of these areas are

[2] Harold Rush, "Organizational Development: A Reconnaissance," The Conference Board, Research Report No. 605, 1973.

production problems, market conditions, and technological changes. Both management and the worker can collaborate to do problem solving in these areas. At the very least, they can try to understand each other's limitations. It is fair to state that this collaboration establishes an increased feeling of individual worth in the worker. He is offered a chance to learn and expand on his environment in order to achieve economic effectiveness for his company and himself. It is clear that management still leads, but the worker is given a new role of active participation in the enterprise.

One very important consideration that can characterize scanlonism is identity. Identity is the merging of personal goals with those of the organization. This process of identification occurs when the organization is organized and developed to a point at which it is perceived by all to be the vehicle for achieving goals and rewards that can come from work. Not all firms can expect this form of identity; however, those firms which have achieved identity are a model blend of productivity and good human-resource management.

This goal of identity is achievable only if assumptions about the human resource of an organization are sincerely held by management. These are the same assumptions held to be fundamental in OD. The first is that most of us want to continue personal growth and development, especially if the organizational environment is both challenging and supportive. Again, most of us want to become more than what we are capable of becoming. The second assumption of OD and identity is that, given the first assumption, most of us desire to make higher levels of contributions to the attainment of organizational goals.

Given these two assumptions that characterize scanlonism, and most OD efforts, just how can working groups optimize their effectiveness? Since management cannot possibly perform all leadership functions in all situations at all times, working groups must help each other in ways which aid the entire organizational effort. This kind of cooperation is a form of effective personal and group initiative that frequently requires a change in attitudes and perspectives on the part of both worker and management. This change, often a specific goal of OD, is achievable under scanlonism if the two assumptions of identity are held by most.

Another point to consider is that the motivation to adopt this philosophy is more likely to be associated with well-educated workers and sophisticated managers from firms which are not in financial trouble. Usually these firms wish to improve organizational climates which are already healthy. Thus, the philosophy of the plan and some of the ideas it embraces are merely an extension of the prevailing organizational climate; that is, the plan is perceived as a mechanism to unlock the intelligence now found in quality work forces. Therefore, those firms with good organizational climates see the plan as one of a series of innovative changes fully appropriate for OD.

In part, this philosophy is captured and advanced when we address the issue of organizational development as Rush (1973) defines it: ". . . a planned, managed, systematic process to change the culture, systems, and behavior of an organization, in order to improve the organization's effectiveness in solving its problems and achieving its objectives."

Chapter 8 elaborates further on the topic of OD and scanlonism, but Rush's definition of OD is precisely the objective of the scanlon philosophy. Therefore, this book is about a method of productivity enhancement in which OD can thrive but only with productivity improvement.

1.2 HOW IS THIS PHILOSOPHY TO BE ACHIEVED?

Broad involvement is the key. The philosophy of the plan encourages everyone to be involved with the product or service the organization produces. However, this broad involvement must be a managed process. It simply does not occur by itself, nor does the structure of the plan make it happen. It is the responsibility of management to instill into everyone that wide-ranging involvement is not only good but possible.

Additionally, the philosophy requires "fine tuning," and we agree with Frost et al. (1974) that frequent evaluations of the change processes are necessary in establishing the value of the mechanisms of change as well as the value of the organization's progress toward improved effectiveness.

Perhaps a good way to translate these words into effective meaning for you is to capture representative comments and observations from plan workers and managers. In this way, some of the flavor and context of the plan's philosophy can be presented.

Examples

1. When we approached a worker in a plan company for an interview, we were reminded by the worker that ". . . time is money." This same worker had a great deal of time during the before-plan period.
2. Workers try to reduce unnecessary overtime. We have heard workers say, "It's better to work smarter and not harder."
3. "I can now produce ideas as well as effort."
4. "Communication is a real give and take process around here."
5. It is not uncommon to have workers question "the efficiency" of a particular managerial decision. An interest develops in the rationale surrounding decision making.
6. "Technological change (substituting new machines and methods for human

labor) is better understood and accepted. Often, the suggestion for this technological change comes from the worker."

This philosophy needs a framework in which to carry it out. Thus the other two elements represent the operational parts of the plan. One is the social process of making productivity-related suggestions. We call this the involvement system. The other is a formula for sharing the fruits of productivity on an organization-wide basis. As mechanisms they are important, but without the worker and management committed to the philosophy, they exist only as mechanisms.

1.3 THE INVOLVEMENT SYSTEM—HOW THE PHILOSOPHY IS ACHIEVED

The second element of the plan is the structure and process of the involvement system. Employee participation is the process by which the work force and management communicate via the development and transformation of ideas. These ideas are in the form of productivity-related suggestions which are put into action. This action is accomplished through two levels of committees: the departmental level and the executive level. These committee structures are superimposed on the regular organizational structure and thus become a new mechanism for communication. In the following chapters the various aspects of the involvement system are dealt with in great detail. However, no one can minimize the impact of the involvement system, because, at base, each person in the firm is constantly asked to reexamine his or her work. This reexamination pursues three general avenues: (1) quality improvement, (2) quantity enhancement, and (3) cost reduction. It is a humble reminder to management to recognize exactly how much intelligence exists at all levels of most organizations. Unlocking this intelligence is the objective of the involvement system. How is this done?

Divisiveness, isolation, insulation, and narrowly-defined individual interests take a back seat to cooperation and participation. This occurs because the best interest of the firm becomes the best interest of the individual. The scanlon philosophy becomes intertwined with the involvement system. This philosophy and the involvement system tend to reinforce each other as practical, problem-solving behavior focuses attention away from individual concerns. The individual then focuses attention on broader work areas and ultimately on the organizational objectives. The process by which this is achieved is through permitting honest, well-motivated, and intelligent members of the firm to put productivity-related ideas to work. People, if given the opportunity, will by their very nature strive to increase quality, enhance quantity, and reduce costs.

Naturally they want to be reinforced for these behaviors. The involvement system by itself is a source of social reinforcement. Working smarter can be a way of life. However, the involvement system can also legitimize working harder, but care and diligence, and not just speed, may produce more usable units of a product or service in the long run.

Finally, the involvement system is the most exciting element of the plan as the firm's human resource at all levels is challenged to strive for and reach its full potential by reexamining its work. Thus, this process of putting productivity-related ideas to work is a constant reminder of how cooperation benefits not only the firm but ultimately the individual via increased job security, work satisfaction, and a tangible bonus. The final reinforcement of this process is, of course, the third element of the plan–the bonus formula.

1.4 THE FORMULA

A measure of productivity is necessary in order to pay bonuses for increases in productivity. Before installing the plan, each company seeks to determine its normal labor costs. This norm is typically used as part of a ratio of labor costs to sales value of output produced when starting the plan. The ratio becomes the relationship between total labor costs and the market value of goods and services produced. The key problem, according to all in-depth studies reviewed, is to devise a particular formula which accurately and objectively reflects the productive efforts of management and worker as a team. Chapter 4 discusses this in great detail along with other formulas.

In order to make this measurement of productivity clear, the most commonly applied formula is generalized as:

$$base\ ratio = \frac{labor\ costs}{sales\ value\ of\ production}$$

A base ratio is determined between (1) total labor cost, including factory and salary payroll, vacations, and holidays, and (2) sales value of production, including adjustments for such items as fluctuations in inventories. Before any technical discussion of the formula is undertaken, the purpose of the formula needs some discussion.

The formula is designed to focus the attention of the worker and the manager on variables critical to the productivity of the organization. How? When there is a decline in productivity, members of the organization feel the effects. The shifts in product mix, the changing quality of materials purchased, and the effect of selling price and wage changes are all now felt by the employees. They may not particularly like the negative changes, because everyone is still human, but they learn to understand and accept them better.

What better way to learn about the economics of the business than to be actively involved as they are happening? Certainly they should also understand the difficulty of making some managerial decisions and learn the importance of helping to isolate small problems before they become major.

In principle, the formula shows the historical relationship between costs and the sales value of production. This relationship between the human-resource cost and the value of production is the normal ratio of labor to output, or the *base ratio*. Thus the expected labor cost is derived for any given month and compared with the actual labor bill. If actual labor is lower than expected labor, this amount is a bonus to be distributed to the participating payroll. Usually this is everyone, since this is an organization-wide, productivity-sharing system. Therefore, with the entire organization focusing its attention on this relationship of human-resource investment to productivity, real learning is directed toward more productive behavior in order to improve the actual ratio.

1.5 IS THIS FORMULA DIFFERENT FROM PROFIT SHARING?

Yes and no. The generally accepted definition of profit-sharing plans concerns firms which distribute corporate profits on an annual basis, sometimes through a stock-purchase plan. The scanlon plan is a productivity-sharing plan that captures the true ups and downs of business. Productive behavior should lead to a reward which is reasonably tied to the current organizational performance. Profit-sharing plans distribute profits earned in June but paid in January, although some pay more frequently.

Conversely, the plan pays monthly or even bimonthly. Therefore, it brings to everyone's attention that the bonus followed the productive behavior. We argue that this is a good principle of learning, namely, that rewards should be contingent on performance. Profit-sharing companies should, of course, consider applying many of the principles and techniques outlined in this book. In fact, some of Joseph Scanlon's early installations were profit-sharing plans, and even today some very successful plan companies are either profit-sharing or close to it.

1.6 WHAT THE SCANLON PLAN IS NOT

The scanlon plan is not:

1. A gimmick.
2. A speedup device.
3. A job-satisfaction strategy, though this may be an outcome.

4. A worker-management tribunal.
5. A new and risky idea.
6. A substitute for equitable wage structures.
7. A grievance system.

1.7 WHY PRODUCTIVITY IS IMPORTANT TO SCANLON PLAN COMPANIES

Productivity and its improvement are of great importance to scanlon plan companies, because no bonus is earned unless past productivity is increased. No increase in productivity, no bonus. It is a productivity-sharing plan.

Who shares in this increased productivity? The first logical participants are the employees, who receive direct monetary benefits in the form of a bonus. The company should also be a beneficiary of the scanlon plan philosophy by becoming more competitive in its markets. It can directly receive a share of the calculated bonus. Hopefully, each scanlon plan company is one of the lower-priced, higher-quality producers in each of its markets. But last, and perhaps most important, as more and more companies begin to use their resources more efficiently through application of the scanlon plan principles, the entire country's productivity should increase more rapidly than without the application of these principles. Ideally, the United States could then regain some of its world standing as one of the leading countries in productivity improvement.

The importance of increasing productivity at the national level cannot be overemphasized. If wages are increased by 7 percent per year, but labor productivity is increased by only 3 percent per year, unit labor costs will increase by 3.9 percent (107 ÷ 103), and probably prices also. Our economy must attempt to increase the productivity of all its resources if we want to increase our standard of living without major inflation. The goal is there, and the scanlon plan has proved that its principles can help in the attainment of increased productivity. In scanlon plan companies, we have found that the word "productivity" and its improvement have favorable connotations. This is a favorable finding, because studies have consistently found in recent years that attitudes regarding productivity are quite poor. Over the years, the word "productivity" has earned a poor reputation probably because of the fear that it means only working harder. Productivity improvement with a strong behavioral emphasis must be developed as a common goal.

1.8 WHAT IS PRODUCTIVITY?

A fairly clear understanding of productivity is important, because we use the term repeatedly in this book. Without an understanding of it, you may try to improve the wrong thing. But just what is productivity? In general terms, productivity is the efficient use of resources in the production of goods or services. Productivity can be measured in a variety of ways but often is measured as a ratio of output to input. Perhaps an example might clarify the situation. Assume that a man is working a coal mine in which all the coal is the same. In one week's time, the man mines 80 tons of coal in 40 hours of work so that his productivity is 2 tons per hour (80 ÷ 40). Then, in the next week, assuming nothing else such as equipment or distance from the coal changes, the man produces 88 tons of coal; his productivity has increased by 10 percent (88/40 = 2.2 tons per hour compared with 2 tons in the previous week, or a 2.2/2.0 = 10 percent increase). Productivity calculations are often made with the use of index numbers. This coal-mining example in the calculations in the base and the subsequent period are as follows:

Base period (week 1)

Index of output: $\left. \dfrac{80}{80} \right| = 1 \times 100 = 100$

Index of input: $\left. \dfrac{40}{40} \right| = 1 \times 100 = 100$

Productivity: $\left. \dfrac{\text{Output index}}{\text{Input index}} \right| = \dfrac{100}{100} \times 100 = 100$

Next period (week 2)

Index of output: $\left. \dfrac{88}{80} \right| = 1.10 \times 100 = 110$

Index of input: $\left. \dfrac{40}{40} \right| = 1.00 \times 100 = 100$

Productivity: $\left. \dfrac{110}{100} \right| = 1.10 \times 100 = 110$

or productivity increased by 10 percent (110/100)

In this example nothing else changed. Apparently the man worked harder or smarter (e.g., less wasted time) the second week.

In actual practice, however, gains from working harder go only so far. In fact, gains from working harder over time are probably quite limited, even though short-run benefits can be quite dramatic. How are long-run benefits in productivity to be obtained? Primarily through working smarter along with better resources, including capital equipment such as computers and better materials. Improving the flow of goods through a factory or paper work through an office may yield much greater benefits than a few individuals working harder. Frankly, the number of variables influencing productivity are almost beyond counting. Most companies do not even try to measure productivity except in a very broad way.

In our opinion, although measuring productivity may also be as difficult as isolating the variables that influence it, a scanlon plan company must change employees' attitudes about productivity if the plan is to be successful. All levels of employees from the president down should be thinking about productivity improvement.

But what is productivity improvement? Returning to the coal mining example in which 80 tons was mined in the first week and 88 tons in the second week with the same hours, you would probably agree that the miner's productivity has increased. Right? Do not be so fast at agreeing. What if between the two periods the price of the coal decreased from $25 to $20 per ton? Has the worker's productivity really increased? Yes and no. This confusing answer is explained below in detail. A very useful model in analyzing your company's productivity is introduced now, as it is central to understanding the scanlon plan.

1.9 PERFORMANCE VERSUS FINANCIAL MODELS OF PRODUCTIVITY[3]

In the way productivity is computed by the government (output-per hour), our coal miner's increase in output from 80 tons in one week to 88 tons in the next would be recorded as an increase in productivity. This is true, even though the selling price decreased by 20 percent. In fact, it would show up as an increase in output-per hour independent of how the increase was caused. We call this measure *performance productivity*.

The method of calculation above is how air transport achieved approximately 300 percent above average increase in productivity over a twelve-year period (1960-1971) and yet was still in poor financial condition. Exceptions to this governmental method of computing output-per hour can be found in the governmental statistical calculations, but the emphasis is on performance productivity.

Somewhat unfortunately, most of us relate to the performance measure of productivity. We think in terms of number of pieces produced, reports prepared, employees processed, letters typed; primarily, quantity. Why? Because we can relate to these particular activities of our jobs. To relate to the broader considerations of whether product Y rather than product X should be produced is often difficult, because much broader considerations come into play. Since individuals think in performance-productivity terms, scanlon and other companies are faced with a major problem in changing their way of thinking about productivity.

[3] R. J. Bullock and T. L. Ross, *The Meaning and Measurement of Organizational Productivity,* Scanlon Plan Associates, Michigan State University, East Lansing, 1976.

A company, however, does not think in performance-productivity terms alone. Rather, its top managers think more in financial terms, which is really the correct way. For example, if a company's costs increase by 10 percent because of performance-productivity declines and it raises its selling prices by 20 percent, its productivity has increased. We call this measure *financial productivity*. This occurs while the company's performance productivity, as measured by output-per hour, has decreased. Of course, the reverse could occur. A scanlon plan company should attempt to get more employees at all organizational levels to think more in terms of financial productivity rather than just performance productivity. Almost everyone has heard of some examples that have given the word "productivity" a bad name, including stories emphasizing quantity rather than quality, over- or double counting, wasted reports, and the like. Almost all these result from overemphasizing performance-productivity goals. Be careful not to do this.

This raises an opportunity for scanlon companies. They should develop two types of productivity measures: performance and financial. The former because these are what individuals, such as direct labor employees, relate to most easily. And the latter because they are ultimately the most important to the company's success. Much of the effort should be directed in the long run toward financial-productivity improvement. A scanlon plan calculation should include both performance- and financial-productivity measurements.

Assume that you own a carpet-cleaning service and have teams of cleaners throughout the city. How would you evaluate the performance of the different teams? Chances are that you would determine the total square feet of carpet cleaned over a period and compare this with hours worked. This, of course, is a performance-productivity measurement. Now, what would happen if one imaginative team decided that they would clean only where it was dirty, because no one could notice the uncleaned part? If they took off the remaining time, neither the performance nor the financial productivity, except for supplies saved, would be affected, but if they asked for other assignments, the team's financial productivity would have increased, even though their performance productivity did not (same number of square feet cleaned). Not only could the company start competing better, but it also could afford to pay higher salaries and obtain better employees.[4]

1.10 WHAT TO PAY FOR

The calculations discussed in this book as the equitability payoff for the cooperation and involvement processes normally reward productivity increases

[4] This example was supplied by R. J. Bullock.

independently of how they were generated. For example, these calculations allow for payment of a bonus even if it was the result of volume increases. Some managers disagree with this even if it is a true productivity increase. There are ways to deal with this issue, and they are covered in Chapter 4.

We dislike the idea of paying for only performance productivity (quantity) changes. We like the idea of including at least some of the applicable market prices (selling, wages, etc.) to reinforce identity as part of the educational process underlying the plan. It is, of course, easier to get employees to relate to performance-productivity measures; yet full consideration of both kinds of productivity is the preferred strategy.

1.11 SUMMING UP

This chapter presents an overview of the scanlon plan in terms of what it is and is not. It is an organization-wide productivity plan made up of three elements: (1) the practice of cooperation, (2) the involvement system, and (3) the productivity formula. We talk about these three elements independently, but they must work in concert. When they do, the contribution to total productivity is exceeded only by the even higher levels of pride and involvement in work that inevitably follow this form of organizational development.

This chapter also introduces the concept of productivity and its measurement. The more typical aspects of productivity are described through several examples. Then, performance versus financial models of productivity are contrasted. Treating the dynamics of productivity measurement broadly, the financial model of productivity is introduced as the focal point of a successful scanlon plan company.

Finally, there is no question that the quality of management is a crucial consideration. A desire to work through subordinates combined with respect for the generation of better-educated and highly skilled work forces is the key. This means that quality management listens to its workers and reacts in an open, fair manner. Accepting criticism is essential, because it opens channels toward productivity-related problem solving.

PROGRAM GUIDE 2

This chapter quickly puts into your hands the typical steps leading to the consideration and installation of a scanlon plan. We term this overview on how to proceed the *program guide*. Significant steps of the program are sketched with necessary descriptions. These steps are more fully elaborated in later chapters, but model phases of a scanlon plan installation are flow-charted in Figure 2.1. A brief discussion of the key considerations on how to proceed is introduced in this chapter. Then, a comprehensive chronology of the steps to a plan is stated at the end of the chapter. This chronology is compactly stated and can easily serve as a checklist with which to build a time line for tasks and assignments.

As you review the various phases or stages of a scanlon plan installation, depicted in Figure 2.1, you may wish to evaluate your firm's general position vis-à-vis the plan. For that purpose, we have created a self-scoring checklist. You may score yourself, and task force, on each issue (see Section 2.2).

If top management believes their understanding of the plan and its implications for their firm are sound, staff meetings are usually attempted. This begins phase II. Also, a survey of the entire organization could be considered to provide input to the installation of the plan. For example, we include a suggested questionnaire in Appendix A which covers a wide variety of variables such as job satisfaction, cooperation between individuals, and measures of communication.

Concurrently with the phases indicated in Figure 2.1, an analysis of experience with labor costs can begin. In the section on diagnostics (this chapter and Chapter 4), we illustrate how to analyze your accounting data. At this stage you may very well reject the plan, because your data convince you that it is impossible to assess the true labor cost through the years. This is also

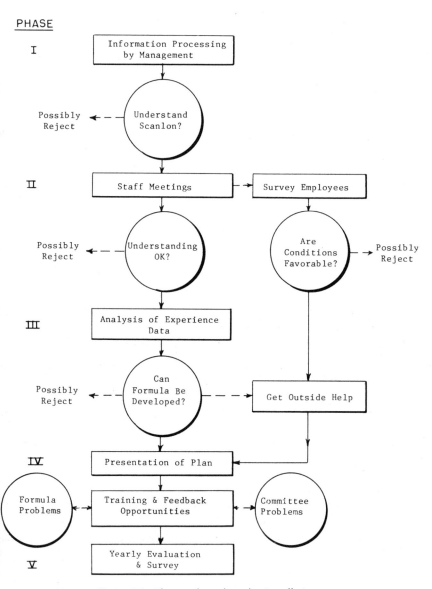

PHASE

I — Information Processing by Management

Understand Scanlon? — Possibly Reject

II — Staff Meetings → Survey Employees

Understanding OK? — Possibly Reject

Are Conditions Favorable? → Possibly Reject

III — Analysis of Experience Data

Can Formula Be Developed? — Possibly Reject — Get Outside Help

IV — Presentation of Plan

Formula Problems ← Training & Feedback Opportunities → Committee Problems

V — Yearly Evaluation & Survey

Figure 2.1   Phases of scanlon plan installation.

a stage to consider outside consultants in order to view your experience data objectively.

All these stages ultimately lead to the presentation of the plan to the entire firm at phase IV. We have some definite suggestions as to how you can do this most effectively. Feedback on how you are doing is critical, and all management and staff should be providing this information for training purposes in all plan meetings.

Finally, a yearly evaluation and survey are worth making a part of your permanent procedures at phase V. At this time you can assess your progress and move into other areas of organizational development and scanlon plan enhancement.

2.1 HOW DO YOU KNOW IF YOU WILL BENEFIT?—PHASE I

As the very first part of phase I, you should review the possible benefits of the plan and evaluate where your firm is in relation to scanlon principles. For example, the benefits of the plan can be listed in terms of the known outcomes associated with the plan (selected studies of the plan are referenced by the annotated bibliography at the end of the book). Here are eleven of the most common outcomes:

1. Everyone produces ideas as well as effort.
2. Changes due to markets, technology, and new methods are accepted, since higher efficiency leads to a bonus.
3. Coordination, teamwork, and sharing knowledge are enhanced.
4. Social needs are recognized, because participation is valued.
5. Attitudinal change of workers occurs, and they demand more efficient management and better planning.
6. Workers try to reduce overtime to work smarter, not harder or faster.
7. Working harder, when needed, is accepted.
8. More flexible administration occurs between workers and the managers.
9. A climate of competence, efficiency, and cost savings occurs.
10. Productivity increases, and the benefits are shared in the total organization.
11. Company gains by becoming more competitive, and jobs become more secure.

All the above benefits are fine, but what is the cost? The apparent costs are the hours invested in formula development by your accounting function; then the hours spent on introducing the plan; and, finally, the hours spent in the committee system administering productivity suggestions. We said "apparent costs," because you can count the hours and compute the wage bill for that. The real cost is to install the plan improperly and fail. Why?

Expectations about cooperation, trust, and the bonus are increased. If a plan is poorly conceived and implemented, failure results. Although management can always say "Well, we tried, and it didn't work," the failure reminds the organization that they could not meet the increased level of expectations. There is no way to compute this "cost," but we believe it is greater than any dollar amount coming from hours consumed.

So we come back to our original question, "How do you know if you will benefit?" If the eleven benefits we listed are objectives you wish to achieve or push to greater levels, honestly work through the checklist. Appraise your organization's condition. Form a task force of key management personnel. Have at least four or five others, maybe even some first-line supervisors, check their appraisal on the list. Combine all the results, and take the average response for each of the items on the checklist. At the end, we show you how to score the checklist. This will help your understanding of the plan in relation to your needs.

2.2 CHECKLIST OF CONDITIONS

Each of the items is to be answered if you have sufficient information or familiarity with the area captured in the item. All the items use a scale of 1 to 7. Each item is asked in terms of your actual situation and then in terms of what should be your situation.

1. Confidence and trust in management.

	Min						Max
Confidence is	1	2	3	4	5	6	7
Confidence should be	1	2	3	4	5	6	7

2. Concern for increasing the quantity of work.

	Min						Max
Quantity concern is	1	2	3	4	5	6	7
Quantity concern should be	1	2	3	4	5	6	7

3. Concern for increasing the quality of work.

	Min					Max	
Quality concern is	1	2	3	4	5	6	7
Quality concern should be	1	2	3	4	5	6	7

4. Concern for decreasing costs.

	Min					Max	
Costs concern is	1	2	3	4	5	6	7
Costs concern should be	1	2	3	4	5	6	7

5. Cooperation between individuals and department.

	Min					Max	
Cooperation is	1	2	3	4	5	6	7
Cooperation should be	1	2	3	4	5	6	7

6. Participation by everyone in the work process.

	Min					Max	
Participation is	1	2	3	4	5	6	7
Participation should be	1	2	3	4	5	6	7

7. Feeling of being informed about information vital to the functioning of the firm.

	Min					Max	
Being informed is	1	2	3	4	5	6	7
Being informed should be	1	2	3	4	5	6	7

8. Interest in and concern for the firm's future.

	Min					Max	
Concern for future is	1	2	3	4	5	6	7
Concern for future should be	1	2	3	4	5	6	7

9. Extent of sharing know-how of the job.

	Min						Max
Know-how sharing is	1	2	3	4	5	6	7
Know-how sharing should be	1	2	3	4	5	6	7

10. Extent of suggestion making, focused on decreasing costs, increasing quantity or quality of product or service.

	Min						Max
Suggestions are	1	2	3	4	5	6	7
Suggestions should be	1	2	3	4	5	6	7

11. Labor costs are competitive when compared with other similar firms.

	Min						Max
Costs are	1	2	3	4	5	6	7
Costs should be	1	2	3	4	5	6	7

12. Technological change is easily handled.

	Min						Max
Change is	1	2	3	4	5	6	7
Change should be	1	2	3	4	5	6	7

13. Current management information systems (MIS) show how productivity is achieved.

	Min						Max
MIS demonstrate	1	2	3	4	5	6	7
MIS should demonstrate	1	2	3	4	5	6	7

The scoring for the checklist is quite simple. If you did not add any questions for your particular situation, there were 13 in all. Subtract the "actuals" from the "should be's".

difference score = should be − actual

Total the difference scores, and divide by the number of the individuals responding. The range of values is 0 to 78, and the total could be anywhere in that range. Let us say that your total average score is 40 or more; that is, a select group of management and staff responds to the checklist, and their average score is 40. The checklist tries to capture the collective opinions as a way to indicate whether there is room for improvement. The magnitude of the average total score shows how far the firm is from its ideal goals. Depending on your management philosophy, the total score should be close to zero. We know negative scores are possible with this scheme, but they can be analyzed separately. Also, difference scores of low priorities may be weighted less than the same difference scores of higher priorities. Nevertheless, if your actual situation is very close to your goals, keep doing whatever it is you are doing.

The analysis of the checklist and a discussion based on the philosophy of the plan should be kept within the original decision-making group. It is important to discuss the firm's goals, personnel, and the plan frankly. Later, when key members have convinced themselves of the merits of the plan, they will be more comfortable and effective in explaining the plan to all concerned. You have now completed phase I referred to in Figure 2.1.

2.3   STAFF MEETINGS—PHASE II

At the end of phase I, basic information on the plan has been processed. Perhaps a management group has participated in responding to the checklist in Section 2.2. You are now beginning phase II. Meetings with the firm's staff are fully appropriate. To get you started, we are suggesting an agenda for this meeting:

1. Review the checklist results with an aim toward understanding the firm's climate and management philosophy.
2. Review the objectives of the scanlon plan. Often, describing how it works elsewhere is the best way to get a discussion going about the objectives of the plan. Case histories are referenced for you in the annotated bibliography.
3. Consider inviting an outsider with plan experience—another firm, a consultant, and so on.
4. What are the costs and benefits for your firm as you see them now?
5. Are the objectives of the plan consistent with your own?
6. Is there sufficient consensus to go ahead and announce management's intention to study the plan?
7. Should you survey the employees?

We firmly believe that each member of the staff or task force should be heard on all the points above. You may also wish to include additional points on the agenda. After careful consideration, the decision to go ahead or not should be made. We suggest, however, that the principles of good discussion be pursued in these sessions; that is, if there is one dominant decision maker, such as the boss, he should try to be objective, listen, probe feelings by reflecting them back to his subordinates, and then summarize the position of the task force. Otherwise, the boss only hears what he wants to hear, with no input from subordinates who can make or break the plan.

If your decision at phase II is to proceed, enlarge the information base to include all levels of management. This book and others in the field are to be read and discussed. Again, we have created the annotated bibliography for that purpose. This, by the way, is also the most exhaustive, comprehensive bibliography ever published, in case certain members of management and staff wish to undertake an intensive short course in the literature.

Discussion sessions within departments and among managers, staff, and interested others can follow the points enumerated earlier. Expect a detailed discussion as to how the plan will work for your firm. By this we mean that managers and staff will begin to operationalize the plan for your specific organization. In a very short period of time there could be some pressure to "quit talking and install the plan." Resist this tendency, because research shows that the more key people who truly understand all aspects of the plan, the smoother going it will have, especially in the critical first year.

As a part of this management and staff preparation you may want to consider bringing in a consultant. This is helpful for some firms and entirely unnecessary for others. *Most firms can install the plan themselves.* There are examples of firms who have done this by themselves. However, it is useful to bring in an outsider for two very practical purposes:

1. Developing the productivity formula.
2. Helping to introduce the plan.

Only a given firm's management can make a determination as to whether they wish outside help. In part, this decision is formulated during this phase of management-staff preparation. How? Usually, healthy skepticism surfaces concerning how the plan can be introduced. Or the controller and accounting function have serious doubts as to the actual construction of the formula.

Encourage the skepticism. Encourage discussion on the formula. These discussions are a necessary part of the preparation. If the sentiment of your key people is that they would like outside help, it is available. In general, our position is that this book anticipates the questions raised by other members of management and the staff.

While staff meetings are underway in phase II, a parallel activity could be considered, that is, a company-wide survey. The survey technique could provide useful information on job satisfaction, pay, company policies, and so on. Many firms have an annual morale survey just to "take the pulse" of their employees. In this special case, a survey can provide base-line information with which to compare the impact of the plan over time; that is, if all or part of the survey is repeated after the trial period of the plan, comparisons can be made as to whether feelings about the job, company pay, involvement with work, and use of one's talents have changed as a result of the plan. For this reason, we have included a prototype questionnaire in Appendix A.1.

If the survey is attempted, the task force of management and staff could mold their thinking to take advantage of the survey results. Also, the accounting function is now beginning to shift into phase III. The survey results can help shape their efforts toward analyzing costs, especially with reference to overtime, redundancies in work coverage, materials wastage, and so on.

2.4 ANALYSIS OF EXPERIENCE DATA ON LABOR—PHASE III

A diagnosis of your experience with labor costs generally shows if a stable ratio of labor to output can be ascertained. It has been estimated that a long-term profile of labor to output tends to emerge in at least nine out of ten manufacturing firms (Rucker, 1973). This ratio varies by industry and by firm but stays in balance for an amazingly high percentage of firms for very long periods of time.

Granted, product design, price increases, capital investments, method improvements, and a host of other productivity-related factors, and so on, all have their influence. Nevertheless, hundreds of firms have analyzed the relationship of labor to output and have established this ratio.

The basic purpose of the diagnostic analysis is to investigate the financial facts of your company. But the primary goal is to develop a formula that generally fulfills the following criteria: Is it

1. A good measure of performance over time?
2. Likely to be perceived as fair?
3. Understandable by those who try?
4. Flexible enough to meet changing conditions?
5. Easily administered?
6. Useful in isolating problem areas?
7. Oriented so as to direct all employees' efforts in the desired directions?

Although these criteria are never completely attained, they should be kept in mind when designing the bonus formula. We suggest ways of testing the criteria later in the book.

Companies normally begin their scanlon plans by applying the *ratio method* of calculation shown in Table 2.1. Why? The basic reasoning is that it

Table 2.1 Formula Exercise

Step	
1. (Definition)	$\text{base ratio} = \dfrac{\text{total personnel costs}}{\text{sales value}} = \dfrac{\$2,000,000}{\$10,000,000} = 20\%$
2. (What it means)	20% means the normal or expected value of the labor going into sales value of product or service.
3. (How constructed)	Total personnel costs = 1 $ straight hours
	2 vacations
	3 fringe
	4 etc.
	$\overline{\ \$\,2,000,000\ }$
	$10,000,000
4. (How constructed)	Sales value = 1 $10,000,000
	Less: Sales returns 2
	Allowances 3
	Discounts 4
	Net sales $
	Plus: Increases to
	inventory $
	Total sales value $10,000,000
5. (Bonus determination)	Expected personnel cost for month = 20% of total sales value
	Subtract actual personnel cost for month = −(amt)
	Bonus pool $(amt)

23

generally fulfills most of the criteria listed above. Companies normally start by making a detailed analysis of cost relationships over a series of years. This can be accomplished by preparing a schedule for the last five years with sales on the first line across the top. To this we add any increase in inventory, or deduct any decrease, from one year to the next to yield *sales value of production.* Next, all the cost items are listed down each year's column. As fine a detailed breakdown as possible is desirable for obvious information purposes on past performance. Specifically, each of the labor-cost items should be broken out separately.

After this is done, you compute the percentage of each labor account to sales value of production and analyze how much the cost items have increased or decreased in percentage of sales value of production. For the immediately previous year you try to do the above steps for each month or at least quarterly, since more recent periods are more reflective of current business activities. Next, you decide which cost items you want to include in the ratio. Add up the percentages of those items, with adjustments being made to reflect long-term productivity, and you have your ratio. Although the actual steps to developing the ratio are somewhat more complex, the principles are not. All the steps to follow are extensively discussed in Chapter 4 along with the questions you should ask and other calculation methods.

2.5   EXPLAINING THE FORMULA

Before phase IV actually begins, the formula must be understood by management and staff (or the task force). Experience has shown that if a few key people understand the productivity formula, others will accept it by virtue of the judgment of a very few. Therefore, management and the task-force members must have a uniform understanding of the formula.

No one can predict which few employees will test the formula. However, we can assure you that the one best way to a thorough understanding is to prepare the task force formally so that they can help prepare others with consistent information. Therefore, use Table 2.1 as an exercise in the formula.

The exercise in Table 2.1 can be developed with your own figures or dummy figures. It takes the formula through five basic steps. Chapter 4 has a detailed breakdown of the formula, but Table 2.1 provides a relatively simple exercise for the task force to fall back on when asked to explain the formula. At later stages of the development the work force will ask questions about the formula which can only be answered from Chapter 4 and your own accounting function. The questioning represents an opportunity for management to teach business principles and the economics of the marketplace. Therefore, having a core of management or staff that can work this exercise is the first step to future exchanges about what makes the American business system work.

2.6 PRESENTATION OF THE PLAN—PHASE IV

Gossip has already spread the word that "something is up." Key management and staff have already studied the plan and undertaken formula construction. It is now time to introduce the plan to the work force formally, as phase IV calls for.

Based on our observations and participation, there is one best way to introduce the plan. Depending on the size of the organization, departmental meetings should be addressed by management. The plan is introduced by explaining the formula and the involvement system. Questions and answers are dealt with face-to-face in small groups. After all the departments and shifts have been contacted in this fashion, a memo covering the formula and involvement system should be distributed and posted. Supervisors will start bringing in additional questions. Each manager and staff person should help the supervisor deal with these questions.

After these departmental meetings, it is very helpful to call a formal, organization-wide meeting for plan discussion and a vote. Some firms actually adjourn and meet at a nearby facility such as a motel. The cafeteria is fine as well. If the firm is too large for this, this meeting will be held in sections.

During this meeting the plan is discussed in terms of the formula and involvement system. All questions are answered, and a secret vote is taken. Everyone can then return to work. The ballots are to be counted immediately. If 80 percent or better vote yes, this acceptance should be announced as quickly as possible so that departments may hold elections for representatives of the production committees. It is a wise practice not to announce the actual percentage but to state in advance that at least 80 percent approval is required. We suggest that, to avoid problems, all ballots be destroyed. Let a blue-ribbon committee count ballots until they reach 80 percent and then destroy them.

2.7 THE INVOLVEMENT SYSTEM

By popular vote, each department or area elects two or three of its own to join with the first-line supervisor in the formation of the production committee. This committee meets at least once a month and evaluates suggestions. These suggestions are to be productively-related; that is, they are to focus on reducing cost, increasing quality, or increasing quantity.

Initially, a very high percentage of suggestions could be irritants of work. For example, a suggester wants ventilation fans installed. Although this suggestion may be accepted, it is the task of the committee to learn and then teach its peers what kinds of suggestions increase productivity.

The second aspect of setting up the involvement system is the screening committee. One-half of the screening committee is handpicked by management. For sure, the president or plant manager, controller, and personnel manager will be on the committee. Also, technical expertise must be represented. The functional areas should have representation in the screening committee.

The other one-half of the screening committee may be made up of the highest vote getters of the production-committee elections. These are individuals who are liked and trusted. Their informal feedback of screening-committee meetings to their fellow workers can be instrumental in the continued acceptance of the plan. Chapter 3 presents detailed procedures for committee representation.

It is not difficult to imagine how a production committee operates. A suggestion made is committed to paper, and the committee makes a determination if they can accept and put into use, reject, or forward the decision to the screening committee. Basically, the production committee is an informal process. However, the screening committee is vastly different in its areas of concern.

Three things will happen in every monthly screening-committee meeting:

1. New and old suggestions are evaluated.
2. Bonus results are analyzed.
3. A true educational process develops in economics and business practices. More understanding "sinks in" about the competitive climate in which the firm operates.

Although analyzing bonus results is a key function of the screening committee, committee meetings also permit an exchange of information by management as to what areas the workers can focus on to improve individual and departmental productivity. It is not uncommon for the workers on the screening committee to request additional information on products, pricing, and market conditions—a domain often considered to be of management's interest only. Screening-committee meetings facilitate a rapid increase in technical knowledge across departments. Also, it is common to hear detailed discussions concerning economies of scale to be attained via capital investment of equipment. In the past, there were no incentives to know the practical problems of other departments or of management's long-range needs.

Chapter 3 provides reporting procedures for the committee involvement system. However, presenting the structure of the committee system is straightforward. The process of what goes on within this structure is really crucial to a successful plan installation. Our guidelines, therefore, are intended to provide you with not only procedures but advice on what types of problems to expect and possible solutions. As indicated in Figure 2.1, there will be many opportunities to discuss the formulas and to solve problems concerning productivity-related ideas. However, each firm has its own organizational climate and managerial style. Thus, our strategy in Chapter 3 is to make clear what has worked elsewhere and to give you some idea of the options you may have during this first critical year under the plan.

2.8 YEARLY EVALUATION AND SURVEY—PHASE V

Whenever your trial year ends, you must evaluate where you stand. Figure 2.2 diagrams how you might formally connect your evaluation with a company-wide survey. If you surveyed before starting the plan, you may now analyze some of the changes which were presumably enhanced by the plan. Granted, the trial year produces a "halo effect," but some attitudinal data may bolster your financial data on the plan. Again, Appendix A has sample questionnaires for this purpose.

The steps for evaluation, whether a questionnaire is used or not, are outlined in Figure 2.2. Make a list of expected benefits. Review these at the departmental level. Ask for recommendations, either from everyone via the questionnaire or through groups via the committee system. Compile these results. Report them out.

Figure 2.3 shows how you could report your survey results of attitudinal data. This should be accompanied with a recap of the scanlon year financial results, that is, bonuses paid, productivity data, and ideas processed. You can report the same results informally just by announcing them in the screening committee and allowing the production committees to pass the information along. This could be followed up with a formal memo to all employees.

2.9 COMPREHENSIVE CHRONOLOGY OF INSTALLATION STEPS

1. Assign readings (particularly books; e.g., see Section 3.1 and Bibliography).
2. Based on organizational size and complexity, develop a task force for installation consideration; include at least the president, plant manager, personnel administrator, controller, and hopefully at least a foreman or departmental supervisor and lower employee or union representative if appropriate (see Sections 3.1 to 3.3).
3. After readings are completed, use the Section 2.2 checklist to determine tentative outcomes of an installation, and visit area scanlon installations if possible (i.e., known ones in your area).

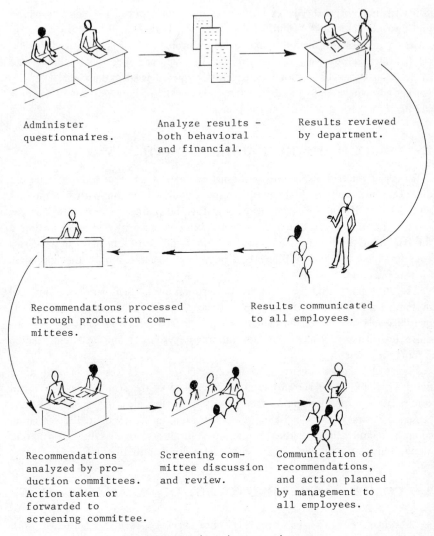

Administer
questionnaires.

Analyze results –
both behavioral
and financial.

Results reviewed
by department.

Recommendations processed
through production com-
mittees.

Results communicated
to all employees.

Recommendations
analyzed by pro-
duction committees.
Action taken or
forwarded to
screening committee.

Screening com-
mittee discussion
and review.

Communication of
recommendations,
and action planned
by management to
all employees.

Figure 2.2   Yearly evaluation and survey.

4. Start the diagnostic analysis (see Section 2.10 checklist and Section 4.10 to
   4.15).
5. Consider an employee survey to isolate possible behavioral and pay-
   inequity problems before installation (see Appendix A.1).
6. Consider an outsider to administer questionnaires and review calculation
   in order to achieve more objectivity.

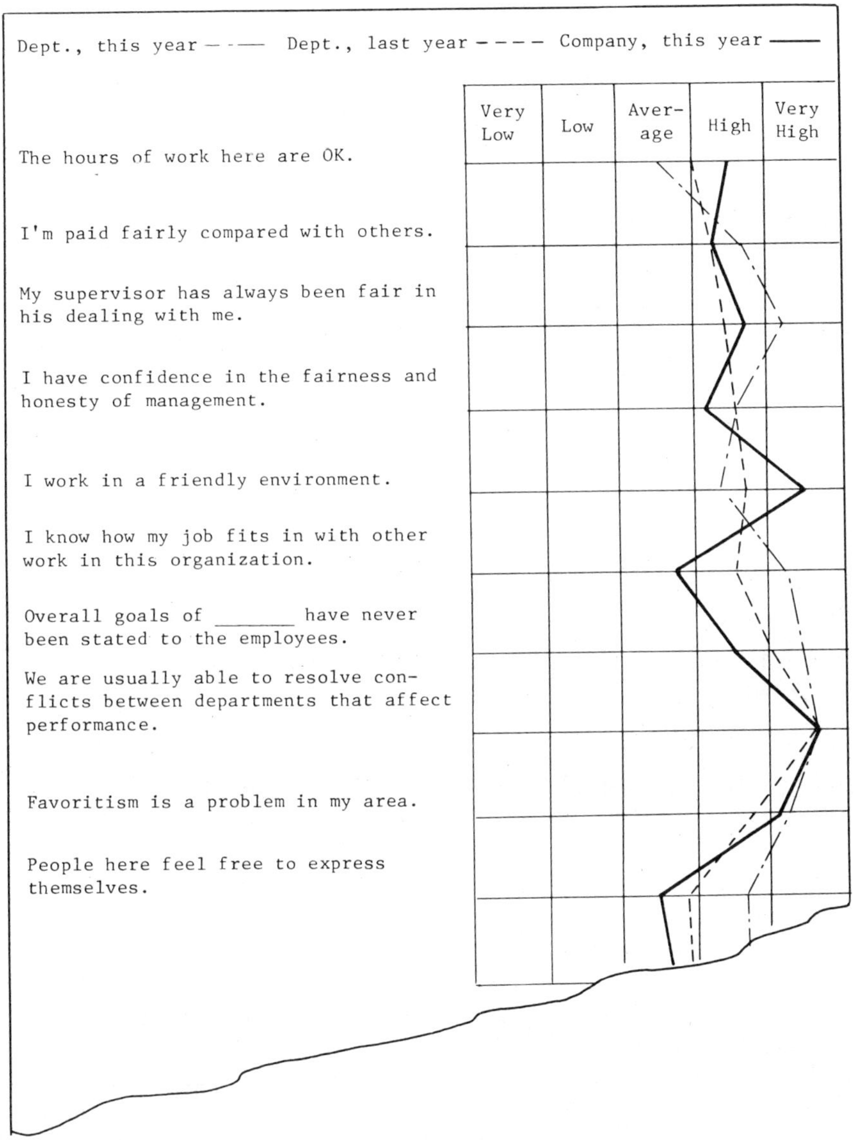
Dept., this year
Dept., last year
Company, this year
Very Low
Low
Aver-age
High
Very High
The hours of work here are OK.
I'm paid fairly compared with others.
My supervisor has always been fair in his dealing with me.
I have confidence in the fairness and honesty of management.
I work in a friendly environment.
I know how my job fits in with other work in this organization.
Overall goals of _______ have never been stated to the employees.
We are usually able to resolve conflicts between departments that affect performance.
Favoritism is a problem in my area.
People here feel free to express themselves.

Figure 2.3 Typical feedback of results.

7. Expand meetings to include more staff, supervisors, and union representatives regarding expectations and problems (repeat use of Chapters 2 and 3).

8. Work on elimination of current problems such as wage inequities and grievances, as well as feedback results of survey if applicable (Appendix A.1 may help).

9. Review calculation in detail, and obtain consensus from the task force.

10. Decide on target dates, and develop a plan of action for possible installation.

11. Develop committee structure, election procedures, and suggestion-system procedures (see Sections 3.4 to 3.7).

12. Develop a memo of understanding, and obtain agreement from the task force and union approval if applicable (see Appendix B) and establish policies (see Chapter 5).

13. Call in all foremen and supervisors to explain details of the plan with the task force.

14. Distribute the memo to all employees to announce the plan (see Section 3.3).

15. Hold departmental meetings, using the task-force members to discuss more details (see Section 3.3).

16. Vote on installation at least 80 percent for a trial period of one year (see Section 3.4.)

17. Hold committee elections, and install the plan in a favorable period (see Sections 3.4 to 3.8).

2.10 COMPREHENSIVE CHRONOLOGY OF FORMULA-INSTALLATION STEPS

1. Assign the diagnostic analysis to the appropriate accounting person or group (normally controller) (see Section 4.4).

2. Analyze financial sophistication and attitudes (see Appendix D).

3. Establish a deadline for the preliminary analysis to be completed.

4. Task force review the preliminary diagnostic analysis and review alternate calculations and options (see Sections 4.7, 4.10, 4.14, 4.17 to 4.21).

5. Decide on which productivity-sharing ingredients are most important at the beginning (see Section 4.2).

6. Decide on objectives of an equitable sharing system and other related objectives (see Chapter 4).

7. Decide on which costs to include in the calculation and rationale for their inclusion and possibly exclusion (see Section 4.5).

8. Consider possible future problems and how they will be considered in

alternate calculations—product mix, capital expenditures, interplant transfers, fluctuating selling and input prices, and inventory valuation (see Section 4.14, Chapter 6, and Appendix D).

9. Select a calculation that looks best for you (see Chapter 4).
10. Obtain consensus if possible from the task force and union representatives if applicable (see Sections 4.7, 4.10, 4.17 to 4.20).
11. "Normalize" the calculation—consider materiality of fluctuations, timing, equitability (see Sections 4.4 and 4.9).
12. Test the calculation for several periods, backward and forward in time (see Section 4.4).
13. Determine timing of distributions—monthly, moving average, and so on (see Sections 4.2).
14. Determine the division of the bonus pool (see Sections 4.10 and 4.12).
15. Determine reserve requirements (see Section 4.11).
16. Consider the best installation period (see Chapter 3 and Section 4.4).
17. Importance of monitoring over time—factors to consider (see Chapters 4, 6, and Appendix D).

2.11 SUMMING UP

This chapter reviews, in brief fashion, the most common phases of a scanlon plan installation. Each phase we have discussed may not occur in the sequence we outlined in Figure 2.1, or necessarily in the comprehensive chronologies. However, each of the phases and checkpoints is likely to be passed through in the course of an installation.

Information processing begins management's first steps toward considering the plan. Staff meetings and company-wide surveys occur to test the chances of the plan. "Go or no go" decision making is reviewed carefully at these early stages. Then, an analysis of experience data is attempted by the accounting function to see if a productivity-measurement formula is not only worthwhile but possible.

At this stage, management decides if they want to install the plan or request outside help. Either way, the presentation of the plan leads to acceptance or rejection by democratic vote. If the vote is better than 80 percent in favor, the trial year begins, and renewed interest in work and productivity occurs.

A year-end evaluation is made, and a survey could be made. Management and staff, direct and resource employees take stock of the year's experience. If it was favorable, most organizations vote to adopt the plan "permanently." This vote is not binding, but it is an excellent way to symbolize the commitment for the plan.

MANAGEMENT AND STAFF PREPARATION 3

For all organizations, the preparation of the management and staff is a critical first step. This chapter deals with those areas which are logically first. For example, we believe that background reading and molding proper attitudes are initially necessary. Then, too, planning for the installation, the setting, and materials required for a smooth first year are all of immediate consideration. Last, this chapter introduces the plan and its record keeping in the same chronological manner you would introduce it to the workplace.

3.1 READING ASSIGNMENTS AND DISCUSSION

Since it is likely that some rudimentary understanding of the plan does exist, it is wisest to deal with whatever plan knowledge is held in the minds of staff and management. In fact, initial attitudes should be freely discussed. Skepticism should be openly tolerated. Management and staff should treat plan preparation as a feasibility study. Therefore, depending on the organization's situation, the merits of the plan can be honestly evaluated.

Normally a task force is selected for this feasibility study. We suggest that the president in small companies and the plant manager, controller, personnel manager, and at least three others from representative areas of the company be chosen. The key idea for selection and formation of this group is that representation be made from important functional areas of the firm as well as positions of leadership. For example, in some firms the maintenance function may be greatly affected by a high rate of suggestions triggered by the plan. Also the formation of opinion about the plan by an informal leader (e.g., from the R and D group) could be enhanced by placing such a person on the task force.

No one wants to be told what to read, and yet only the management and staff are equipped to put forth the effort of reading about the plan. We can honestly report that one comprehensive set of information that all designated management and staff should read consists of two other books and one booklet. These are

C. F. Frost, J. H. Wakely, and R. A. Ruh, *The Scanlon Plan for Organization Development: Identity, Participation and Equity,* The Michigan State University Press, East Lansing, 1974.

F. G. Lesieur (Ed.), *The Scanlon Plan: A Frontier in Labor-Management Cooperation,* Technology Press, Cambridge, Mass., and Wiley, New York, 1958.

The National Commission of Productivity and Work Quality, *A Plant-Wide Productivity Plan in Action: Three Years of Experience with the Scanlon Plan,* Washington, D.C., May, 1975.

All other references are listed in the comprehensive bibliography. We know of managers who have read every article on that list. That kind of effort certainly is not entirely necessary. We encourage you to read the sources mentioned above as a minimum. However, keep your discussions centered on your organization and the plan, not what Parker Pen did or what Atwood Manufacturing did. What works for one firm may not work for you. But you also can get valuable assistance by learning from other's efforts and mistakes.

It is reasonable that the designated management and staff begin with this book in this fashion:

1. Skim the entire book to familiarize yourself with its organization and contents.
2. Develop discussions based on the steps required for installation as outlined in Figure 2.1.
3. The accounting functions should be assigned Chapter 4 specifically. All members of the task force should review its general contents.
4. Begin discussion sessions based on the checklist of conditions in Chapter 2; that is, the results of Section 2.2 lead to general discussions concerning where the firm is and where it should be. Have everyone answer the checklist. Consolidate the results. Focus meaningful discussion on those areas in which management objectives and practical realities differ. Let us take a concrete example:

DISCUSSION LEADER. Our total average score from the checklist is 48. We feel that is good enough but we'd like to improve on some of those factors. Here is the breakdown.

(He hands out an item-by-item analysis.)

We show the greatest difference between the feeling of being informed about information vital to the functioning of the firm. That's number seven on the checklist. Since we are the guys who filled this out, let's pursue some current examples which the scanlon plan would have handled.

At this point, the discussion leader acknowledges that perceptions between the ideal and actual are far apart. He attempts to focus attention on how the structure of the plan, not individual personalities, might decrease this discrepancy. At the end of this discussion the leader should summarize the information and feelings that surfaced. We suggest taking each point in the order of greatest discrepancy. List the areas in which agreement is unanimous. List the areas in which honest disagreement occurs. Save this list for future discussion.

Remember that the checklist shows discrepancy and magnitude on the scale. Thus, you as a discussion leader may be totally unhappy with the consensus if it occurs in the below-average range. Probe as to why expectations are so low. What could be done to raise them? Would the plan help in raising them by giving everyone a stake in the rewards?

3.2 MOLDING PROPER ATTITUDES

Management is always driven by the idea that things could be better. Conversely, the workers often feel that their situation could be better. Thus, it is the mutual acknowledgement that higher levels of cooperation, participation, communication, and productivity are obtainable. If enough members of the firm believe this is so, the molding of proper attitudes is a viable task. It reinforces the climate of productive work attitudes.

Just how is this done? Initially, we are referring to management and staff only. Thus the status quo or equilibrium of yesterday is going to be examined for a new kind of future. Change itself is a powerful force. However, the change contemplated here is a structural one that superimposes itself on the regular organization. Expect those skeptics and those with low expectations to adjust their attitudes as definite assignments within the structure of the plan are made. For example, in Section 3.3 we deal with planning for installation. There are assignments to be performed that require a good manager to act professionally, regardless of his inner beliefs. It has happened in other scanlon companies that lukewarm managers catch on fire when they are called on to carry out assignments for plan objectives. This happens because of the identity of personal goals merging with corporate goals. Research consistently shows managerial attitudes increasing favorably toward the plan over time.

As a responsible leader of the firm or of the task force, ask each member of the firm to set aside narrow self-interests in favor of improving the firm's overall productivity. Perhaps company loyalty is an outdated term, but making employment count is only achieved because the firm is an instrument for cooperative work behavior. For example, we all understand selfish behavior. Yet, individuals and businesses are not completely selfish, because we believe in rules about fair play. Our value system reinforces the notion of teamwork, coordination, and winning through the specialized efforts of others. Thus, just as the whole is greater than the sum of the parts, the firm is the perfect instrument for productive teamwork because of its special division of labor. Careful and complete understanding of this premise molds proper attitudes at all levels of the firm. What is good for the firm is staying competitive. True job security is only offered by the firm that is viable in its markets. Thus, the scanlon plan is a development system that maximizes the chances for both job security and cash bonuses.

3.3 PLANNING FOR INSTALLATION

Since the management and staff discussions are favorable, it is important to consider how the scanlon plan can be introduced, explained, and hopefully installed. The following steps assume the firm handles its own plan and does not bring in outside help.

Remember Figure 2.1? You are at stage II but moving quickly into stage III. As we indicated in Chapter 2, some employees know that there is "something coming up." Thus, nothing you do of a formal nature will be complete news to them, but it will help to dispel some false perceptions.

We recommend the employee survey before you announce the plan. Appendix A is suitable, but you may modify it any way you wish. Since the survey is to be repeated yearly, design it carefully so that you may make comparisons over time. For example, do not change the wording or scales of the items you plan to repeat. The benefits of an annual survey are many, but it is a valuable aid in evaluating the impact of the scanlon plan on the quality of work. Chapter 7 provides you with an evaluation strategy.

If you do not decide to use an employee survey, the next step is to prepare for the presentation of the plan. In addition to the comprehensive chronologies in Sections 2.9 and 2.10, Chapter 4 has been pursued parallel by your controller and his staff. They have reported that the formula is constructed. After review with the management-staff task force, it is clear that only timing is left as a factor. The plan should be started when there is a good chance for a bonus in the trial year only. For example, let us say that January, February, and March are poor business months but April is normally a good business month.

In the trial year it is a good idea to start the plan in April so that a bonus can be experienced. In the following years the plan should be on a twelve-month basis.

Now, we recommend the following procedures in presenting the plan:

1. Call in your foremen or middle-level supervisors to announce and discuss the plan.
2. Distribute a memo concerning your announcement of the plan and your intentions. Key ideas to incorporate in your memo should center on:

    What is the scanlon plan?
    Why does management wish to try it?
    Who started the plan?
    Assumptions underlying the plan.
    How the bonus works.
    What is a production committee?
    What is a screening committee?
    How do you participate in the scanlon plan?

3. Visit each department or break the work force into small groups, and further discuss the plan.
4. Indicate that the personnel manager, or other designated person, will handle follow-up questions. Also, hand out a brief memo of understanding. Announce that a larger, complete version is being developed to explain company policy and will be available for reading in draft form in the personnel office (in Appendix B we give you a model memo of understanding).
5. If there is another scanlon plan in operation nearby, request permission to visit the plant, and possibly attend a screening-committee meeting. The authors, the Scanlon Plan Associates, and interested consultants can advise you of nearby scanlon plan firms. It is advisable to take two or three respected employees along. Their opinions and feedback will help sell the plan.
6. After these steps, you will have ample opportunity for all to discuss the plan.

However, now that the formula is ready, place a large copy of it in a conspicuous place, such as the cafeteria. Hope that some of the employees will push some numbers through the formula. Our experience has shown that if two or three employees out of 200 understand the calculation in detail, that may be all that is necessary. Their opinion as trusted experts will be sought out. In the beginning, building trust in the calculation is more important than understanding.

3.4 THE ELECTION AND RECORD KEEPING

This section deals with how to organize a scanlon plan election and how to handle records associated with the election meeting.

Announce a formal meeting after the events in Section 3.3 have occurred (i.e., the memo about the plan, the small-group discussion meetings). This formal meeting serves the purpose of final discussion and a vote to try the plan for a trial year. If at all possible, let this meeting include everyone. Showing the work force the importance of this meeting by concentrating everyone together at the same time is a clear demonstration of the plan's importance.

Meet in the cafeteria or, better yet, in a nearby facility. Your agenda, again, is to discuss the plan, answer questions, and then vote.

As to the vote, be prepared to count the votes quickly with a blue-ribbon committee. Agree that 80 percent must be the cutoff point for acceptance of the plan. Establish this 80 percent figure in advance so that the counting committee can destroy the ballots as soon as they reach the cutoff figure; that is, if there are 200 employees in total with 185 present, the cutoff is 148, or 80 percent of those present. Announce the results as soon as possible.

3.5 COMMITTEE STRUCTURE

Assuming a positive vote, the next step is to have an election for production- and screening-committee membership. A description of the production and screening committees, their governing procedures, and guidelines for handling suggestions should be distributed. This will aid the work force in determining their vote. Decide on the number of production committees needed and the number of committee members that will give you good representation in departments, shifts, and so on. Whatever numbers you decide on could be changed later if circumstances dictate (terms of office are covered in Chapter 5). The principle governing numbers is that you want adequate representativeness of the entire work force by work function.

It is unrealistic to expect people to campaign or volunteer themselves for the first production-committee vote. It is simply too early in the game for the structure of the plan to be understood. Therefore, persuasion of key employees in each department is a wise consideration. Although the vote for members of each production committee should reflect the wishes of the employees, someone must be on the ballot. At least for the first year, select people who you feel would do a good job. Talk to them, and get them to see you genuine concern about getting the involvement system off to a good start.

One concern you should have is to get good representation of all areas of the

firm reflected in the committee system. Structure the production committees as
you would a sampling plan. Be sure that departments, shifts, and functional
areas of the firm are represented by their own production committees. The size of
these committees could be the supervisor plus two other elected members, but in
some very large departments more representatives may be needed or, perhaps,
two committees set up along functional lines. Remember small committees work
best. With this in mind, the size of the screening commitee should never exceed
20.

Tenure of production-committee members is usually for one year. Plan to
rotate people through the screening-committee assignments. Consider limiting
scanlon office holding to a two-year period in order to guarantee maximum
exposure to scanlon committees to as many responsible employees as possible.

Natural first questions about serving on production committees tend to focus
on what to do and whether is there a change in the authority system? The
foreman is still the supervisor and the manager still the boss, but the involvement
system seeks input from all employees, as channeled through the production
committees first. Employees serving on these committees do not overrule the
foreman or acceptance or rejection of suggestions. Any divided opinions will be
cleared up in the screening committee. Thus the emphasis is on collaboration and
participation in the processing of suggestions. For these reasons you can see how
important it is to guide the selection of trial-year production-committee
members. Make sure your first election is a guided, organized event.

The ballot results give you two outcomes: (1) members of the production
committee; (2) the highest vote getter by department should be considered for
screening-committee membership. However, management should exercise care
and deliberation as to whom to select for membership of the screening commit- ·
tee, especially in the trial year. A description of committee functions follows:

1. *Description of Production Committee.* In order to make use of the
ideas people have about how to do their jobs better, the scanlon plan sets up a
production committee in each department. The production committee is made
up of the supervisor of the department and at least one employee elected by the
people to represent their ideas. Suggestions for improved operations are
presented to the supervisor, assistant supervisor, or representative. In order to
keep suggestions from being lost or forgotten, they should be written, and the
suggester should keep a copy. At least once a month the employee representatives and the supervisor sit down and go over the suggestions which have been
submitted. Suggestions which do not affect other departments and which do not
require more than specified dollar amounts are put into effect at the department level by the production committee. Suggestions which affect several
departments or require more than the specified amount are referred to
the screening committee. Also, any suggestions rejected at the production-

committee level often receive "another hearing" by the screening committee.

2. *The Role of Production-Committee Representatives.* Production-committee members have extremely important roles to play in the successful operation of the scanlon plan. They have been elected by the people in their departments to help them get action on their suggestions for ways of doing their jobs better and making bigger bonuses. There are many reasons why ideas people have do not get acted on. People may sometimes be too shy to offer suggestions, or they may be embarrassed at not being able to express themselves well. They may feel that their supervisor does not want them to offer suggestions (for information concerning the role of supervisor, see Chapter 6). It is the job of the production-committee representatives to do their best to see that these things happen as infrequently as possible. More specifically, production-committee representatives should do the following:

1. Ask the people they represent to submit suggestions.
2. Discuss suggestions with the people who submit them in order to make sure they are understood and, if possible, improve on suggestions.
3. Inform the supervisor as soon as possible of suggestions on which they may wish to take immediate action.
4. Follow up to make sure suggestions are acted on as soon as possible.
5. Inform the people concerned of the status of suggestions and the reasons for any delays.
6. If a person disagrees with the treatment his suggestion receives, take his objection to the supervisor and, if necessary, the screening committee.

3. *The Role of the Screening Committee.* The screening committee has three activities that make up its principal role. These are:

1. Review and evaluate suggestions
2. Review and discuss the bonus (or deficit) and,
3. Discuss economic principles affecting the viability of the firm

The greatest amount of time is spent on evaluating suggestions. The screening committee must evaluate all suggestions referred by the production committees.

The purpose of this evaluation is to process all relevant information (task-force committees can pursue the feasibility of a given suggestion) and to insure that collective points of view intersect at the point of decision. *The decision, however, is the plant manager's.* The procedure for processing suggestions is spelled out in Section 3.7.

The second principal activity of the screening committee is the review and discussion of the bonus (or deficit). Facts and figures used in the calculation of the bonus are carefully delineated by the controller or accounting function. While Section 3.7 and Appendix C.2 show how to catalog this information, this review of the calculation with key personnel offers deeper understanding to those involved as representatives of the plan.

The last principal activity of the screening committee is to discuss economic principles affecting the viability of the firm. This activity grows over time, but becomes one of the most important facets of the screening committee's role. Mature scanlon companies know that discussion of why a firm can and can't do what it wants to do surfaces within the screening committee meeting. As it happens, the screening committee becomes a task oriented classroom for merging individual goals with corporate goals to achieve success. This identity becomes crystallized in the screening committee discussions of the economic facts of life surrounding each firm.

The committee-function descriptions may be copied or modified by you for distribution to the work force. They are also suitable for inclusion in your memo of understanding. And now, since the plan was voted in, it is appropriate to print this memo. Remember Appendix B presents a model memo. Also included are forms for handling suggestions and reporting minutes of the screening committee (see Appendix C).

3.6 MEMO OF UNDERSTANDING—PRINCIPLES

The memo of understanding is a document suitable for printing as a company booklet. In it (see Appendix B, for example) you want to cover these points:

1. What the plan is.
2. How and why it got started (historically and at your firm).
3. Principles of the plan.
4. How the bonus calculation works.
5. How the committee system works.
6. Procedures for handling suggestions.

Additionally, if your firm is unionized, you will review it with the union. Acknowledge its existence in both the union contract and cross-reference this acknowledgment in your memo of understanding.

3.7 PROCEDURE FOR HANDLING SUGGESTIONS— THE INVOLVEMENT SYSTEM

We cover this last in this chapter, but it should be included in the memo preceding the committee elections. Also, this discussion belongs in the memo of understanding. Although we offer concrete procedures for handling suggestions, it is the process of handling them that ensures the involvement system; that is, every effort should be made to deal with people face-to-face on all aspects of suggestion handling. The procedures that follow should not become a bureaucratic device that interferes with clear communication.

1. Someone with a suggestion should submit it in writing to the supervisor or representative.
2. The representative or supervisor should discuss the suggestion with the person making it, and others who may be affected, and take appropriate action as soon as possible.
3. At least once a month the production committee (supervisor and representatives) should meet. In this meeting they should review the status of previously discussed suggestions, expedite delayed suggestions, and discuss any new suggestions.
4. Suggestions which involve more than the specified amount in costs should be referred to the screening committee.
5. The production committee should assign the responsibility for following through on delayed suggestions to one of its members.
6. The production committee should keep records of its activities. These records should include all the suggestions submitted to the committee and the status of these suggestions—action taken, action proposed, and so on (see Appendix C for record keeping).
7. By a certain date of each month the production committee should submit all the suggestions it has received during that month to the screening committee.
8. All suggestions and the actions taken by the production committee will be published each month before the screening-committee meeting.

The production committee can take one of five actions on suggestions received. These five dispositions are:

1. Accept the suggestion and use it.
2. Reject the suggestion with carefully stated reasons.
3. Accept the suggestion and place it under investigation. (Suggestions are normally placed under investigation when there are insufficient facts to make a decision or when it is necessary to ascertain if net savings offset the cost of putting it into effect).
4. Accepted by recommending to the screening committee. (These suggestions normally are those which a production committee feels should be placed into effect but cost over a specified amount to implement).
5. If committee members cannot agree on acceptability of a suggestion, these are referred to the screening committee.

3.8 SOME THOUGHTS ON INVOLVEMENT-SYSTEM PROCESS

Let us consider how the involvement system works with people. First, the purpose is to produce productivity-related suggestions. Complaints, grievances, and safety suggestions simply do not belong. This must be communicated effectively through the production committee. This means that during the trial year your committees may indeed accept suggestions which are not productivity-related. They do this to encourage involvement. But let us be practical. Bob Smith submits suggestions all the time, even before scanlon. He can tolerate harder evaluation. Susan Black never says "boo" to anybody, and she submits a weak suggestion after three months. The production committee must understand its primary objective is to reinforce and teach Susan Black to submit more and better suggestions.

Second, it is a sound policy to permit your production committee to accept any suggestion if it meets these two criteria:

1. It costs less than x amount. This amount depends on the size of the organization and cost constraints. This amount places some discretion into the hands of the departmental or production committee.
2. It does not affect other departments.

All suggestions not rejected or meeting these two criteria are sent to the screening committee. One ground rule for the trial year is that when in doubt as to the disposition of a suggestion, refer it to the screening committee.

Third, the screening committee is normally made up of one-half management and one-half workers. These meetings are to be held monthly and also coincide with bonus announcements. The first meeting will be the toughest and longest. Here is what you can expect:

1. Everyone will expect the president or plant manager to listen to each suggestion and make Solomon-like decisions.
2. There may be hesitancy and reticence to speak freely.
3. Some may be defensive about the usefulness of suggestions from their area or speak disparagingly of them, and so on.

All suggestions should be typed in the format specified (see Appendix C). The agenda for each meeting will cover current business, expectations about bonus possibilities, and these suggestions. However, let department representatives explain their suggestions. Develop an agenda that is comfortable with your management style. For example, encourage full but concise participation.

If a production-committee representative has not prepared a suggestion properly, ask questions that will point this out. For example:

1. Did the suggestion maker "talk up" his suggestion with others to get their opinion before writing up the suggestion?
2. Did the authors of the suggestions state the problem well?
3. Is all the relevant information included, or could the suggester assist in its development?
4. Is the suggestion going to influence productivity through cost savings, quality or quantity improvement?

This first meeting will set the tone for all the others. Sometimes the first meeting takes half a day. Clearly, management's role is to make every attempt to hear out each suggestion. You may notice your blue-collar colleagues on the screening committee start to wilt toward the end of a long meeting. Do your best to give every sincere suggestion the benefit of good discussion.

Let us summarize the first meeting. Since we encouraged you to get the involvement system going as soon as possible, there may not have been time for a bonus period. If there was, announce it in the meeting. We believe it is a good idea to have a prescreening-committee meeting with departmental supervisors, since most of them will not be in the screening-committee meeting. In fact, large organizations could have as many as 400 supervisors. The screening committee should be of manageable size, about ten to twenty people. However, by reviewing the bonus announcement before the screening-committee meeting, this puts some positive communication into the hands of first-line supervisors. It is advisable for the supervisor to announce the bonus or deficit in their department. In this way, the supervisor is not being bypassed by some screening committee members who could be in a given supervisor's department. Also, it provides an opportunity for the supervisor to explain why a bonus or deficit occurred. After this supervisors' meeting, immediately begin the screening-committee meeting by announcing the bonus or deficit and begin reviewing suggestions.

Persuasively discuss why some suggestions are productivity-related and others are not. Ask what the expected savings are. Ask when the benefits will offset the costs. Ask if choices were offered, which suggestion should be funded from limited resources. Never be timid in tabling a suggestion for further study. Appendix C demonstrates one excellent way to handle and report the minutes of the screening-committee meetings.

Please note that a careful analysis of many years of suggestion making shows that irritants are a common type of suggestion. They will disappear as you communicate through the screening committee (see Section 6.4).

3.9 SUMMING UP

This chapter deals with providing the management and staff just the amount of necessary information to get started with the scanlon plan.

Although we say "just the amount necessary," you may even feel overloaded with information right now. However, we are putting into your hands key information and principles. Generally, we refer you to other areas of the book for more specifics. If we do not, in our judgment the material is pertinent now.

To that end, reading assignments and a discussion model are offered. Those assignments, as well as the material on molding attitudes, require careful interpretation by you for your situation.

Last, the material on installation of the plan, elections, memo of understanding, and the involvement system are all synthesized from many successful scanlon firms. Again, the ideas and descriptions in Sections 3.4 to 3.6 work well elsewhere. Your task is to evaluate this information in the context of your firm's environment.

EQUITABLE SHARING OF BENEFITS
Formula Calculations

4

This chapter covers a number of major areas and is perhaps the most difficult chapter, because it deals with measurement. It is also one of the most important chapters, because we cover how the productivity-improvement aspects of the scanlon plan are tied together. In condensed terms, we discuss how you can proceed through a diagnostic analysis. We also present several possible formulas. Go through the chapter slowly. Remember that decisions will have to be made on a large range of variables and that ultimately many of these will be discussed with employees. Unfortunately, we do not have any simplistic techniques that solve all your measurement problems with one sweep of the hand.

Before beginning our detailed discussion, a few comments might serve a useful purpose. Among "students" of the scanlon plan, both advocates and critics, considerable disagreement exists on the role of measurement in the scanlon plan. Some experts feel that too much emphasis on measurement will ultimately cause the plan to fail. After extensive studying of the scanlon plan and working with actual scanlon plan companies, our perceptions in this area differ considerably from those of these experts. Since the scanlon plan is a productivity-sharing plan, a fairly accurate measurement of productivity is essential to the success of the plan. You must find something that works for you.

But at the same time, a fairly accurate measurement does not ensure success if the practices of a particular installation are manipulative. Hence, the measurement system should be viewed as hygienic—a necessary but not sufficient cause of ultimate scanlon plan success. Our study of the scanlon plan literature generally confirms this belief. Few individuals would take a simplistic view of the organizational variables in operation under the plan; the same should be said of the measurement variables of the plan.

The scanlon plan typically is associated with only the so-called ratio method of calculation briefly discussed in Chapter 2. We feel this is unfortunate, because over time many successful plan companies move away from this method of calculation by generally becoming more sophisticated in their sharing-of-benefits measurements. This is true more recently than in the past and is probably due to the higher inflation rate. Additionally, this method of calculation does not work for some organizations. Some of you might wonder whether they are still the scanlon plan if the ratio method is not used. The answer is yes. Hence, one of the goals of this book is to get people to realize that the principle of equitable sharing and all others related to the involvement, accountability, and identity processes are the important variables, not just the method of calculating the bonus. The bonus is just one of the payoffs for these processes.

Do not expect all employees ever to completely understand the bonus calculation and all the variables that influence it. It takes years to educate the majority of employees regarding the facts of life of the scanlon plan calculation. Because of this fact, building trust in the reliability of the calculation is an extremely important and a formidable task. This general area is extensively discussed in Chapter 6.

We hope that at least the members of the task force read this chapter. The accountants involved must analyze it in detail to determine which measurement system is best for your company. Appendix D also presents valuable tools to help all managers evaluate the accounting function. Do not skip over it, since it contains some valuable ideas that will help you establish objectives for the scanlon plan.

4.1 DIAGNOSTIC ANALYSIS

Why make a diagnostic analysis? The most commonly mentioned reason is to develop a productivity-measurement model; the scanlon plan is a productivity-improvement plan. Until some sort of system is developed to measure productivity, the scanlon plan will not be ready for implementation. Coupled with this purpose is a related one of finding out about yourselves by asking a series of questions on system sophistication.

You will have to make a large number of decisions regarding the type of calculation that would be most appropriate under the circumstances and what to include and exclude from the calculation. It may be appropriate at this point to review Appendix D on the economic facts of life as well as your accounting system's sophistication. One quick glance at this appendix will tell the accounting function whether these topics and our advice are pertinent to your situation.

Additionally, you will have to decide who will do what when the scanlon plan progresses toward the implementation stages. All these are essentially management decisions. The diagnostic analysis should be assigned to the controller, with deadlines established. If deadlines are not established, a firm's accountants can always find enough other work to keep them more than amply busy in today's financially oriented, rapidly changing business climate.

4.2 INGREDIENTS OF A PRODUCTIVITY-SHARING CALCULATION

In simple terms, the scanlon plan is normally thought of as a productivity-sharing plan, even if we define productivity either very narrowly or broadly. When we talk about productivity sharing, we must by necessity discuss measurement and, in this case, productivity measurement. Now you might ask a question whether a productivity-measurement model can ever be developed that is a perfect measure of productivity? The probable answer is no, simply because we can never agree on what specific criteria should be met in attaining such a system. Of course, this is essentially the same problem confronted in designing any financial-information system. At the same time you should keep certain criteria in mind when designing your productivity-measurement system. What do you really want from the system, and how best can this be achieved? Monitor it over time if for no other reason than to isolate possible problem areas. You should also keep in mind that all the criteria are never attained at the same time and that some of them are quite subjective. Basically you should not disagree with our criteria. Naturally you may add any others you feel are important. In designing and maintaining the system over time, however, they are all important criteria to keep in mind and monitor.

An extremely important point should be made. Since the bonus system is essentially a reward system, or reinforcement for good performance, employees at all levels will adjust to the calculation you install. So remember, try not to install a calculation that may encourage personnel to react in a way you really do not desire. Monitor what is happening so that corrective action can be taken. More on this later.

The remainder of this section contains brief discussions of the criteria of productivity-sharing calculations. Each of the measurement systems discussed in the remainder of this chapter is evaluated in light of these criteria.

4.2.1 Is the Calculation a Good Measure of Performance over Time?

As you will see in later sections in this chapter, what starts as a good measurement may rapidly deteriorate. Attainment of these criteria depends on the sophistication of your measurement system and on what is included in your calculation. At this point you may or may not have a good idea of the objectives you hope the scanlon plan will assist in attaining. Here we are discussing financial rather than behavioral objectives. We provide information to assist you in setting objectives, but we encourage you to start with most labor costs. Because of the nature of your operations, you may decide on a broad calculation such as labor and material or even profit sharing. Perhaps you may decide on a narrower one such as direct labor. We discourage using material and direct labor as starting points.

You must establish your objectives. Are you willing to pay for an increase in labor productivity based on an increase in volume? Do you want to include market prices or only cost savings? Do you really want a form of profit sharing? You must decide what your performance goals are, or you might later say, "That's not what I really wanted."

A word of caution is appropriate at this point. Do not be sold "down the road" on a standardized calculation (e.g., the single ratio) that does not fit your organization. Remember, you must live with the calculation; you must have the information to adjust it when necessary; and you must perceive that you can "control" the calculation by understanding what is happening to it over time. If you have a fairly satisfactory profit-sharing plan and want to use the other scanlon principle "to get things going," so be it. Decide on your objectives early. Nothing is more discouraging than hearing a controller say,

> I can't get a good feeling for the calculation. How can I really tell whether it's accurate or not? If I don't feel that it is accurate, how can I convince other managers and employees?

Take great care in designing your system. The remainder of this chapter is directed to help you in this activity. But remember, when determining your objectives and calculation, think about what could happen in the future. Do you think you can live with it?

4.2.2 Is the Calculation Perceived as a Fair Measure of Performance?

This undoubtedly is the most problematic area for many scanlon companies. Why? Numerous reasons can be found in practice, but perhaps the primary reasons are that the measurement system is normally designed and maintained by accountants and that not enough care was taken when the calculation was originally established. Although financial information has grown in importance and influence in recent years, many individuals still have a natural dislike and distrust in anything financial. Accountants make various changes in the calculation over the years and make errors requiring revision of previous calculations.

These latter problems can develop the feeling that the scanlon plan calculation is manipulative. This is why frequent changes in the calculation are not advisable unless economic conditions change drastically. All changes should, of course, be made carefully and be well explained. For example, it is relatively easy to have a trade-off between differing qualities of material and labor. Be careful in this area, because employees soon figure out the "game" that you are playing. Your strategies must be clear and fair.

Traditionally, some accountants and other measurement personnel have done a poor job in educating managers and employees as to the economic facts of life regarding the calculation. One frequently hears accountants in scanlon plan companies making such comments as: "They (employees) just won't accept the facts as they are," or "I won't talk to him again, he just won't listen," or "Why should I spend my time talking to employees who are not rational and don't trust anything I do." These comments are symptomatic of lack of trust and ultimately could result in the downfall of the scanlon plan.

A desirable direction to take is to develop the feeling that the measurement personnel are really working for the scanlon plan, because they are its resource workers. If employees can get the feeling that these experts are there to help them and the scanlon plan, relations can improve greatly from both employees' and measurement experts' points of view.

Building this trust in and understanding of the calculation begins at the top corporate level and moves down the organization. It is an important challenge for accountants, other measurement experts, managers, and employees alike.

4.2.3 Is It Too Complex for Employees to Understand?

This criterion takes considerable educational efforts on the part of accountants and other interested personnel. Complete understanding by all employees is never possible, nor should it be a goal, since the effort probably would not be worth the costs involved. You must also be on guard against creating a calculation which becomes a "monster" and impossible to explain. Complaints about lack of understanding are most common when bonuses are declining or negative. We will show you many techniques that have been tried over the years by scanlon plan companies. These techniques will assist you in achieving your goals of increasing the understanding of the calculation and variables that influence the calculation.

4.2.4 Is the Calculation Easily Administered?

You should not install a productivity-measurement model that cannot be calculated on a timely basis and without excessive man-hour requirements. Ideally, a desirable goal is to make the calculation, even if only roughly, on a weekly basis. You do not want a calculation that you may lose control of. You can judge each of the calculations, discussed later in this chapter, in light of your own accounting system's sophistication and plan objectives.

4.2.5   Is the Calculation Flexible Enough to Meet Rapidly Changing Economic Conditions?

Scanlon plan companies hopefully become among the most competitive in their industries. When designing a productivity-measurement system, you do not want to adopt a system that seriously hinders this goal. Do not put yourself in a straitjacket by losing control of what is happening in both the internal and external economic environment. The first necessary step in preventing this from happening is realizing that this is a possibility with some of the common calculations.

4.2.6   Is the Calculation Useful in Isolating Problem Areas in Directing All Employees' Efforts in Resolving Them and Increasing Productivity?

Here you can run into the problem encountered by some scanlon plan companies of having either a calculation so general or broad that few can relate to it or too narrow so as to lose flexibility. Ideally a large, multidivision company should have one scanlon plan for the entire company, but the average manager and employee have a great deal of difficulty relating to such a calculation. The motivational impact may deteriorate, as will the other criteria discussed above.

If this is true, you might wonder, "Why not install individual incentives?"— the other side of the incentive continuum. The simple fact is that too many interdependencies and measurement problems exist. For example, direct labor could increase its productivity at the expense of more quality control. How do you measure the productivity of a personnel or accounting employee? You cannot have a total, organizational incentive system, such as the scanlon plan, based on individual incentives because of measurement problems. It also defeats one of the main goals of the scanlon plan—increasing productivity through better coordination and cooperation.

If we cannot or should not measure all individual performance, how can you establish a productivity-measurement system? The scanlon plan is almost always established on the basis of past cost relationships. If you increase volume without a proportional increase in inputs (normally only labor), you increase labor productivity. For example, if you increase sales volume in constant dollars without a proportional increase in labor costs, the "financial" productivity of labor has increased. It may be due to employees working smarter or harder, capital expenditures, technologies, or general business conditions. The calculation should isolate the areas and departments which are contributing to this changing productivity along with isolating problem areas so that corrective action can be suggested. Although a calculation provides valuable information to improve decision making, it may also make management's job more difficult. If the calculation does not provide the information, other accounting information should do so.

4.3 BEGINNING THE DIAGNOSTIC ANALYSIS

In this part we recommend a straightforward diagnostic approach that most manufacturing companies find useful in developing the ratio method of calculation. In later sections of the chapter we discuss diagnostic procedures for other calculation methods which can even be used by firms in the service industries. We suggest, however, that all potential scanlon plan companies read through the remainder of this chapter for possible ideas.

Before beginning the quantitative diagnostic analysis, you should evaluate your accounting system sophistication. Additional ideas on your economic facts of life and attitudes regarding the financial function are found in Appendix D.

4.4 DIAGNOSTIC ANALYSIS FOR THE RATIO METHOD OF CALCULATION

Most companies installing the scanlon plan normally start with the ratio of personnel costs to total sales value of production, as we discussed briefly in Chapter 2. They start by developing the following ratio from historical records:

$$base\ ratio = \frac{total\ personnel\ costs\ to\ be\ included}{sales\ value\ of\ production}$$

In any subsequent period, whenever the actual labor costs included are less than the allowed labor costs (i.e., actual month sales value of production times the base-ratio percentage), a bonus is earned. This section covers only the procedures you use in developing a base ratio. The next section discusses the rationale of including or excluding certain items when developing the calculation, and following sections cover detailed methods of calculation, ranging from the single ratio of labor method to profit sharing.

At this point, you probably have a basic question: Why do most companies start their scanlon plans with this method of calculation? Partly from tradition; that is, the scanlon plan has historically been associated with the allowed-labor-percentage calculation as opposed to a profit-sharing or *value-added* calculation. Other reasons are that it may be a fairly good measure of performance over time, it is understandable, and it is easily administered. Finally, what better way is there to start such a system than by making this basic statement, "Beat your past performance and you will earn a bonus." You can normally say this more easily with a labor-only calculation than a broader one based on profit sharing because of the number of variables that influence the latter.

Now, how do you get started in developing a base ratio or percentage? You get started by preparing an analysis to compare past labor costs with *sales value of production*. Figure 4.1 shows the basic steps that are involved. By now, you should have a good idea of the steps involved. For the time being, we assume that you do this for a plant or company as a whole and not worry about such things as product mix and so on.

In preparing the analysis, you may be surprised to find, as do many companies, that the total labor cost is a reasonably constant percentage of sales value of production. Indirect or resource workers or fringe benefits may replace

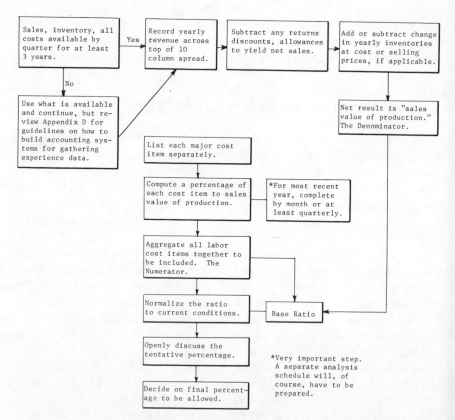

Figure 4.1   Steps to development of allowed-labor percentage.

direct labor over a period of time or vice versa, but the total percentage remains fairly constant. If this is not true, you, of course, could have problems.

In preparing the analysis, the normal tendency is to lump a large number of costs together or take the totals directly from the aggregated financial statements. This is a mistake, since you are losing a good opportunity to investigate cost relationships and trends over time. The more detailed analysis, the better. These might require some digging through old general ledgers. Time spent before installation may decrease problems later in the evaluative process.

Additionally, if your company is a manufacturing concern, we suggest that you consider valuing inventories at selling prices in the diagnostic analysis and in computing the monthly bonus. The reason for this is that you do not have to worry about inventories, just production based on selling prices. For example, if something is one-third completed in a month, you would allow one-third of the final selling price for that product in that month. This also increases the smoothing of the bonus results, since sales normally are more cyclical during the year than production. If significant amounts are added to inventories during different times of the year, you should be reluctant to give full credit until the product is sold, that is, until a final selling price is determined. If you sell merchandise at significant discounts during certain times of the year, you do not want to give full credit until sold. Additionally, you will not be able to get your analysis to reconcile to net income if you value inventories at selling prices.

All these variables are considered when determining the original base ratio so that problems should result only when major changes are made in your marketing strategy. If you want to include inventories at their selling price in the analysis, a good estimate can be obtained by adding the normal average markup to total product costs for each of the years. If no estimate is possible for earlier years, you must use costs instead of selling prices. Some firms use selling prices for finished goods and cost for work-in-process inventories. Independent of which method is used, you should be consistent in both the analysis and after the plan is established. You should also realize that technically this is sales value of production only if inventory is valued at selling prices.

On with the analysis. Table 4.1 presents a three-year analysis in summarized form. A five-year analysis is preferred. Your organization may not be this complex, or you may not have the old records in as much detail. For this example, we are assuming a manufacturing firm with moderate complexity and fairly detailed records. Work with your records in as much detail as possible to obtain a general feeling of trends. For the immediate past year, prepare the analysis by month (or quarter) on a separate sheet. You will be able to see what would have happened if you actually had had the calculation installed. You can use back-up sheets for some of the details, such as manufacturing costs. Although the details are not presented in Table 4.1, you might find it desirable to separate out the variable and fixed portions of all costs over the

Table 4.1 Sample Diagnostic Analysis Three Past Years (in $000)

	Year 1		Year 2		Year 3 (Most Recent Year)	
	$	%	$	%	$	%
1. Gross sales	10,000	100	13,000	110.3	10,500	99.0
2. Less: Sales returns	(200)		(200)		(400)	
3. Sales discounts	(200)		(240)		(300)	
4. Other allowances	(100)		(75)		(200)	
5.	(500)	(5.0)	(515)	(4.4)	(900)	(8.5)
6. Net sales (1–5)	9,500	95.0	12,485	105.9	9,600	90.5
7. Net change in inventory during the year at cost or selling price (+ for increases; – for decreases)	+500	5.0	–700	5.9	+1,000	9.5
8. Sales value of production (6 ± 7)	10,000	100.0	11,785	100.0	10,600	100.0
Less: Actual labor-related costs:						
9. Direct labor	800	8.0	890	7.5	868	8.2
10. Factory indirect	200	2.0	220	1.9	222	2.1
11. Overtime premium (factory)	40	0.4	80	0.7	32	0.3
12. Factory supervisory (foremen, etc.)	200	2.0	220	1.9	230	2.2
13. Engineering	100	1.0	110	0.9	118	1.1
14. Maintenance	110	1.1	140	1.2	135	1.3
15. Receiving and shipping	140	1.4	170	1.4	160	1.5
Factory fringe benefits:						
16. FICA	95	1.0	107	0.9	114	1.1
17. Unemployment	65	0.6	69	0.6	76	0.7
18. Workmen's compensation	50	0.5	60	0.5	54	0.5
19. Hospitalization	70	0.7	80	0.7	89	0.8
20. Vacation, holidays, retirement, etc.	110	1.1	130	1.1	140	1.3
21. Total factory labor costs (9 to 20)	1,980	19.8	2,276	19.3	2,238	21.1
Other labor costs:						
22. Research and development salaries	150	1.5	155	1.3	159	1.5
23. Selling salaries	100	1.0	120	1.0	135	1.3
24. General and administrative salaries	330	3.3	345	2.9	315	3.0

Table 4.1   (*continued*)

	Year 1		Year 2		Year 3 (Most Recent Year)	
	$	%	$	%	$	%
25. Taxes and other fringes on above (detailed)	100	1.0	125	1.1	130	1.2
26. Total other costs (22 to 25)	680	6.8	745	6.3	739	7.0
27. Total labor (people) costs (21 + 26)	2,660	26.6	3,021	25.6	2,977	28.1
Less: Other actual costs in detail:						
28. Material used	4,500	45.0	4,850	41.2	4,700	44.3
29. Other manufacturing costs	500	5.0	510	4.3	550	5.2
30. Other R and D expenses	400	4.0	420	3.6	430	4.1
31. Other selling expenses	200	2.0	210	1.8	230	2.2
32. Other general and administrative expenses	400	4.0	415	3.5	425	4.0
33. Total other costs and expenses (28 to 32)	6,000	60.0	6,405	54.4	6,335	59.7
34. Total normal costs and expenses (27 + 33)	8,660	86.6	9,426	80.0	9,312	87.8
Net before interest, taxes, etc. (8–34)	1,340	13.4	2,359	20.0	1,288	12.2

years analyzed if records permit. Finally, be careful of a lack of consistency which may affect comparability over the years. For example, changes in policies regarding interplant transfers, charges for corporate staff, or changes in inventory valuation methods among others may affect comparability.

Although Table 4.1 may appear complex, it is not. You may find it quite detailed because of the three years of figures shown (remember, you should prepare at least five years and break the most recent down by months if possible). This analysis was made somewhat complex because of significant inventory fluctuations. In actual practice you could use cost of goods sold for factory costs if inventories did not fluctuate significantly in percentage from the change percentage in net sales. This could, of course, be a major problem area but in practice seldom is. Note also that since ideally you should be using actual costs, you should be able to continue the analysis and reconcile to total net income, assuming that inventories are valued at costs rather than selling prices.

From Table 4.1 you can note a large number of interesting details. First, a large number of the costs vary quite closely with production. For example, when sales value of production (line 8) increased by 17.8 percent between years 1 and 2 (11,785/10,000), total labor costs (line 27) increased by 13.6 percent between the two years (3,021/2,660). This, of course, is what financial productivity is all about.

In this particular firm production is more stable than sales, as is often the case. Labor costs (line 27) are a large percentage of sales value of production (line 8) and fluctuated between 25.6 (year 2) and 28.1 percent (year 3). Year 3 (most recent year) is a major problem. Sales are dropping off about 20 percent in current dollars, and if we assume that the selling prices increased, the physical volume is probably decreasing even more. This could be the result of a recession or competition. In year 3, various returns and allowances (lines 2 to 5) increased, as might be expected in a poor year.

You should at this point see the usefulness of such a long-run analysis. One can get a good feel for the company over time. This same type of analysis can, of course, be made by major product lines or divisions. Section 4.15 of this chapter details the use of this analysis for product line or division.

Now let us assume that we determine that year 1 was our normal year and decide to include all people costs in the calculation. What would we establish as our base ratio? Look at Table 4.1. The total labor costs are 26.6 percent of sales value of production (line 27), so that this would be our base ratio. If we did set the base ratio at 26.6 percent, what would be the gross bonuses in years 2 and 3? First, try to figure it out on your own. However, the answer follows:

Gross Bonus Calculation Used in Table 4.1

Year 2

1. Sales value of production – year 2 (line 8)	$11,785,000
2. Allowed people costs (26.6% of (1))	3,134,810
3. Actual people costs (line 27, year 2)	3,021,000
Gross bonus (allowed − actual)	$ 113,810

Year 3 (Most Recent Year)

1. Sales value of production – year 3 (line 8)	$10,600,000
2. Allowed people costs (26.6%of (1))	2,819,600
3. Actual people costs (line 27, year 3)	2,977,000
Deficit (allowed − actual)	$ (157,400)

In this example, the gross bonus would be $113,810 in year 2 and a deficit of $157,400 in year 3. A number of points should be made here. When sales increased by 30 percent between years 1 and 2, apparently productivity of the work force did not significantly increase, as was discussed earlier; sales value of production increased only by 17.85 percent. Notice that the gross bonus looks small in year 2. If we assume the company actually went to the scanlon plan in year 2, the leverage is normally much greater than it might appear, because some employees do not participate in the bonus results. And, of course, bonus is not paid on fringe benefits.

Between years 2 and 3 production did not drop so much as sales (about 10 versus 20 percent respectively), which explains why the deficit in year 3 was not larger. In actual practice you might expect year 2's bonus to be much greater, and if costs were not better controlled than in the example, year 3's deficit would be greater. From this detailed example, we cannot tell whether the firm's labor performance productivity (output-per hour) is increasing or decreasing. Labor's financial productivity (dollar value of output ÷ dollar value of input) is increasing in year 2 when compared with year 1 and is decreasing in year 3, the cause of which is indeterminable from the example.

Now, what if year 3 (most recent year) were selected as the base year? Would bonus earnings possibilities be higher or lower than normal? From Table 4.1 you can see that the base ratio would be 28.1 percent so that the bonus earnings possibility would be above average. What about year 2? If year 2 were selected, the bonus would be more difficult to earn, because you would have a lower base ratio.

From the above discussion, you should be able to understand the following general rule: select a normal period for establishing the base ratio, and do not install the plan during a downturn in business if possible. Some firms use an average of the last three years if nothing major has happened in the areas of mix, technology, or relative value of input.

No major problems should result if the plan is installed anytime during a business expansion or a stable period. If it is installed during a contraction, you will want to control inventory buildup and then production. You may be laying off lower-seniority personnel, who probably are also lower paid, so that the average wage rate will be increasing. Additionally, work will be expanding to fill the time available which will also decrease productivity.

Acceptance and enthusiasm about the plan will be much greater if early bonuses rather than deficits are earned. This is, of course, only human nature. Or stated somewhat differently, behavioral problems are normally greater during hard times than good times. Logically, then, use an average of the two or three most recent years of labor costs as a percentage of sales value of production to establish the base ratio. There may be a good reason why such an average is not used. Some good reasons would include significant changes in (1) product mix requiring much more or less labor, (2) capital additions reducing labor (remember that you may be substituting indirect for direct labor), or (3) selling prices caused by major fluctuations in the prices of input at much different percentages than labor. In such instances you may find it unfair to either the employees or the company to establish a base ratio on an average of the last three years. Consequently you may wish to establish the base ratio on the most recent experience. You definitely *must* establish the ratio at a break-even position for the company.

The key variable is fairness to all parties. Does the base-ratio percentage make it too easy to make a bonus, or is it the reverse if set too low? You, your fellow managers, and union representatives, if applicable, must answer this question because you will have to live with the consequences. In the long run, no one gains if either extreme is true. In all likelihood, greater behavioral problems will result if the ratio is established at too low a percentage. If employees feel that they have increased productivity in the early months of the plan, especially the first one, but the bonus calculation does not show it, they are likely to become discouraged. An important point should be made here. If a consultant is hired to help install the plan, including the establishment of the base ratio, be careful that he does not encourage setting too high a ratio percentage. Consultants know that having early bonuses help to sell managers, union representatives, and other employees as to the merits of the scanlon plan.

In addition to the above analysis, you may also desire to do other ones for a variety of reasons, with the best reason being to isolate any future problem areas. For example, you might want to analyze the effect that product mix has had on costs. This can be easily done by preparing the analysis down to and including direct costs, at least direct labor and material, by product line. Over time this should give you a good feel for what has happened to product mix (see Section 4.15).

Some firms like to look at the effect that capital expenditures have had on costs. Sometimes you can just analyze the percentage changes by year in gross and net fixed assets and compare these with the percentage changes in sales value of production to give you a good feel for trends and effects. But, at other times, a more detailed analysis by major assets is necessary.

Other firms find adjusting all major revenue and cost items by price indexes a useful analysis when the information is available; you may be limited to average price and wage changes because of the unavailability of data. This analysis sometimes can be useful in determining an approximation of physical volume changes and relative value of inputs.

For divisionalized companies with numerous interplant transfers, you must of course develop a good grasp of these items and how they have and will effect the analysis and calculation. Some firms give credit for these items based on standard cost, or at least standard times, with some incentive to improve efficiency. The magnitude of this problem (interdependencies) may ultimately result in combining more than one plant into a single scanlon calculation or avoiding the ratio of "sales" calculation.

Whatever the analysis and problems, keep careful line-by-line details on how the data were obtained. Why? You would be surprised regarding how many questions are asked about the source of some figures; or, three years later, the question is raised regarding how come this or that was done. Without good notes and details the accountants may look arbitrary and manipulative, or, years later, they may be unable to determine how the calculation was determined in the first place. Needless to say, do not get carried away with the diagnostic analysis, or you may find yourself forever making analyses and never getting on to the business at hand. Use common sense.

We are sorry that we cannot devise a rule book for establishing a base-ratio percentage. In many situations it is relatively easy, once the diagnostic analysis is made, but in others it is somewhat difficult. Only the diagnostic analysis tells you if it is possible at all. Remember, other analyses and calculations are still to come for other calculations. At times other calculations are much preferred, as discussed later in this chapter. Only after the accountants have prepared the analysis and others have extensively viewed the results can you analyze the problem areas and establish a fair ratio percentage. If you cannot say it is fair, you are going to have difficulty convincing others of its fairness. A good union relationship and acceptance of the calculation would certainly help ensure plan acceptance. No productivity-measurement system is set in stone. Economic conditions and cause-and-effect relationships change as should the ratio percentage. Whatever diagnostic analysis is made to establish the base ratio (a detailed one we hope), we strongly recommend that you continue the same analysis at least quarterly after the plan is installed to help determine the reasonableness of the ratio over time. We present more on monitoring the plan over time in this chapter and in Chapter 6.

After you decide on your calculation method in detail, you will want to test it under actual conditions for several months. After you decide what to include and exclude, how to compute, and so on, you will want to use it for several months without actually having the plan installed to get a good feel for the calculation. Some companies have sufficiently reliable information to go back in time, but others do not. Use your own best judgment in this area, but do become comfortable with the calculation before the plan is formally installed. Do not be overly eager to install it formally before the accountants obtain a good understanding of it.

4.5 ITEMS TO INCLUDE AND EXCLUDE—RATIONALE

Sections 4.5 and 4.6 are organized around two principal areas of concern.

1. Rationale for including and excluding certain labor costs with a discussion of specific costs involved.
2. Adjustments to derive sales value of production (e.g., inventory).

As we stated in Chapter 1, the plan is a total organizational involvement system directed toward productivity improvement. Consequently, you might feel that any system of bonus calculation might be acceptable. Theoretically, then, some sort of profit sharing would be the preferred calculation to install, since most items of input influence profit and everyone's effort should be oriented in this broad direction. A firm with existing profit sharing may of course decide to keep it. Perhaps this should be the ultimate goal, but until this philosophy is developed throughout the organization, the risks of installing such a broad calculation are significant. You should be able to envision getting employees to understand and relate to the difficulties of such a broad calculation by thinking about the following comments.

Month 5 screening committee representative's comment:

Why didn't we earn a bonus? We all worked hard and really got a lot of production out.

Comment by president:

We know everyone worked hard, but we had a 6 percent increase in raw material cost last month, and that really ate into the bonus.

Month 7 representative's comments:

Now we are really interested in what you are going to tell us this month. We helped solve a large number of problem areas, made eighty suggestions, and worked hard and still no bonus. When are we going to get some payoff for our efforts?

Comments by president among others:

We know everyone is doing a great job. Material prices are still going up rapidly, and energy costs are going through the roof—we must start conserving better. . . .

Month 8 representative's comments:

Now things are a mess; we didn't get much produced at all, even though shipments were high, and we earn a 26 percent bonus. We just don't understand this damn system.

Comment by president:

Boy, isn't it exciting to earn a bonus for all of our hard work. Purchasing made some good buys; we were finally able to increase our selling prices a little; and our depreciation expense accrual was a little high earlier in the year, so we adjusted for that.

This sequence of events demonstrates the difficulty of getting employees to relate to a profit-sharing type of system (and also that the president was not really listening). On the other side, employees would learn about the company and the variables that influence it.

At the same time you should see that you would really like to get employees to relate to the economic environment in which the company operates. This climate takes years to develop. Most non-scanlons never accomplish this even to a small degree. Most scanlon companies do, however, have a profit-sharing plan as part of the retirement system, which makes considerable economic and practical sense in helping to develop this broader commitment. Generally speaking, another problem of profit sharing is that if it is a deferred form of compensation, the amount is normally limited to 15 percent of average compensation for tax purposes. This method of sharing probably provides little incentive to perform; perhaps it does provide incentive to remain with the organization, however. If paid out to the employees immediately, no such limitations on amounts exist. Many profit-sharing companies would in fact be well advised to apply the other principles underlying the plan as of course many have. Another problem with profit sharing per se, at least in the beginning, is the delay in getting the results out to employees and computing on a weekly basis. On the other side, having a profit-sharing system helps decrease problems of inequitable formula construction; that is, if they do not get the reward from the bonus calculation, hopefully they will get it through the profit sharing.

Given these considerations of profit sharing, this is why we recommend that you start with a labor-only type of calculation. By limiting your calculation to labor items, you will have a manageable portion of the firm's costs to get employees to concentrate on and establish goals for. And it is the one thing employees can partially control—their own productivity.

An important point is that while the calculation may directly consider only labor costs, our experience has shown that employees can and will get involved in increasing the productivity of areas such as materials, energy, and capital investment. Over time they realize that if they can help the firm increase its competitiveness, everyone gains. These gains come from areas other than just labor savings. Discussion later in this chapter deals with including items other than labor in the calculation.

If we assume that you are going to establish your plan based only on labor costs, what labor costs should be included? Traditionally, companies have established ratios based on all employee costs from the president's salary down to most payroll fringe benefits and taxes. As a general rule, we feel that all labor costs should be included if employees directly or indirectly influence those costs. For the most part, employee benefits have been going up faster than wage and salary costs. By including them in the bonus based on a historical percentage, the scanlon plan tends to pick up part of the increases over time, assuming that selling prices have not been increasing at even a greater percentage, and the company, hopefully, becoming more competitive as a result.

Which labor items should be considered for inclusion? First, the following items normally should be included:

1. Direct and indirect factory labor.
2. All other wages and salaries (selling, R and D, engineering, shipping and receiving, administrative, etc.).
3. Overtime premium, vacation, and holiday pay.
4. Hospitalization and workmens' compensation (employees indirectly control by their health and safety records plus you want to involve them in decisions to increase health benefits).

Second are some of the items to be considered for exclusion:

1. Salesmens' commissions. Normally excluded, since it is a separate reward system. If salesmen are on total commissions, they are normally excluded from the plan entirely, even though they play an important role in the success of the plan's bonus-earning opportunities (without sales, no long-term productivity would occur). If they are on part salary, that portion can be included, and they can share in the bonus on that basis.
2. FICA (employer's portion of social security contribution). We are indifferent on this rapidly increasing cost. It is a continual drain on the bonus, because it is continually increasing and employees really cannot influence it in any way.
3. State and federal unemployment insurance. No real reason can be found to include other than it is a cost of having employees. Additionally, it penalizes the plan in the early months of the calendar year, even though it is insurance for the entire year.
4. Various pension systems. These items can be included or excluded, depending on who controls them and the future objectives of the system. If it is a negotiated item, it should be included, since employees indirectly control it. Other situations might yield a different decision.
5. Various other miscellaneous employee costs. Particular companies may have a large number of additional employee-related costs which may be quite large in certain circumstances and numerous (e.g., a hospital's training costs). Examples might include types of training costs to items such as Christmas hams and Thanksgiving turkeys. Basically, the same logic should be considered, although hard and fast rules cannot be encouraged. Can employees influence; do you want to influence; or should they be trying to influence? If the answer is yes to any one of these, logically they should be included, since the purpose is to start trying to control all the relevant costs.

After you have decided which items to include and exclude, you compute the ratio percentage as discussed in the previous section.

6. New costs after the installation. If the scanlon plan is installed, certain new costs could be incurred. These could include outside consulting directed toward improving the operation of the plan or membership dues in an organization such as the Scanlon Plan Associates (a cooperative group of scanlon plan companies headquartered at Michigan State University). These should be charged against the plan, since they are related to its improved operation, even though the allowed percentage normally does not include them.

4.6 DETERMINING SALES VALUE OF PRODUCTION

After reviewing Sections 4.1 to 4.4, you should have elected to deduct sales returns, allowances, and perhaps discounts from sales independent of the calculation method you ultimately decide on. Why? For the obvious effect of getting employees involved in increasing quality. As stated earlier, this is an important area of stress at most scanlon plan companies. After these items are deducted, you arrive at net sales. From net sales, firms with inventories should add (for increases) or deduct (for decreases) the net change for the period. If you do not have significant inventories to which labor is added, you can skip the next five paragraphs.

Manufacturing firms in particular must give careful consideration to inventory fluctuations. Why? Because the scanlon plan is normally considered to be a production-sharing plan, and consequently you want to reward increases in production rather than increases in sales. If the bonus were paid solely on sales or shipments, bonuses would likely be more volatile and not directly related to employee performance. However, a significant number of scanlon companies do base their calculations on sales rather than production (e.g., many profit-sharing companies).

Finished-goods inventories are normally not a major problem, because most companies maintain perpetual records for at least quantities. Work-in-process (WIP) inventories often present a greater problem, because perpetuals are often not maintained and many companies experience significant monthly fluctuations in WIP inventories. You should develop a mechanism to give the plan credit (normally a percentage of the total base ratio at various major checkpoints) before completion to decrease bonus fluctuations if the production cycle is long. Production records can often be used, but companies frequently find it necessary to take monthly counts of WIP inventories to·ensure that the plan does receive credit as close to production as possible and to reward performance as it occurs. Normally, the finished and especially the WIP inventories are valued at cost rather than selling price for two main reasons: (1) most companies maintain inventory records by costs and not sales value, and determining exactly when sales value is added would normally be quite difficult to ascertain, and (2) only when the product is sold does the plan receive full value. This latter reason helps protect the company's cash resources by not paying out the full bonus until the product is actually sold. Finished goods, of course, could be valued at selling price and WIP inventories at cost, which would more closely approximate sales value of production. If you previously did not maintain records on WIP inventories, an estimate must be made in order to determine a base ratio, although rarely is this a major problem, because WIP inventories do not normally fluctuate greatly on a yearly basis. Companies normally prepare monthly financial statments so that this is no longer a major problem for most firms.

If you have not maintained any records on either finished-goods or WIP inventories and fairly accurate estimates are not possible, you will want to delay implementation of the plan until a fairly accurate history is developed. You might question the cost of such procedures, but many scanlon plan companies have learned to streamline their inventory-taking procedures. The costs are considered acceptable, since they result in more accurate information for financial reporting, and of course the scanlon plan picks up the cost of the inventory taking.

As we discussed in Chapter 2, you can eliminate the inventory-taking problem entirely if you maintain accurate production records; that is, as production is completed (for short production cycles) or as it passes certain checkpoints (for long production cycles), credit can be given the plan as a percentage of the base ratio. But the credit given probably must be the full sales price or percentage, if at a checkpoint, rather than cost. This method works quite well for companies with stable selling prices but not for some others. If you often give discounts to move goods, you will not wish to give the scanlon plan full credit until the product is sold. Remember that the discount and other factors are built into the original base ratio.

Needless to say, the method of inventory valuation (e.g., LIFO, FIFO) can be a problem in developing the base ratio. You will probably encounter the greatest problems if you are on LIFO and not adding to inventories over a period. Just remember that you may have to make an adjustment in deriving the base ratio to yield a value of production based on fairly current costs.

4.7 THE SINGLE-RATIO CALCULATION—A WAY TO GET STARTED

Sections 4.7 to 4.12 deal with interrelated factors of the single-ratio method. Areas reviewed are:

1. Normalizing the ratio.
2. Smoothing costs.

3. Division of the bonus pool (company and employees).
4. Bonus reserve.
5. Monthly and yearly distribution plan.

After you have completed your diagnostic analysis and decided what you want to include in the bonus calculation, you are ready to consider which bonus calculation best fits your particular needs. Sections 4.7 to 4.12 must be read even if you do not use the single-ratio calculation. The remaining sections of this chapter provide alternatives. No one calculation is the preferred method. The selected calculation depends on the sophistication of your accounting system, type of operation, and the ability of management and employees to understand and relate to the relevant variables. We provide our own thoughts on the different calculations where applicable.

4.8 THE BASE RATIO

Many companies discover from a diagnostic analysis that total personnel costs as a percentage of sales remain fairly constant over long periods of time. This is especially true for manufacturing films, even though gradual shifts may occur in the different labor categories. When this is validated through the above diagnostic analysis, companies feel quite comfortable installing the relatively simple bonus calculation based on the relationship of total labor costs to sales value of production, or in formula form:

$$base\ ratio = \frac{total\ personnel\ costs}{sales\ value\ of\ production}$$

We have made several references to this method of benefit sharing, and the diagnostic analysis emphasized this calculation. You should at this point have a good idea of how you can establish this base ratio.

We will continue to refer to this as the single-ratio method of calculation. The base ratio or percentage becomes the allowed payroll in each month. When is a bonus earned? Whenever actual payroll costs are less than the allowed payroll costs. An example follows in Section 4.9. Important note: Much of the discussion in Section 4.9 is relevant even if you do not install the single-ratio method of calculation.

4.9 NORMALIZING THE RATIO AND WHEN TO INSTALL

As we discussed in Section 4.4, your analysis should disclose the normal fluctuations that might occur in the bonus results. Probably it is easier to earn a bonus during some months of a year than others, as well as during expansionary cyclical periods. No method of calculation can or should eliminate economic reality. But getting the scanlon plan off to a good start with early bonuses can help to sell the philosophy as much as anything. You should install the plan when bonus opportunities are favorable.

When developing the base ratio, three things should be kept in mind: materiality, timing, and equitability. At the time of implementation, only material adjustments and changes should be considered. If you attempt to analyze and adjust the ratio for every minor fluctuation, you might never establish the scanlon plan or might assume the calculation to be more accurate than it really is. In reality the single-ratio calculation is a measure of productivity only in a crude sense. By constantly adjusting it, you might give the impression that you are manipulating the calculation. Timing of installation should be considered in terms of both seasonal and cyclical fluctuations, since early bonuses help sell the plan. Some companies even adjust the calculation in early months to ensure a bonus. Overall, your calculation should be perceived to be equitable by both the employees and the company. Chapter 6 covers all these items in more detail from a long-run point of view. Do not expect a great deal of knowledge about the calculation's details during the early history of the plan. Perceived equitability is very important, however. A favorite story of one of the authors is a company that had installed the plan but did not earn a bonus the first month. Everyone from the president down agreed that production increased and everyone worked hard. The controller had made an error in the calculation which in reality doomed this installation to limited success and contributed to ultimate failure.

4.10   A TYPICAL MONTH'S CALCULATION

Sections 4.10 to 4.12 present a typical month's single-ratio calculation in a series of steps along with discussion of decisions to be made. The single-ratio method is summarized and critiqued in Sections 4.13 to 4.16. For illustrative purposes we assume a base ratio or percentage of 20 percent computed as follows:

$$base\ ratio = \frac{total\ personnel\ costs}{sales\ value\ of\ production} = \frac{\$2,000,000}{\$10,000,000} = 20\%$$

STEP 1   *Determining Sales Value*

The sales value is typically computed as follows:

Sales	$1,100,000
Less: Sales returns,	
allowances, discounts	25,000
Net Sales	1,075,000
Add: Increases in inventories	125,000
Sales value (of production)	$1,200,000

The adjustments to sales for returns, allowances, discounts, and inventories depend on how the ratio to determine sales value of production was originally established (see Sections 4.5 and 4.6).

STEP 2 *Determining the Bonus Pool*

Now, continuing the example, the sales value of production is multiplied by the base ratio to yield allowed personnel costs as follows:

Sales value of production (from step 1)	$1,200,000
Allowed personnel costs: 20% of sales value	240,000
(base ratio)	
Less: Actual personnel costs	210,000
Bonus pool	$ 30,000

The actual personnel costs of all the included items are subtracted from the allowed personnel costs to develop the base ratio used in determining the bonus pool. Should a detailed breakdown of all the actual costs be included on the bonus calculation sheet given to employees? Normally no, since it just clutters up the calculation, but the accountants should be prepared to discuss any of the particular items when discussing the bonus results, especially any problem areas.

One item should be noted. Rather than charging the actual costs of vacations and holidays against the plan when they are incurred, you should accrue a monthly amount over the full year. This helps decrease fluctuations in the bonus during months with a high percentage of vacation or holiday days in them. Adjustments in the monthly accrual can be made during the year as conditions change and actual dollar costs are updated. This approach also can be used for other costs that are bunched during a certain part of the year. It makes sense to do this spreading, because even though the costs are paid at certain times, they are incurred over a longer period. Do not get carried away with this "smoothing" however. Note that separate accounting records are not normally required because of the plan; all the calculations are normally completed on work sheets. Many firms accrue applicable taxes on the bonus, which generally decreases bonus fluctuations.

STEP 3.   *Division of the Bonus Pool*

How should the bonus pool be divided? No easy answer exists to this question, but we can make a number of suggestions.

Some consultants advise setting up the reserve first and then giving the company a percentage of the remainder (the company has an interest in the bonus reserve). By allowing the company to take its share off the top, its continued profitability is more assured, and inventory pricing and establishment of bonus-payable liability becomes easier to accomplish. (That is, how can a company have a liability to itself?). Deficits are normally charged against the reserve.

In the continued example that follows, you can see a fairly common bonus-pool distribution: 25 percent is returned to the company, and 25 percent is reserved for deficit months, with the employees receiving the remaining portion.

Bonus pool (from step 2)	$ 30,000
Company share (25%)	7,500
Subtotal	22,500
Reserve for deficit months (25%)	5,625
Employee share—current distribution (75%)	$ 16,875
Participating payroll	$168,750
Bonus percentage ($16,875 ÷ $168,750)	10%

Optional information: amount of bonus reserve or deficit to date, number of suggestions, labor savings, capital expenditures, backlogs, and so on. This type of information dissemination normally increases as employees request it, or you ask them if they want it. Do not overload them with information.

Should the company receive any portion of the increase in labor productivity as computed by the single-ratio method? Percentages returned to the company vary from zero to 50 percent. Normally, the latter percentage is used for those companies which have a larger formula by including more items than labor in the calculation (expanded calculations are covered in Sections 4.17 to 4.25). Profit-sharing companies normally allow even less to go to the employees or give a certain percentage depending on size; that is, 50 percent of the first $200,000, 30 percent of the next $50,000, and so on.

There are companies which believe they obtain a more dedicated work force by giving their employees all the increase in productivity as measured by the ratio of labor method. Some companies believe they obtain their return through a work force that is less resistant to change and better utilized capital resources. You should remember that the labor savings are often only a small portion of the total savings that are possible. Based on past experience, a 25 percent company split, as shown in Step 3, is fairly common. The probable solution to the decision of the split lies in the area of the company's external environment and the extent of labor savings and capital expenditures that are anticipated.

First, regarding the external-environment variable, some companies operate in an environment in which material and other costs, as well as volume, fluctuate considerably in the short run. Add to this a very competitive climate in which increasing selling prices is difficult, then allowing the company a certain percentage would make considerable sense for competitive reasons. This permits viability without the need to make frequent adjustments in the base ratio because of rapidly changing intermediate input prices and subsequent adjustment of selling prices.

Now the second item of labor-saving expenditures is considered. Productivity increases result from a large number of variables; some are behaviorally oriented and others technologically, method, or market oriented. For highly technological or significant labor-saving investments, a scanlon plan company would probably not desire to absorb all the benefits of the labor savings. Why? If none of the benefits accrue to the plan participants, the company may soon be confronted with a decrease in the number of suggestions as well as an increase in resistance to accept such equipment. The scanlon plan company must maintain its competitive posture if the equipment is externally developed and hence available to every company in the industry. A partial solution is to allow the company to retain a certain portion of the bonus, which also would decrease the need for frequent adjustments in the base ratio when major investments are made.

Scanlon companies solve these problems in a variety of other ways. For example, some companies have required the plan to pay for any specific labor-saving equipment over a certain dollar amount before receiving any credit. After the equipment is paid for over a certain time span, the plan receives the full credit. Another approach sometimes used is to not adjust the ratio if the savings resulted from a suggestion but to adjust it for any externally available equipment purchased. If the single-ratio method is used, you must have good records to make such an adjustment possible.

4.11 BONUS RESERVE

A strong argument can be made for establishing a bonus *reserve* for possible future deficit months. The strongest part of this argument is that it protects the company. After the end of the year, any bonus reserve is distributed to the remaining employees in the form of a "jackpot," with any deficit normally being absorbed by the company. The percentage you elect as the bonus reserve should depend heavily on the degree of production and sales fluctuations that occur over a year's time, giving consideration to forecasted conditions for the next year. A company with a high degree of seasonal fluctuations in either sales or production might elect to establish a reserve as high as 40 to 50 percent. A company with stable sales and production might elect to reserve only 20 percent and pay out all the bonus earned once the total reserve reaches a certain monetary amount.

Whether you establish a formal bonus-reserve liability (on the balance sheet) depends on the size of the bonus and its volatility. If the size is large in percentage and labor is a significant part of inventory cost, not recording the reserve-bonus expense and liability during the year can result in significant year-end adjustments. Interim financial statements will also be incorrect. The actual amount payable (e.g., the previous month's bonus to be paid in the next month) should normally be established as a liability.

If the bonus is expected to fluctuate greatly, with some months positive and others negative, it may make less sense to accrue the bonus reserve as a liability during the year. Independent of what is done, the bonus, including any year-end reserve, is a cost of producing the inventory and, according to Internal Revenue Service rulings, must be added to year-end inventories for valuation purposes. The factory labor part normally is determined as a percentage of direct labor. This, of course, is a problem primarily for companies on a first-in, first-out (FIFO) inventory-valuation basis or those adding a last-in, first-out (LIFO) layer for the year. Generally speaking, companies handle the scanlon bonus for inventory purposes in a manner similar to overtime premium (i.e., normally included in overhead) without undue difficulty.

4.12 DISTRIBUTION TO EMPLOYEES

If you examine the bottom of the recombined example, Table 4.2, you can see that when the employee share of the bonus ($16,875) is divided by the participating payroll, the bonus percentage is determined. Here are some factors to consider. The participating payroll costs (line 12) are normally less than the actual payroll costs (line 7), because some fringe benefits are included in the latter (line 7) and because companies normally establish a one to six-month waiting period before employees become eligible to participate in the bonus. As discussed in Chapter 5, this is a policy matter that you should carefully consider. Also, the bonus is not normally paid on vacations and holidays, but on productive labor.

Table 4.2 Typical Scanlon Plan Bonus Calculation—Month X

1. Sales		$1,100,000
2. Less sales returns, allowances, discounts		25,000
3. Net sales		$1,075,000
4. Add: Increase in inventory (at cost or selling price)		125,000
5. Value of production		$1,200,000
6. Allowed payroll costs (20% of value of production)	$	240,000
7. Actual payroll costs		210,000
8. Bonus pool		30,000
9. Company share (25%)		7,500
Subtotal		22,500
10. Reserve for deficit months (25%)		5,625
11. Employee share (75%)—immediate distribution	$	16,875
12. Participating payroll costs	$	168,750
13. Bonus percentage ($16,875 ÷ $168,750)		10%

Optional information: Amount of bonus reserve or deficit to date, number of suggestions, labor savings, capital expenditures, backlogs, etc.

Just how long does it take before an employee reaches an average productivity level? In any respect, older employees have a clear motivation to assist newer employees in becoming productive because of the latter's possible negative bonus effect. How much motivation to become productive will new employees have if they must wait six months to share in the benefits? Hence, a 30 to 60 day period should probably be the maximum waiting period for new employes, with the other employees being able to vote their earlier bonus participation if the circumstances merit such consideration.

When and how should the bonuses be paid? They should be paid as soon as possible in the month following the performance measurement unless unusual problems prevent such action. Normally a common monthly date is established. Payment should be by seperate check to differentiate bonus earnings from regular earnings. The obvious reason for this rapid payment is the motivational effect of quick feedback.

But a short digression is also appropriate here. We have noted in some firms the tendency to emphasize short-run performance too much. As we said earlier, just expect employees at all levels to adjust to the system you install. So, how can you reinforce a longer-term point of view regarding performance? Firms have tried at least three approaches when it is perceived as a problem. One way is to install a profit-sharing plan also, even if small. This often is a deferred type of plan when combined also with a normal scanlon calculation. This allows a firm to talk about the long-run effect of actions without sounding "hollow" and also to emphasize cost savings other than just labor. Firms having profit sharing as the only calculation are of course not normally confronted as much with this problem. The second way is to pay the bonus over a moving three-month period. In fact some firms only compute the bonus quarterly, which probably is a mistake. You also should note that the bonus reserve is the third method, and most common, used to reinforce this longer-term attitude.

Any bonus reserve at year end should be disbursed early in the new year, based on the percentage of each remaining employee's participating bonus wages for the year. An example should help. Assume total bonus reserve is $100,000 and participating payroll is $2 million. Every employee would receive a 5 percent year-end bonus as a percentage of his participating payroll for the year. A recent employee would receive less than an employee who was there the whole year.

Managers also frequently comment that they can see no reason why the company should not keep the part earned by the employees who have left the firm. We can see a certain logic in this thinking, although this is not normally done. As said earlier, if the bonus is large (year end or monthly), some firms also accrue the employer's share of payroll taxes rather than charging them all against the subsequent month's bonus. If a month's bonus is very small, say less then 2 percent, it should be deferred until the next bonus-earning month. Some companies on a calendar year end the first year on November 30 so that any bonus reserve can be distributed before Christmas.

4.13 SINGLE-RATIO SUMMARY

What are the main advantages of the single-ratio method of calculating the bonus results? Three come immediately to the forefront: simplicity, ease of understanding, and lack of any elaborate new accounting records. Additionally, if sales prices, wages, and intermediate input prices such as materials and energy fluctuate fairly close together, this calculation should provide a fairly accurate measure of labor's financial productivity. For these reasons, you should seriously consider adopting this method of calculation or the version discussed in Section 4.14 as a starting point. As you build trust and understanding in the scanlon philosophy, more sophisticated calculations can be selected. These are discussed in more comprehensive calculations sections of this chapter (Sections 4.17 to 4.25).

4.14 SINGLE RATIO—CRITIQUE AND EXPANSION

Sections 4.14 to 4.16 deal with potential problem areas of the single ratio and reflect years of careful financial evaluation. Therefore, we encourage you to review the pertinence of these sections for your own situation:

1. Single-ratio problems such as product mix, inflation, and so on.
2. Split-ratio approaches.
3. Base-ratio adjustment problems.

How well do you feel the single-ratio method works in terms of our evaluation criteria discussed early in this chapter? Frankly, the single ratio works great in some companies and terrible in others, ranking as a significant contributing factor for many plan failures. Some companies use the single-ratio calculation as one of their primary control techniques for labor—something it was never intended for. They lose control of what is happening. When we have asked some scanlon plan managers how productivity is progressing, many do not know. Larger companies generally do not fall into this trap, perhaps because of more sophisticated information systems to help control and isolate problem areas along with determining when to make necessary adjustments to the ratio. Smaller companies are probably the ones that should consider changing from the single-ratio calculation the earliest (i.e., within two to three years after installation or sooner).

To continue the evaluation of the single-ratio in detail, we list the criteria and our subjective estimate of its ranking at the time of installation (A for excellent and F for flunking) on the average and three years after installation. A brief outline of the possible problem areas is given in Table 4.3.

As Table 4.3 indicates, the single-ratio calculation leaves a little to be desired as a measurement system. It probably worked better in the past than it does today. However, if the price relationships between the various inputs (labor, materials, capital, energy) and the final selling price remain fairly constant during inflationary times, and product mix and technology do not radically change to require significantly more or less labor per unit of output, the single-ratio calculation works quite well. This is true even if a switch occurs from direct to indirect labor. Also, if the labor part of the final selling price has remained fairly constant over long periods, it should serve quite well. If you are willing to change the ratio when necessary, the single-ratio method should be an acceptable payoff for the involvement process. This assumes you have adequate records and acceptance from employees. Since this is a practical guide, we feel that awareness of the possible problems is the important part of solving them as they occur. Section 4.15 discusses some of these problems in more

Table 4.3   Critique of Single-Ratio Calculation Method

Criteria	Ranking at Installation	Rank Years Later	Possible Problems
1. Soundness as a measure of performance	B	B–D	Inflation, product mix
2. Perceived fairness as a measure of performance	A	C–D	Inflation, product mix
3. Ease in understanding	A	B–D	A fooler at times
4. Easily administered	A–B	A–B	Inventory taking
5. Flexibility to meet changing economic conditions	B–C	B–D	Used improperly as a control tool
6. Useful in isolating problem areas and properly directing attention	D	D–F	No real assistance—too gross of measurement; may conceal problem area; no separation of financial and performance productivity

detail and presents some alternatives of how scanlon plan companies have resolved them over time with varying types of measurement systems.

4.15   PRODUCT-MIX PROBLEMS AND A SOLUTION

Often one of the first problems encountered is changing product mixes. Table 4.4 covers one possible outcome of changing product mixes. You can easily see that the one-ratio calculation did not reflect the shift to a less labor-intensive product line. Although the shift was quite radical, are such shifts over time unusual? Probably not. The bonus in this example was certainly not earned, nor was the decline in productivity in product line A accurately reflected to permit corrective action to be taken. Other accounting records might have reflected more accurately what was happening. Nevertheless, the bonus calculation did not. The reverse could, of course, also occur if a shift were made over time to more labor-intensive products.

As a result of the above, some companies establish separate allowed amounts by major product lines within a few years after installing the scanlon plan. This could be easily accomplished when the plan is originally established but seldom is at that time. The actual procedures include finding the direct labor by product line and allowing this amount as a percentage of sales value of production. Indirect labor, manufacturing, general, and administrative labor costs are allowed as either (1) a percentage of sales value of production for each major product line or (2) based on total sales value of production. Some method of allocating indirect labor is required in determining the base ratios if determined on each product line, or overhead labor costs can be based on total production value (i.e., a separate allowed percentage for all the indirect, manufacturing, general, and administrative payroll in total). Which method should be used? If indirect expenses do not fluctuate greatly by product lines, one total allowed percentage for these items is best. If they do fluctuate greatly, a separate allowed amount or percentage for each line would provide useful information for control purposes. Both methods along with hybrids (indirect percentage based on sales) are found in practice. A more detailed diagnostic analysis by product line should indicate the preferred method. Allocating the indirect costs to product lines is somewhat arbitrary and difficult to explain to employees, even though we see it commonly practiced. Hence, a separate allowed amount for at least general and administrative labor based on total production value may be preferable in most instances.

Table 4.4 Bonus Calculation under One- and Assumed Split-Ratio Method

Period 1	Typical One-Ratio	Split Ratios		
		Product A	Product B	Total
Sales value of production	$1,800,000	$1,200,000	$ 600,000	$1,800,000
Allowed payroll costs:				
One-ratio: 20%	360,000			
Split-ratio: 10% product A		120,000		
30% product B			180,000	300,000
Actual payroll (assumed)	300,000	140,000	160,000	300,000
Bonus pool	$ 60,000	$ (20,000)	$ 20,000	$ 0

Assumptions:
Period 0
    Two products (A and B) are produced with equal quantities and selling prices. Sales of product A = $600,000; sales of product B = $600,000.
    Labor costs allowed = 20% in total; A actually = 10%, B = 30%.
Period 1
    Sales of A increase by 100% ($600,000 + $600,000); B's remain the same ($600,000).
    Total sales now equal $1,800,000.
Split-ratio calculation
    When determining the original allowed amounts, indirect payroll costs were allocated to products based on sales and this continues for actual costs in subsequent periods.

4.16 PROBLEMS OF BASE RATIO ADJUSTMENTS AND OTHER PROBLEMS

Another alternative to adjusting for changing product mixes would be to adjust the base ratio. Although we cover the management of adjustment procedures in Chapter 6, a brief discussion of the mechanics of the various adjustments might be worthwhile at this point. Are there problems with changing the base ratio? Yes. Changing the allowed percentage (the base ratio) often presents a difficult behavioral problem for the scanlon plan company. This is one reason why some companies seldom change the percentage. An important goal is to build trust in and understanding of the calculation of which the allowed percentage is an important part. Hence, when an adjustment in the percentage is contemplated, employees tend to look on the change with distrust, particularly if changes are made on a fairly regular basis. However, careful explanations enhance acceptance of the change, and management needs to consider remaining flexible, since changes will be required. Long periods of no change might actually work against acceptance when one becomes necessary. This is particularly true in unionized organizations. Changing the percentage allowed is normally quite difficult to accomplish in an accurate way for product-mix changes, because some shifts are made to more labor-intensive products and others to less labor-intensive products. Consequently, adjusting the one-base ratio calculation is sometimes difficult to accomplish, and ultimately distrust may tend to build. Therefore the split-ratio method normally may be preferable, because you have more information to help isolate problem areas and needed ratio changes. This also helps to explain why a detailed diagnostic analysis is important before the plan is installed. After you start the plan, isolating these variables is sometimes quite difficult. We suggest that you keep good records on the original plan and get representatives involved when a change is contemplated even if the change may be a management decision.

Does this split-ratio calculation solve your problems? No. Even this split-ratio calculation tends to deteriorate for a variety of reasons. A primary problem is probably one of rapidly changing input prices. For example, assume that material costs increase by 20 percent in a year and that they are 50 percent of a particular product line's selling price. Assume also that the company is able to increase its selling price to offset the increase in material costs or raises them by 10 percent (50 percent $\times$ 20 percent). If the allowed labor percentage is not reduced, the allowed labor (and bonus) will increase significantly without any increase in labor's productivity. The difficulty of adjusting the allowed percentage was briefly discussed above. The reverse could, of course, happen, and the employees might soon perceive that little they do as a group influences the outcome of the bonus.

Although the above varying conditions might provide a valuable lesson about the free-enterprise system, they also can contribute to the failure of the scanlon plan philosophy if not considered and properly handled by an imaginative and perceptive managment team. Additional problems with the traditional single-ratio calculation that should be considered are:

1. The allowed percentage may have to be adjusted for major capital investments, but determining the amount of the adjustment may be difficult for some companies (see Section 6.6 for procedures).
2. Allowing the same amount for all products may result in problems when cost-reduction goal setting is attempted. The information flow should expand considerably under the scanlon plan, but behavioral problems can result when employees discover that it is impossible to earn a bonus on some products.
3. Physical inventories may be required, especially for work-in-process items if not presently maintained, and this may reduce productivity. This is normally a problem and required only for companies with long production cycles in order to decrease bonus fluctuations and reward performance as it occurs. In practice, this does not tend to be a major problem once procedures are streamlined.
4. One is practically guaranteeing that labor cost varies directly with sales in the long run independent of what happens in the company's internal and external environment. This may make marginal decision making difficult (e.g., reducing prices to obtain additional volume in some markets). It also assumes no adjustment in the ratio percentage. Consequently you will share in changes in volume.
5. Nonprofit organizations such as hospitals may have difficulty using the ratio method because of rapidly changing economic conditions.

Many of these problems are eventually confronted by companies that elect to install the scanlon plan based on the single-ratio and sometimes split-ratio calculation. Would your company? Maybe or maybe not, depending on what your diagnostic analysis found and what happened over time. If the resulting problems are minor, companies cope with them without substantial difficulties. But if they become major, they may cause the failure of the scanlon plan from both productivity and behavioral standpoints. Success depends primarily on managers' and especially accountants' abilities to adjust the calculation to changing conditions and still convince other employees of the equitability of the entire bonus system.

However, in the end, many scanlon plan companies have found that as adjustments are made in the one or more ratio methods, they lost control of the calculation and experience increasing difficulty with explaining the bonus results to employees. As a summarizing criticism, a calculation to help organizational development and productivity improvement should provide useful information to assist in these activities in addition to measuring performance. Unfortunately, the typical single-ratio method of calculation often does not provide such information over the years without significant difficulties. Of course, the single-ratio was not intended to perform such functions; unfortunately, companies try to use it for this purpose. A calculation should be more than just a scorecard. Do numerous "authorities" on the scanlon plan disagree with this last sentence? Yes, because to them the philosophy is the important variable. But our experience has shown us that a good measurement system can help to develop this philosophy especially in small companies.

4.17 MORE COMPREHENSIVE CALCULATIONS

Sections 4.18 to 4.20 deal with:

1. Multicost calculations and profit sharing.
2. Value-added calculations.
3. Allowed-labor calculations.

From here on, the going becomes a little more difficult. Why? Up to this point we have discussed the pros and cons of the basic measurement plan normally associated with the scanlon plan. The expanded, split-ratio method discussed in the previous section does not really change the basic measurement process, but it does help to solve the problem of product-mix changes. Many of the remaining problems are still present. How can these be at least partially resolved?

The resolution for any given situation may be based on some variant of one of the three generic comprehensive calculations listed above. For example, the idiosyncracies of service, retail, or other nonmanufacturing organizations might require broadening the calculation; or if accounting systems are sophisticated to provide necessary information, the calculation constructed could be more flexible to changing conditions. Sometimes the primary objective of the organization may be to measure and improve labor productivity. Given this, more comprehensive calculations help to satisfy these conditions. In almost all instances, one adaptation of the three basic calculations in Sections 4.18 to 4.20 are used.

4.18 MULTICOST RATIO AND PROFIT-SHARING METHODS

One approach already mentioned is to broaden the calculation to include more items, the ultimate being profit sharing. Probably the best calculation from a long-run point of view would be something like return on investment even with its problems. This of course would consider not only profit but also the capital that it took to generate that profit. From a sociological standpoint, this would be desirable and perhaps should be the direction a scanlon plan company ultimately moves toward. The diagnostic analysis would be the same as presented in Sections 4.1 to 4.5 but just include more items. Let us assume that we determined from a diagnostic analysis that a cost ratio of 80 percent would be appropriate, with depreciation, interest, taxes, and profit being excluded. A month's actual calculation might look as shown in Table 4.5. Existing profit-sharing plans would be an even broader calculation.

By including most costs in the calculation, you solve many of the deficiencies of the single-ratio (labor only) type of calculation. You could, of course, also do this by product line, and so on, just like the labor-only ratio. For example, problems regarding product mix and inflation are decreased considerably and in fact practically eliminated. By including more items in the calculation, potential savings also expand.

This type of calculation somewhat guarantees the company a certain return when the multicost-ratio percentage is established. Additionally in the example you can see that 50 percent of the bonus was allocated to the company— something probably essential for competitive reasons (we suggest even more). A straight, profit-sharing firm normally pays out even a smaller percentage. You may remember our earlier mentioning that in deferred profit sharing you are limited to 15 percent of average compensation. This could enable the firm to purchase capital equipment and maintain its competitive posture. If established

Table 4.5 MultiCost Ratio Calculation—Month X

1. Value of production (sales ± inventory, allowances, etc.)		$1,000,000
2. Allowable expenses (80% of #1)		$ 800,000
3. Actual expenses:		
Labor (all employee costs)	$120,000	
Material and supplies	500,000	
Other costs (energy, etc.)	160,000	780,000
4. Bonus pool (#2 − #3)		20,000
5. Company share (50% × #4)		10,000
6. Gross bonus		10,000
7. Reserve for deficit months (20% × #6)		2,000
8. Bonus pool (#6 − #7)		$ 8,000
9. Participating payroll		$ 80,000
10. Bonus percentage (#8 ÷ #9)		10%

properly in the first place, little reason can exist to change the ratio unless of course objectives change.

We strongly recommend that the typical company not start with such a calculation. Why? The basic reason is that employees have difficulty relating to and understanding the calculation. They are happy when there are bonuses and upset when none exist but normally have little feeling other than this. However, they have no influence over the price of materials and supplies and other costs of production, such as the cost of energy. Another possible problem with both multicost and profit sharing is the increase in information that must be disseminated when requested on areas other than labor. Some firms are hesitant to give out this type of data.

As a company develops its scanlon plan philosophy and data information system (to isolate problem and cost-saving opportunity areas), this type of calculation makes much more sense. Without this sophistication, you are probably asking for trouble with such a calculation; you cannot use it as a control system. Some scanlon plan companies have used such a multicost calculation with varying degrees of success over the years. Many straight profit-sharing firms can and have applied the scanlon principles while maintaining their profit-sharing systems; many others should be encouraged to do so.

4.19   VALUE-ADDED METHODS

This method subtracts intermediate (outside) purchases from sales value of production. You must subtract items used rather than items purchased. An example should help you see what we mean. We use the same figures in Table 4.6 as were used in the previous example of multicost-ratio calculation (Table 4.5).

What advantages does this method of calculation have over the simple-ratio calculation and others? One advantage would be that the value-added approach does give some consideration to changing product mix and inflation. For example, if material or some other outside purchase increased in price significantly and product selling prices were increased to offset the changes, the ratio of labor, assumed 41.17 percent in the example, would not have to be adjusted. It is automatically considered by subtracting materials used. Still, if quantity used decreased, the plan would receive the credit as intended. This probably would make it useful for such difficult firms as job shops.

Overall, then, this method could fulfill our criteria quite well if your accounting system is adequate to provide the information necessary for control of what is happening. It may be a fairly good measure of overall financial productivity of labor, quite understandable, probably easily administered, fairly

Table 4.6 Value-Added Calculation Method—Month X

1. Value of production (sales ± various adjustments)		$1,000,000
2. Less: Outside purchases (material, supplies, energy)		
Material and supplies	$500,000	
Other outside purchases, nonlabor costs	160,000	660,000
3. Value added (#1 − #2)		340,000
4. Allowed employee costs (from diagnostic historical		
analysis)—(#3 × 41.17%)		140,000
5. Actual labor (employee costs)		120,000
6. Bonus pool (#4 − #5)		20,000
7. Company share (50% × #6)		10,000
8. Employee share (#6 − #7)		10,000
9. Reserve for deficit months (20% × #8)		2,000
10. Bonus pool (#8 − #9)		$ 8,000
11. Participating payroll		$ 80,000
12. Bonus percentage (#10 ÷ #11)		10%

flexible to changing conditions, and useful in isolating problem and opportunity areas if computed by major product line or product division.

What is the primary disadvantage of such a system of measurement? Inability of employees to relate to such a measure may be a problem. This problem would depend on the nature of the organization's operations. It too shares some of the motivational weaknesses of profit sharing. Generally speaking, it may be a desirable method for a job shop type of firm to consider along with perhaps some retailing types of organizations.

4.20 ALLOWED-LABOR CALCULATION

What factor is causing many of the heretofore mentioned problems? Including revenue in the calculation. Think about it. If revenue could be dropped from the calculation, most of product-mix and inflation problems could be eliminated. Over time more variables influence sales and the firm's total financial productivity than just payroll costs. Sales just allow labor productivity to occur. All costs are of course eventually influenced by sales, but in the meantime historical and current costs are all intermingled, with the company at times losing control over the variables that influence the bonus. Consequently it seems logical to exclude sales directly from the calculation, at least until the firm has developed the scanlon plan philosophy to a significant degree. But remember that this drops one of the important variables that sets the scanlon plan apart, including market prices (sales) in the calculation.

Some scanlon plan type of companies eventually come to this conclusion if the primary objectives of their plans and calculations are to measure and increase labor productivity. Usually they are satisfied with the results, although the calculation is not without its problems. The allowed-labor calculation is also a significantly better measure of labor productivity and provides vastly improved information to get more employees more involved in the cost-reduction aspects of the plan. Simply stated, it can help to develop the scanlon plan philosophy and accountability. Now how do they do it? Remember you must develop a system that includes broad labor costs, from direct labor employees to most fringe benefits, and indirect resource employees from the president on down. At the same time, a system must be developed that does not unduly emphasize individualistic behavior.

4.20.1   Rationale Underlying the System

In manufacturing firms most costs are related to production at least in the long run. Without production the firm, of course, eventually goes out of business. Similarly where there is production, someone (direct labor) or something (machine hours, patients, tests performed, hours billed, etc.) is involved in getting the production out. Often in many manufacturing firms without direct labor there is no long-term productivity. Consequently if the objective is to measure and improve labor productivity, why not base the measurement system on direct-labor productivity rather than on sales? For some firms another direct measurement variable (e.g., machine hours) may be more suitable than direct labor, but most manufacturing firms do have some such direct measurement variable. By using this point in the production-and-sale cycle, you have decreased product-mix problems and practically eliminated the influence inflation has on the typical ratio calculation discussed earlier. How is it done?

Most companies have a fairly accurate measurement of the time involved to accomplish a particular direct-labor task. These measurements are tied into a standard cost system and accumulated by each department or job for a period such as a month to determine how efficient a particular department, job, or employee was by comparing actual times (and costs) with standard times (and costs). Variance analysis normally provides information regarding why allowances were or were not attained. Even if a standard cost system has not been developed, most companies do account for all direct-labor hours. The allowed times may be developed from past experience or engineered, and may be detailed by each operation or just a total for a department. Our preference is to use actual past times, because it can then be said that the target to shoot for is actual past performance—a very important point. Engineered times could be acceptable if based on normal capacity. Both time and dollar allowances are normally reviewed annually for changed conditions. This method of calculation then proceeds along the following lines:

1. Use the actual times it takes to produce each product in each department. Often an average of the last three times is used. An allowed time to produce the particular product is established for each department. If standard times are used, they should ideally be adjusted to actual normal times when the new calculation is installed to ensure equitability (i.e., set at normal capacity). The only time that these allowed times are changed is when conditions change, such as a major investment in laborsaving equipment or obvious error. They are the new allowed times and will remain the same, with any betterment being paid in bonus. This is essentially what is said in the single-ratio calculation—beat past performance and a bonus is earned. This type of measure is similar to the government's output-per-hour calculation. Each month you would take each department's equivalent output by product; multiply by the allowed time of each product; divide by actual direct-labor hours; and multiply the sum by 100 to yield a productivity index which you could plot over time. This can be a good measure of performance productivity of direct labor.

2. Each allowed time is multiplied by the average labor rate in the department when the calculation is established. This wage rate must of course be normalized for fairness. For example, if you have just hired a significant number of new workers, your average wage rate will be below normal. The reverse is true if you are in or just coming out of a recessionary period. Now, the actual labor cost is subtracted from allowed time; the amount of the bonus contribution and financial productivity of direct labor is determined. For example, if the allowed time for a particular product in a particular department is 2.5 hours and the average wage when the calculation is implemented is $4 per hour, the allowed labor is 2.5 × $4, or $10 per item produced. If 500 are produced in a particular period and actual labor costs are $4,500, the total allowed payroll is 500 × $10 or $5,000. This permits the calculation of a productivity index:

$$\frac{\$5,000}{\$4,500} \times 100 = 111.1 \text{ percent}$$

or if the base period is 100, you experienced an 11.1 percent increase in productivity for this product for the period. The productivity of products produced by department or overall plant could be easily charted in the plant over time for additional feedback on even a daily basis if the records provided the data on such a regular basis. These figures would be tied directly to the bonus calculation shown later. The allowed times and dollars could be provided to the employees before production began to increase involvement in productivity improvement. The details are presented in Table 4.7 in the form of an example.

3. Based on the direct-labor allowances, similar allowances are established for all the other indirect costs to be included in the calculation. This is accomplished by dividing the actual costs of the indirect items in the base period by the total direct labor allowed in the same period. Some companies, where indirect-labor costs vary considerably by product line (e.g., selling, delivery, or administrative labor expenses), use a separate indirect allowance for each of the costs by every major product line to ensure equitability and flexibility. Other companies allow percentages of budgeted sales for some costs. A careful diagnostic analysis of the particular company should disclose which alternative is the most applicable. Depending on the sophistication of your analysis and records, you may determine that direct labor may be acceptable for some items, sales for other items, and some other variable for still others. The analysis made in the diagnostic section would be expanded to compare all labor costs with direct labor in addition to sales value of production. You may decide that certain indirect costs vary more with sales than direct labor.

4.20.2 Observations Regarding the System

You should immediately note that this calculation appears to be somewhat contrary to the philosophy we have encouraged you to develop, that is, the philosophy of teamwork and cooperation. On the surface this calculation does appear to be more individualistic, and it will probably become so if you encourage such behavior. It certainly expands accountability significantly. For if cooperation is lost to competition, problem isolating and solving to finger pointing and criticism, surely the system will fail. We encourage you to not establish the allowances on an individual employee basis where possible to help prevent certain supervisors from taking such actions. Remember if you beat employees over the head with their performance results, you will ruin the plan's philosophy. Help them to see how they can improve their jobs and performance. The goal should be to develop self-control and accountability.

Several scanlon companies have adopted such a system without overly developing the individualistic behavior, but they have guarded against such behavior in a variety of ways. These techniques include not even collecting individual performance data (the company uses engineered allowances); monitoring suggestions closely (watching for decreasing numbers or ones emphasizing individualistic behavior); and not giving one department's performance to other departments (working with only that department in the beginning). Can you say you are ready for such a system? See Appendix D for help.

Table 4.7 Calculation of the Equity Bonus by Percentage of Allowed Labor, Incentive, and Calculation, Month of _____

	1 Percentage of Allowed* Direct Labor	2 Labor Allowed	3 Actual Labor	4 Bonus Contri- butions	5 Productivity Index $(2 \div 3 \times 100)$
Direct labor:					
Department or product A		$ 5,000	$ 4,200	$ 800	119
Department or product B		6,000	5,600	400	107
Department or product C		7,000	6,100	900	115
Direct labor		18,000	15,900	2,100	113
Indirect payroll allowances:					
Indirect labor (by department?)	25	4,500	4,100	400	110
Overtime premium	7	1,260	1,400	(140)	90
Holiday	6	1,080	1,200	(120)	90
Vacation	5	900	1,000	(100)	90
Workmen's compensation	5	900	800	100	112
Other taxes and insurance	10	1,800	1,900	(100)	95
Manufacturing overhead					
(supervisor, etc.)	20	3,600	2,900	700	124
Selling	10	1,800	1,500	300	120
R and D	5	900	1,000	(100)	90
General administrative	25	4,500	4,000	500	113
Returns and allowances	2	360	450	(90)	80
Indirect allowances	120%	21,600	20,250	1,350	107
Total		$39,600	$36,160	3,450	110

Company share (assume 20%) $ 690

Participants share   2,760

Reserve for deficit months (assume 25%)   690

Pool for immediate distribution $2,070

Net bonus percentage to be distributed this month:
  Bonus ÷ participating payroll = $2,070 ÷ $28,000 = 7.4%

Gross bonus before reserve: $\dfrac{\$ 2,760}{\$28,000} = 9.9\%$

Cumulative total in bonus reserve: $10,500
Optional information:
  Allowed payroll costs ÷ sales value of production = $39,600 ÷ $158,400 (assumed actual) = 25%
  Backlog: $380,000 in sales, $40,000 standard labor

* Some method other than direct labor could be used to determine indirect allowances if appropriate.

Regarding complexity, this fluctuates greatly from firm to firm. Some can do it easily, and others take quite a while to work out the details. Only you can answer the question of whether it is too complex for you or whether your system is sufficiently reliable in the aggregate.

Another obvious use of this approach to the calculation is when an organization does not establish market prices; that is, it may be the only practical calculation for a plant at which all or a significant part of its output is just transferred to another unit of the company. Either this approach or combining two or more units into one plan are the only logical alternatives.

But until you have developed the organization both from a financial data sophistication and reliability standpoint and from a behavioral point of view of openness and trust, *we strongly suggest that you not use such a system.* Why? Management at all levels is not likely to be able to resist using the data in an improper way, giving the participants a feeling of manipulation. It is of course proper to use such data in monitoring of the bonus calculation.

Other comments can be briefly summarized as follows:

1. We suggest feeding back to the screening committee and employees only allowed labor minus actual labor in the beginning. Then, work with additional feedback to individual departmental foremen, and provide more details as you develop the organization. Go slowly with the large quantity of additional information. Nothing is really gained by giving one department's performance to another, and much can be lost in terms of confidence.
2. Converting a ratio calculation to an allowed-labor type is discussed in Appendix E.
3. Establishing a formalized system (committee) for an annual review of direct allowances and setting a minimum variance (e.g., 15 percent) before a change is considered, and then only for good reason, normally only for previous errors or capital expenditures. Hopefully, the committee includes a foreman and a screening representative. Do not allow nit-picking or concentration only on tight allowances. Make sure that you keep track of how many you give and take on. Top managment must make the decisions on final changes.
4. Establishing a general policy for capital expenditures (when to adjust allowances) and wage increases. For example, allowances are not normally adjusted for merit increases with across-the-board increases dependent on economic and competitive conditions. Other variables often requiring adjustment include timing differences between direct and other wage adjustments, and the working off of backlog before adjustments are made.
5. If separate allowances are established in all the separate indirect fringe areas such as workmen's and unemployment compensation, bonuses or losses will be incurred on these items which can be allocated on some

reasonable basis (both allowance and actual cost). Bonus in these areas are earned even with the single-ratio calculation, but the amounts are not separately calculated (i.e., are all aggregated together). Over time some firms take out a few of these items to clean up the calculation somewhat (see earlier discussion of items to include and exclude).

6. Materials, supplies, or energy could easily be added to such a calculation by isolating the price variance so that only the quantity directly affects the calculation.

7. Productivity indexes can easily be computed either on a performance or financial basis. Additionally you should be able to see how this calculation should force an increase in productivity if a shift occurs from direct to indirect employees.

8. Rather than using the continued actual wage (pay for performance productivity only), we suggest that firms allow the allowed wages (actual average when established) plus any adjustments over time. This hopefully gets employees involved in the trade-off of higher-skilled and higher-paid employees who must be the most financially productive. Allowing the actual wage would decrease problems during expansionary times, becuase you hire lower-waged employees than you are allowed. During recessionary times, however, you average actual wages will be greater than allowed if employees are laid off. This latter effect may cause wider bonus fluctuations during a business cycle, depending, of course, on the productivity of older and newer employees.

9. In order to bring in the market-price considerations and all the other variables that influence profit, you should consider also installing some form of profit sharing, even if small in percentage.

A couple of very important final notes must be made. First, all adjustments must be decided on competitive conditions at the time changes are considered. This is true of technology, wage adjustments, and other changes. Second, consider materiality, timing, and equitability in your deliberations. Do not allow nit-picking to build up, and do not give the company away. Also, do not be arbitrary and unfair, or the whole system will fail. Building overall trust and equity are certainly more important than what calculations you have.

4.21 OTHER CALCULATIONS

Some companies have experimented with or installed still other calculations. What has directed them to these unusual variations? Perhaps the conviction that volume changes should not be rewarded with bonuses. In other cases, perhaps the conviction that all levels of employees should be held accountable not only for profit but also the resources that it took to generate those profits (e.g., return on investment). Other organizations have tried to use regression analysis to isolate cause-and-effect relationships and included only these in the calculation.

We suggest that you avoid these calculations at least in the beginning. Employees have sufficient difficulty relating to some of the more common and simple calculations to start with.

4.22 NEWLY FORMED ORGANIZATIONS

A question sometimes asked is how do we set up a scanlon plan measurement system for a new firm or a new plant? Intuitively, you could certainly find considerable merit in starting a plan at a newly formed organization, because it may reduce friction, decrease resistance to change, and get all employees off to a good start. So, ideally, we can see certain merit in wanting to start the organization out with a scanlon plan.

But, from a measurement standpoint, we normally say in the scanlon plan, "Beat past performance (however defined) and earn a bonus!" What past performance? Naturally, you have no past experience, and to use some other plant's experience could be a serious mistake. About the only thing that might work reasonably well would be a very broad calculation such as the multicost or profit-sharing types. You could set up all the other principles of the plan (e.g., suggestion system, committees, identity) with the commitment that if everything was progressing smoothly, the bonus system would be installed. With some likelihood, the enthusiasm for the plan would probably be less than that normally experienced because of this action.

4.23 OVERALL EVALUATION AND QUALITY CONSIDERATIONS

You can probably evaluate the systems we have discussed yourself, but we have prepared Table 4.8 to give you some assistance. The five systems in the table are (1) single-ratio, (2) split-ratio, (3) value-added, (4) allowed-labor, and (5) multicost and profit sharing. Our evaluation is somewhat subjective and varies from situation to situation. It is based on our logic and experience in the field. As with many activities, trade-offs do occur. You must evaluate your own trade-offs.

We have not said much in this chapter about quality. In any system a trade-off can occur among price, productivity, and quality. For example, if management establishes a plan based on the single ratio, it could in some cases substitute lower-quality material which would penalize the plan if no adjust-

Table 4.8 Critique of Measurement Systems: Ranking A (Excellent)—F (Very Poor)

	Single-Ratio		Split-Ratio		Value-Added		Allowed-Labor		MultiCost and Profit	
	At Instal-lation	3–5 Years	At Instal-lation	3–5 Years	At Instal-lation	3–5 Years	At Instal-lation	3–5 Years	At Instal-lation	3–5 Years
1. Soundness as a measure of performance	B	B–D*	A–B	B–D	A–B	B–C	A	A–B	A–B	A–B
2. Perceived fairness as a measure of performance	A	C–D	A	B–C	B	B–C	A–B	B–C	A–B	B–D
3. Ease of understanding	A	B–D	A	B–C	B	C–D	B	B	B–C	C–D
4. Ease of administering	A–B	A–B	B–C	B–C	B	B–C	A–C†	A–B	B	A–B
5. Flexibility to meet changing economic conditions	B–C	B–D	B	A–C	B	B–C	A	A–B	A	A–B
6. Usefulness—isolating problem areas and directing attention	D	D–F	C	C–D	C	C–D	A	A–B	C	C–D

* Some companies that use the calculation as a control system seem to have more problems than large companies that have the data and staff to adjust when it is required.

† This of course will depend on the availability of data and its accuracy.

ment were made. Likewise, employees could start putting out lower-quality merchandise to increase short-run bonuses. The returns are normally charged against the plan, but you must establish a goal of at least monitoring the same level of product quality, or in the long run the plan and the company suffer. Many scanlon firms have found that in the long run quality goals have become as important as productivity goals.

4.24 CALCULATIONS FOR SERVICE, RETAIL, AND OTHER NONMANUFACTURING ORGANIZATIONS

The remaining sections extend productivity measurement to new areas.

1. Service-area measurement problems.
2. Sample service-industry models, such as hospitals.
3. Calculation alternatives.
4. Quality-merchandise alternatives in the service industries.

As the country continues to move toward service-oriented companies, application of the principles underlying such organizational approaches as the scanlon plan should increase in importance. Many organizations from retail stores, financial institutions, and educational and governmental units could be classed in this grouping. Some individuals do not feel that calculations such as we have already discussed work well in service and other nonmanufacturing-oriented organizations. We disagree quite strongly, although we were asked this question quite frequently. We do feel that many nonmanufacturing firms can use one of these approaches to equitable sharing of benefits.

For the most part, even service organizations have fairly specific outputs. If that output is not of sufficient quality and economic benefit, purchasers will go elsewhere or cease buying it altogether if possible. The measurement problems confronted by many service-oriented firms are not that dissimilar from those of a manufacturing firm with 10 percent of its labor cost direct labor and 90 percent indirect resource employees. Why are most service, financial, professional, or retailing organizations any different? This could be true for organizations from banks, schools, retail stores, to many governmental units (the plan has been applied in government units). Naturally, we agree that in some instances measuring productivity in terms of output would be difficult at best. However, nothing should prevent them from attempting to apply other principles underlying the plan.

Both types of organizations must develop a way to include all the resource employees in the calculation (output not directly measurable in terms of performance productivity). You, of course, will not have difficulty finding exceptions to this logic in those organizations for which measurable output is extremely difficult.

But why could not the single-ratio or straight allowed-labor methods of calculation work as well in service-oriented and other nonmanufacturing firms as in manufacturing firms? In fact they may work better, because labor is often a larger percentage of total costs and technology may influence the organization less. We know, for example, that the single-ratio has worked well in a distribution center. The particular calculation method would depend on the objectives of the scanlon and measurement systems, the particular type of organization, and what the diagnostic analysis would show. Regression analysis could be helpful in isolating interrelationships. You must analyze your situation based on the calculations discussed earlier.

Continuing, the value-added or multicost approaches may be particularly adaptable to retail types of establishments (because of rapidly changing outside purchases, and selling prices, low profit margin). The single-ratio method may be useful in consulting and other professional firms. The allowed-labor method may be the most useful for organizations such as large repair shops and educational institutions. To be sure, problems of quality, and so on, would occur, but if they are not considered before the plan is installed, perhaps the management deserves to be severely squeezed competitively or in other ways. Many individuals do not feel that the quality of services and efficiency is terribly high in all instances now. Developing the scanlonism principles is of paramount importance to the quality and productivity of all service and other firms, with the measurement of the outcomes often being less difficult than in manufacturing organizations. The idea seems novel, since the plan has been installed more frequently in manufacturing firms.

One type of service organization in which the scanlon plan per se has been tried numerous times is hospitals. In following sections we discuss an approach to installing a scanlon plan measurement system in a hospital. We feel that it has significant merit to hospitals and that the general approach has applicability to many other types of service organizations.

4.25 HOSPITALS—A SAMPLE CALCULATION FOR SERVICE ORGANIZATIONS

You will undoubtedly agree that increasing hospital costs have become a major United States problem. The reasons for this are not difficult to find and include general inflation, increased hospital size, shorter workweek, traditionally low wages, higher technology and skill levels, new facilities, and malpractice insurance. Probably no industry has been confronted with more problems at one time, which helps explain why in a recent 10-year period, hospital costs per inpatient day have risen about four times faster than the consumers' price index. Some individuals, however, question whether hospitals have done everything possible to increase productivity and quality. We feel that hospitals will be forced to install good management principles if cost control is ever to be attained. This is true partly because of the rapidly changing skill level and employee expectations. These management principles include the same ones underlying the scanlon plan.

Based on the above comments, you would think that hospitals would be particularly interested in plans such as scanlon with its sharing of benefits. As a matter of fact, successful installation of the scanlon per se have been few and far between, although hospitals are active users of many of the principles of scanlonism. Why the lack of success?

We feel that hospitals and their administrators perceive that two significant problems confront the installation of scanlon type of plans; they are (1) developing a fair measurement system and (2) maintenance of quality. We discuss both in depth.

4.25.1 Developing a Fair Hospital Measurement System

On the surface you might wonder why hospital measurement is any different from other organizations. In fact they look easier, since they do not have problems with inventories, as would a manufacturing or retailing organization. We do not believe that they are necessarily more complex, but we do believe that installing the single-ratio method would create problems.

When the scanlon plan per se has been installed, normally the single (multi-cost) ratio has been used; that is, a ratio of revenue to labor costs and sometimes other costs has been established and used in subsequent periods to determine allowed labor. The results have not generally been encouraging. Unfortunately, we do not know all the reasons why, but the calculation formula often played a role. One reason for the single ratio's not working well in hospitals is that total hospital costs per day have been rising about twice as fast as payroll costs; that is, payroll costs are a decreasing percentage of total revenue. Consequently, by allowing a certain percentage of revenue with revenue rising faster than payroll costs, a hospital would probably find its costs increasing after installing the plan rather than decreasing. Not a very exciting prospect. Profit sharing does not work in most hospitals, because if the system looks remotely like a profit-sharing plan, the hospital will lose its tax-exempt status and, of course, many of its donations.

As hospitals move toward prospective rather than retroactive reimbursement programs, perhaps some sort of budget approach will work if adjusted for volume. Something like the following could be employed:[5]

$$contribution = budget\ dollars \times \frac{actual\ volume}{anticipated\ volume} - actual\ dollars$$

Of course you would have to do this by department or service. Its success would depend heavily on the budgeting process (dollars and volume). Each year's bonus would depend heavily on anticipated activity. Frankly, we are uncertain regarding how well it would work, but we are not optimistic regarding its success over time.

The value-added approach discussed in this chapter should work fairly well; that is, subtract from revenue the outside purchases, including supplies, physicians' fees, insurance, energy, and perhaps depreciation, to yield value added. Then determine a historical relationship of wage costs to this value added, and allow this percentage. Although we are not aware of a hospital that has used this calculation, it should work considerably better than the single-ratio calculation.

We feel that as hospitals develop their information system with the aid of computers, the allowed-labor method of calculation will work quite well. You would have to make a comprehensive analysis to determine the appropriate unit of measurement for the respective service. Then several easily measured departments could be carefully monitored for a trial basis. Some examples are the following:

1. Laboratory—tests.
2. Radiology, anesthesiology, EKG and EEG—procedures.
3. Nursing units, food service, maintenance and security, accounting, administration—patient days.

You would continue on until all departments are assigned a physical measure of output. You would break it down as detailed as possible for monitoring and control purposes. For whatever periods you have past records for, you would find past times requirements per unit of measurement; that is, the average lab test took 15 minutes, the average operation one hour (in total or by type if mix has changed significantly over time and records are available), and continuing on until all departments are analyzed and an average physical measurement time is obtained. Another approach would be to use minutes of utilization, although this might result in wasted time. Use the essential ingredients in Section 4.5 for guidelines along with the detailed discussion of the allowed-labor

[5] This approach was suggested by Larry Redoutey, of Bon Secours Hospital, Grosse Pointe, Michigan. Other approaches might include regression analysis by department in attempting to establish the best output measure.

calculation method in Section 4.20. Establish the average wage rate per unit of measurement when installed, and when multiplied by the allowed time, you would have the total allowed per unit of output. You could even adjust for wage differences. In any period, you would compute the allowed labor as follows:

$$\begin{array}{l} total\ allowed \\ labor\ per \\ department \end{array} = \begin{array}{l} number\ of\ items \\ performed\ in \\ month \end{array} \times \begin{array}{l} time\ allowed \\ per\ item \end{array} \times \begin{array}{l} average \\ wage\ per \\ item \end{array}$$

In abbreviated form the calculation could look like Table 4.9.

Table 4.9　Hospital Bonus Calculation—Month X (Brief Form)

Departments	Allowed Labor	Actual Labor	Bonus Contribution	Productivity Index
Direct Departments:				
Radiology:				
Month's procedures × time allowed per procedure × average wage per procedure				
OR:				
Number of operations × time allowed per operation × average wage per operation				
Dietary:				
Number of meals				
Nursing units (in detail):				
Patient days				
Indirect Departments:				
Accounting:				
Patient days ($ per)				
Fringe benefits:				
Detailed—% of payroll				
	XX	XX	XX	XX
Organization's and others' (Blue Cross, etc.) share			XX	
Participants' share			XX	
Reserve for deficit months			XX	
Current bonus			XX	

This type of calculation would offer significant advantages over the other types discussed, and most of the earlier comments to the allowed-labor method would be applicable. It recognizes the interdependencies of the typical hospital. Performance (hours) and financial (dollars) productivity measures can be easily computed for most departments. It can be easily adjusted to changing conditions and meets the other essential ingredients discussed in the first part of this chapter. The biggest problem of measurement is data requirements. Most hospitals now have much of the information or could fairly easily obtain it with existing computer capabilities. You could also include supplies in the calculation by isolating the price variance when purchased so that only quantity and not rapidly changing supply prices influence the bonus. Remember not to feed back too much data too fast. Refrain from distributing a summary sheet of all departments' contributions to all employees or the screening representatives.

Important point: You might at this time ask a basic question. What is to prevent employees from performing more procedures, and so on, in order to increase allowed labor? Generally speaking, staff doctors determine the quantity of procedures performed. The hospital and its employees determine the efficiency (productivity) and quality of these procedures. Consequently, no major problems should result in the performance of extra, unneeded services.

A final comment is in order. Rather than applying this measurement system to the entire hospital at once, you might elect to use it in certain departments that are not so interdependent with others on a trial basis, particularly if past data are currently inadequate. Good candidates may include laboratory and dietary departments. Theoretically, you should of course include everyone in the calculation or at least soon after a test period.

4.25.2 Quality Maintenance for Hospitals

Now comes the difficult part. The consequences of not having a quality measuring and monitoring system when such a plan is installed could be significant. You could imagine a lawyer's line of questioning in a malpractice suit if such a system were not in use. For it is likely that hospital productivity could be increased significantly if such a productivity-improvement system were installed.

Any organization, including a hospital, that does not maintain its quality after installing the plan discovers its customers soon finding other suppliers. As a matter of fact, quality consciousness and improvement normally becomes an important goal of scanlon plan organizations. As they develop the scanlon plan philosophy, they normally place quality high in the list of priorities. We feel that hospitals are no different, especially with the malpractice threat.

Hospitals are in fact some of the most thoroughly organized institutions in the country. Part of this is the result of hospitals performing very similar activities, which makes standardizing systems among hospitals possible. The American Hospital Association is an exteremely important contributor to this activity. One unfortunate fact is that some hospitals do not use what is available to them.

Some examples of quality control programs are the following:

1. CASH approach—Commission for Administrative Services in Hospitals; concerned primarily with administrative and patient care.
2. PAS—Professional Activity Study; concerned with medical services performed.
3. Internal nursing and other audits.
4. Patient surveys (for such items as food and service).[6]

These monitoring activities would, of course, be done on a sample basis, and once they are systematized, the cost of collecting the data should not be too great. This cost would have to be absorbed by the scanlon plan, just as the inventory taking is in a manufacturing firm.

Frankly, we do not feel that the quality-maintenance program required by the plan is difficult, and we think hospitals should be doing many of the activities already. But because of the severe consequences, the penalties of not maintaining quality must be more severe in a hospital compared with some other firms. Consequently, if it is determined that quality is not being maintained, the plan bonus calculation should be temporarily or permanently discontinued. The remaining principles could, of course, continue to be applied. All participants should understand this quality commitment from the beginning or it should not be installed.

4.26 SUMMING UP

This is a long and complex chapter. You cannot digest it all in one reading, but we feel that problems others have encountered should help you avoid or at least cope with them.

We begin the chapter by discussing a way to prepare a diagnostic analysis, including some guiding criteria for installing such reward systems. We present a method of establishing the single-ratio calculation. Next, we discuss the rationale for including and excluding certain variables from your scanlon plan calculations.

---

[6] Additional ideas and details can be obtained from the American Hospital Association and some of its publications such as *The Management of Hospital Employee Productivity*, American Hospital Association, Chicago, 1973.

The remainder of the chapter primarily discusses alternative equity-measurement systems, starting with the traditional single-ratio method and proceeding along to develop some useful, more complex calculations. We say and try to show why we do not think that measurement in nonmanufacturing firms is necessarily any more difficult than in manufacturing firms.

To summarize, we feel that you must answer the following general questions with regard to measurement: (1) will the elected measurement system of rewarding performance work well for you based on your objectives, and (2) will it orient everyone's attention in the direction you desire? Although they are not easily answered, we have provided a significant amount of assistance to help you answer them. A key point to remember in developing a calculation is what problems you will encounter in the future, and how you will cope with them? Although the problems are often not that great, anticipation is important.

Appendix D is concerned with your company's economic facts of life and sophistication of accounting system. It should be of considerable assistance in evaluating your company's current status and to help set goals for the scanlon plan.

Note that Appendix E is concerned with converting a single-ratio calculation to an allowed-labor calculation.

This chapter deals with policy considerations brought about by the adoption of the scanlon plan. Another term for policy is "conventional wisdom." Nevertheless, though we may not be able to prove each of the following considerations which should be dealt with in the manner we are suggesting, we can say the following policies work well for many scanlon firms.

5.1 PARTICIPATING PAYROLL—WHO SHOULD PARTICIPATE

Most firms include everyone on the participating payroll with these exceptions:

1. Summer and part-time workers are excluded.
2. New employees must wait through a probationary period before they may join the scanlon payroll.
3. Sales forces on their own incentive system are normally excluded.

New employees wait for a very good reason. Their contribution to productivity is not up to full speed at first. Thus the plan does not carry them through their learning period. On an average, the probationary period is 60 days for most scanlon firms, or new employees sometimes are voted in on an exception basis.

Why is everyone included on the participating payroll? Scanlon is a total, company-wide plan. Its philosophy is to increase cooperation by giving everyone a share. Since all employees are part of a total system, no distinction is made as to who shares in the gains of a productive firm. Granted, the bonus system is superimposed on the regular pay structure. It does not replace the concept of differential rewards. Top management should get more salary, because their contribution is supposed to be worth it to the firm. Therefore, if a monthly bonus for the participating payroll is 10 percent, the plant manager receives a 10 percent bonus based on his monthly salary.

We know of at least one plant manager in a multiplant corporation who gave up executive corporate benefits in favor of sharing in the scanlon bonus. In a sense he cut his ties with the centralized corporation in favor of sharing in the gains and losses of his own plant. Remember, the key idea is that everyone shares in the fate of the firm. The more inclusive the participating payroll, the greater the bond of cooperation.

You might ask about perceived equity of the participating payroll. We tested the notion that perhaps workers might see the bonus system as inequitable, since everyone gets differing absolute amounts of bonus. We surveyed 140 workers with an open-ended question, "In general do some people get a better deal than others as far as the bonus is concerned?" (see Appendix A so that you may test this in your own evaluation).

Only 4 percent wanted the bonus divided equally. This small percentage wanted everyone to get equal shares. Ninety-six percent saw the bonus system as equitable. Many volunteered the belief that higher levels of management or skill get paid more because they contribute more; therefore, it was appropriate that they receive more absolute dollars. This is precisely what Joe Scanlon felt was fair also.

Another factor that concerns the participating payroll is overtime. Everyone learns very quickly that periods of high productivity can be associated with overtime. If a person worked 40 hours, with 5 hours of overtime, his bonus check was higher than the person working only 40 hours. Therefore the overtime person received more absolute dollars in a bonus period because of the combined effect of overtime and the bonus. This is perceived as fair by others, since the overtime person expended more effort during periods of high productivity.

Two very interesting policy considerations occur because of overtime. First, everyone wants overtime to be justified, because it affects the formula in a way to reduce the total amount of the bonus. This causes vigilance over the abuse of overtime. Second, it also focuses attention on suggestions to improve methods so that overtime can be eliminated. Now, both of these instances affect policy, because people in department A want to know more about people in department B, because B may be getting more overtime. In the past, there was no need to know about other departments. As a matter of policy, you should encourage company-wide sharing of information. However, we suggest the policy that any suggestion relating to other departments must go to the screening committee.

Policy can be reinforced in imaginative ways. Consider the following example from a plan company that developed a questionnaire on the knowledge employees had about the bonus (the entire example is found in Appendix A.3).

SCANLON PLAN QUESTIONNAIRE

(Excerpt)

Underline the one correct answer, or fill in the blanks as instructed:

1. If labor earned on total production is (more, less) than the actual payroll, a bonus is earned.
2. Products with a higher labor content are easier to make bonus on than those with a lower labor content (true, false).
3. If the inventory decreases, it is still possible to earn a bonus (true, false).
4. If we are able to produce the same amount of product with less payroll, the bonus is (more, less).
5. If, with the same amount of payroll, we are able to increase the amount of labor earned in production, the bonus is (more, less).
6. Overtime is part of the participating payroll (true, false).

As you can see, understanding of the bonus calculation is directly connected to the policy of who should be on the participating payroll; that is, with everyone on the payroll, it pays to understand how labor costs influence the bonus.

5.2 BONUS AND GOOD COMPENSATION PRACTICES

Differential rewards are a part of life. The Roman Empire paid skilled workers more than unskilled. Though Russia professes to have a "pure" communistic system, differential pay structures and incentives are a way of life there. In the United States, it is a positive value to earn according to one's level of achievement, training, or contribution. Often it is a combination of all three of these elements. Thus it comes as no surprise that Americans see differential pay as a legitimate reward of work. Therefore, at no time should the plan be perceived as a wage increase or cost-of-living adjustment. As a matter of policy, your firm's position on wage structures should not vary after installing the plan. The plan is compatible with differential pay systems. Most scanlon firms pay well. If your wage and salary surveys show you are not paying the rates you should pay, be competitive and make your adjustments. Clearly, attracting and keeping the best people with competitive wages is sound policy. This policy will pay off if the plan is working for your firm. Your competition has to pay similar compensation rates but does not have the entire work force pulling together to work smarter, improve methods, raise quality, and control costs. One of the costs everyone tries to control is the labor bill. Selling prices may have to go up because of external influences, but a scanlon firm is trying harder to make its prices lower through improved productivity. Though not exactly a scanlon plan firm, Lincoln Electric Corporation pays competitive wages and pays a huge bonus because of its high level of productivity. Therefore, make it a very clear policy that your prevailing pay policy will not change as a function of installing the scanlon plan.

We would like to point out that your compensation package will be compatible with the plan. The only restriction is that the scanlon plan should not be installed with some other form of incentive plan (excluding profit sharing, which is dealt with next). Why? The scanlon plan alone is sufficient to manage. You will be challenged to explain it and manage it properly. For example, you will want to strike a balance between too much group behavior and too much individual behavior. Your compensation plan should be such that it fits into an individual's achievement, training, and contributions. Conversely, the scanlon plan should be emphasized to enhance cooperation and teamwork for greater productivity by individuals. This balance is only achieved by administering both plans effectively. As far as executive compensation is concerned, the plan is compatible, but reasonable care should be exercised to avoid dual standards. In this way executives should not have motives contrary to the plan.

5.3 PROFIT SHARING

Is the plan compatible with profit sharing? Yes. In fact, many plan firms have both. Historically, profit-sharing plans took off in the fifties. There were many positive reasons for this, but, currently, profit-sharing plans have not done so well, especially those related to stock prices. For public-relations purposes, many firms are reluctant to drop profit sharing. As it happens, a scanlon plan can start after a profit-sharing plan comes into existence. On introducing the scanlon plan, some workers may express concern about the two plans competing for the same profits. If this question occurs, take it as an opportunity to explain how the scanlon plan normally works on labor productivity but profit sharing is more complex as well as more removed from the direct influence of the work force.

Consider, for example, profit sharing's comprehensiveness as a corporation-wide plan. A multiplant corporation could have scanlon plans at the plant level and still have a corporation-wide, profit-sharing plan. This very comprehensiveness of profit sharing could permit the realization of material savings when they may not be shared under the plan (see Section 4.18 for discussion on how material savings may or may not influence the bonus). Therefore, when material savings occur to increase profitability, the profit-sharing plan offers a way to capture that and pay it as a reward once a year.

Though compatible with scanlon plans, profit sharing has a different character. We have argued earlier that profit-sharing plans have weak motivational properties. They may keep people from leaving a firm, but they may not encourage productive work behavior. Conversely, scanlon plans with their monthly bonus opportunities and emphasis on productivity continually reinforce productive work behaviors. Both plans can live together, but scanlonism increases the usefulness of profit sharing, because it is a constant business-teaching device in the hands of management.

5.4 FINANCIAL POLICY

Careful analysis of firms with long years of experience with the scanlon plan show that the average worker has an increased interest in and knowledge of the firm. We believe that is good. We know that nationally the general level of education is rising, and the worker of today is of a much higher caliber than in any other period of American industrial history. Therefore, it stands to reason that with this kind of worker firms committed to organizational development should disclose the kind of financial information that produces problem surfacing and problem solving.

This disclosure can take a variety of forms. First of all, it is hoped that everyone will start interpreting the bonus formula. At some point in time they may push numbers through the formula. One test such as this led to a request to have the controller compute a monthly bonus with and without summer workers. He did. The next suggestion requested management to reduce the summer work force by two-thirds. Management did. This worked out successfully for the firm. Now, communication such as this teaches everyone the benefit of using financial information. Once the process starts, it is difficult to turn off. Your policy goal is to get employees to identify with this type of information. In another example, a batch of a product was produced improperly; rather than eat the loss, R and D and production committees asked management for cost information on storing the batch for rework. At the same time they asked sales to develop a market for the reworked batch. Management provided the input, sales developed the market, and the batch was sold at cost. All this was done to avoid an increase to costs which would affect the bonus.

These examples led their firms toward sharing financial information they had not shared in the past. There is no doubt that successful scanlon firms share financial information with employees on a need-to-know basis. It is also true that accountants have tried to interest employees in financial data in the past, but then no one saw the need for relating to this information.

If you were lucky enough to visit a screening-committee meeting of a scanlon firm before your installation, the chances are very good you heard the president or controller routinely discuss financial information bearing on costs. You may have been astounded to hear a worker asking for cost information and challenging a suggestion as being "cost-effective." Therefore, start formulating your ground rules on disclosure of financial information. In general, the more information, the higher the quality of the involvement system up to a point. A word of caution is in order. Too much information is often worse than too little. Start slowly, and work with people as they need to know information and as they ask for it. Only then can they understand the information. The reason, by all accounts, is that problem solving (not snooping) makes the information salient. Incidently, just because some information is requested, do not automatically provide it without considering the implications.

5.5   ROLE OF MANAGEMENT

It may seem strange to talk about the role of management in a discussion on policy. Nevertheless, there are some general considerations which belong here. For example, informal leadership, recognition, and social esteem emerge from employee participation on production committees. Given that outcome, management should reevaluate its relative contributions to the plan. This examination may well lead to a redefinition of responsibilities for at least three key management roles. These roles are the president or plant manager, the controller (or designated staff), and the personnel manager. Chapter 6 describes in greater detail how these roles become operationalized.

Scanlonism does not change the prerogatives of management. Someone must still be the boss. For example, management decides when a change is needed in the calculation even if others are consulted. The style of management could change, but authority and decision making still reside with management. One expert, Carl Frost, has termed the screening committee as a consultative body and not a decision-making body. Arbitrary rule tends to be the kind of management style that is diminshed over time. Why? The screening committee provides a platform for management's rationale for its acceptance and rejection of suggestions. Disclosure of the president's thinking helps the screening committee work toward more effective problem identification. We argue that if businesses are to run rationally, it does not hurt to be persuaded by rational arguments. Thus, if management is a catalyst for goal setting and quality communication, the style of management is participative, not permissive. You will find further information in Chapter 8 which may affect your policy concerning the ultimate role of management. Scanlon managers are heard to say that the plan does not really change their style. They believe sincerely that the plan permits "good managers to manage better."

5.6 INDUSTRIAL RELATIONS AND SCANLONISM *AND* UNIONISM

The scanlon plan is not a grievance system, and it is an abuse of the plan to try to use it as such. Granted, the involvement system produces suggestions, especially in the trial year, which are gripes—some even more serious as grievances. The memo of understanding or just simply effective communication should make clear that only productivity-related suggestions are to be processed under the involvement system.

Whether union or nonunion, make clear distinctions in the screening committee when explaining why a given suggestion is not productivity-related. You might give some of the benefit of the doubt in the trial year to avoid discouraging enthusiasm. For example, a suggestion asking to rerate a job to make the hourly pay more equitable might have merit in a union company. However, no matter how cleverly the suggestion may be worded to make it sound productivity-related, refer the suggestion to the personnel manager of other appropriate committee for study. Show in the screening-committee minutes that the suggestion is "not a scanlon suggestion."

It is also true that the screening committee can appear to be a bargaining table. Why? Suggestions concerning methods improvements could lead to discussions of pay and job protection. The purpose of scanlon is to keep the firm viable. This does protect jobs. However, if a methods-improvement suggestion leads the discussion to red-circling the pay rate of workers involved, the screening committee has become a bargaining table. This is contrary to good industrial-relations practice. As a matter of policy, set aside suggestions dealing with pay rates, job protection, and general grievances. They are "not scanlon" and should be referred to the proper mechanism in your firm which you already have or should develop. This advice should be followed whether your firm is unionized or not.

Where there is a union, a good policy to follow is to indicate that the company does not intend to negotiate any aspects of the plan. It is a wise practice to structure your scanlon year on a different time cycle from the labor contract year. Thus the contract termination date will not coincide with the scanlon year-end date.

Even though all aspects of the plan would not be negotiated, you should recognize the existence of it in the union contract. Also some realization is necessary, in respect to unions, that they can repeal the plan. Naturally, if the union is in opposition to the plan, it simply nullifies any chance of plan success. Therefore, in the memo of understanding (Appendix B) a provision is made to cross-reference the plan with the union contract for those firms that are unionized. Philosophically, unionism and scanlonism are different. A better job for both can be done by those concerned if they are handled separately. Most unionized scanlon companies operate with this policy so that the advice has a basis in current industrial-relations practices.

The scanlon plan is not designed to replace or supplement the union. When applied to unionized firms, there is usually no problem in complementarity. Some firms, however, see it as a very strong viable alternative to a union for maintaining cooperation, decreasing confrontation, and getting first exposure to grievances. It is true that some companies have found this use very valuable. The reason for this is that the scanlon plan is perceived as a harmony model versus the conceptions of those who view industrial relations as a conflict model.

5.7 TERMS OF OFFICE FOR COMMITTEES WITH IMPLICATIONS FOR TRAINING

It is wise to structure the terms of office for committee membership at the beginning of the plan. Normally a term of office is one year. In the trial year it is possible that the first elected production-committee members may serve out the year, as elections could interfere with so many other new activities. Thereafter, set your policy at a one-year term. Hope to facilitate a rotation of the work force through these assignments.

What does this gain for you? Rotation maximizes exposure to the involvement system and bonus calculation. As more employees serve in the committee structure, they gain valuable experience into the profitable operation of the firm. It is not at all surprising that the plan serves as an informal training program. Many firms report that promotions can now consider other forms of behavior just as valuable as producing units of an output. An example might include working effectively with others. It seems odd, but usual working environments do not have enough facets to them when compared with supervisory roles. Just where is the job incumbent going to get people experience? Ironically, some forms of organizational development simulate these behaviors, because they are not available in the work environment. The scanlon plan structures these roles as a necessary and real facet of work.

Many firms have two employee representatives elected to the production committee, with the senior member in a one-year roll-over basis serving as the screening-committee representative; that is, if two employees are originally elected, the one receiving the most votes will also serve as the screening-committee representative. His term will be one year. At the end of a year (or six months sometimes), a new employee is elected, and the previously elected employee not presently on the screening committee replaces the first one. The process continues on a roll-over basis. If only one employee is elected, he, of course, serves as the screening-committee representative.

5.8   YOUR POLICY CONSIDERATIONS

We have carefully discussed common policy considerations that have evolved in more than 30 years of recorded scanlon plan experience. These considerations will help you to anticipate policy for your organization. If we have guided you carefully, you will be pointed in the right direction to modify these policy considerations for your firm.

From Chapter 2 onward we have offered you checklists and reminded you to keep notes on your discussion of goals, philosophy of management, and formula calculations. Review those now, and make a determination if further policy considerations will surface. After all, your particular organization and personnel will produce its own set of constraints. Deal honestly with those now. The sooner your policies are set and communicated, the easier it will be to achieve the kind of identity you wish to mold. Your policy considerations dealt with now are not an idle process. This review process can be adjusted as you evaluate your progress with the plan. Of course, this is just one more reason why the evaluation techniques discussed in Chapter 7 are useful. With updated information you can check reality in order to form more precisely the kind of policy which characterizes the needs of your organization.

One key element of your own policy considerations is a frank assessment of your position on full employment. If you are already committed to full employment, fine. If you wish you could establish a work force permanently attached to the firm, review the factors which lead to this goal for your situation. Most scanlon firms have a full-employment policy, because it meets one of the principal needs of the workforce—job security. An open and honest statement by management on this policy will be well received, because it has strong motivational value and the reserve account of the formula actually encourages a longer-range, incentive payoff at the year-end meeting.

5.9   SUMMING UP

This chapter brings to your attention policy that you may wish to anticipate for your firm. Of key concern is the role of the participating payroll and your compensation practices. Clearly, the scanlon plan is an augmenter or enhancer to good compensation practices. Profit sharing and the plan are compatible; however, we argue that the plan makes profit sharing more naturally appealing.

Financial policy and the role of management are key considerations. The plan is an information inducer. Management is challenged to open up its style and to provide their rationale for decision making. These two forces feed the involvement system to produce productivity-related suggestions and behaviors.

Finally, the plan is not an industrial-relations scheme. It will help to produce a harmony model of participation and cooperation between management and workers. It should not be used to preempt unions or used on problems which are clearly grievances about pay rates, seniority, and job protection. The plan encourages adaptability and acceptance of change. However, where issues affect industrial relations, they should be labeled as "not scanlon" and referred to other administrative groups such as safety or grievance committees. In this way, your policy is clearly stated, and the integrity of the plan is preserved.

OPERATING THE PLAN OVER TIME 6
Feeding the System

The greatest problem and challenge for management is to deal with the scanlon plan over time. During the trial year, there was much to learn, there was excitement about this new organizational development, and there was great optimism about the bonus. These factors will diminish because of the sheer impact of time and familiarity. How do you develop "true" identity with the organization and its problems and opportunities. Successful plan firms do manage to rekindle that enthusiasm through a sincere interest in organizational development. Another factor which helps to keep the plan fresh is the natural relation of the bonus to the firm's ability to meet its markets effectively. No bonus accrues automatically. The bonus is only achievable if productive zeal increases quantity, increases quality, and reduces costs each month.

At the end of the trial year a vote is taken to adopt the plan permanently. If that vote affirms the plan, it is a strong indication that all employees wish to make the plan work (see Section 6.9). But the best intentions do not make the plan succeed. Management and staff have to provide help. It is analogous to being taught what to search for but not knowing how. This is where management and staff can really serve the firm.

Thus this chapter deals with how to make the plan continue to work over time, well after the enthusiasm of the trial year. One of the key considerations is the continuing role of management. Evaluation under the plan is covered in Chapter 7.

6.1 MANAGEMENT SUPPORT—THE CATALYSTS

Four key roles emerge in support of the scanlon plan over time. These are:

1. Plant manager.
2. Controller.

3. Personnel manager.
4. Departmental supervisor.

Each of these roles has different duties, pressures, and opportunities which shape the quality of plan involvement.

6.1.1 The First Role Is the Plant Manager (or President in Smaller Firms)

It must be remembered that scanlonism does not change the basis of authority. Someone must be the legitimate boss. True, the style of management may change. Thus the plant manager may be explaining the reasons for his decisions in an effort (1) to teach members of the screening committee the why's and wherefore's of the free-market system and efficient management and (2) to help develop identity with the organization. Especially at the time of suggestion rejection (the prerogative of the plant manager), disclosure of his thinking helps members of the screening committee toward effective communication with their peers. Also it does not hurt to be persuaded by a rational argument. Therefore, instead of specifying scanlon beliefs to describe the plant manager's role, we argue it is what this role does, as a set of behaviors, that is important. And the plant manager or president (or both) is a catalyst for goal setting, quality communication, and, above all, a teacher. By seeing these facets of his role in the screening committee, the plant manager is afforded a meaningful opportunity to guide the plan over the years.

6.1.2 The Next Catalyst Is the Controller (and His Assistants Who Work Closely with Employees)

His role cannot be minimized. Almost as a matter of policy, his role will expand enormously. He will maintain a new information system as well as be in demand for visits in production committees. He will discover that he is getting to know more and more people throughout the firm. This is to be expected. If necessary, the controller should shift some of his normal duties to someone else, at least during the trial year.

The controller and his assistants will be explaining the formula often. Every month he will be displaying the results for the bonus announcement, be it a bonus or not. He will be asked to explain why fluctuations occurred. He will be faced with justifying expectations with reality. His role becomes an opportunity to teach the use of cost information to improve productivity. Therefore, as a matter of policy, the controller should expect to be more accessible and open with his time. He should strive to produce examples of the formula that are relevant to his firm's work force. He will become a resource person to production committees, which is something no one ever trained him for. Sure, he may cut some new checks with scanlon printed on them, but he also will find a new audience for accounting data. For example, since the plan focuses attention on cost reduction, the measurement of cost will become a topic for break and lunchtime discussion. We hope he is accessible to workers who want this information. Also, cost consciousness becomes heightened to the point that workers may see the controller as the key to problem solving for the involvement system. One important contribution to production committees is that the controller might indicate high-cost areas for suggestion making. In this way, maximum impact of productivity-related suggestions can be felt.

6.1.3 The Personnel Manager's Role Is a Catalyst Because of What He Must Do to Keep the Integrity of the Plan

Per our discussions on industrial relations, he will strive to separate out understanding on what is scanlon and what is not. The memo of understanding is kept by him, and it is fully appropriate for him to work with that document while counseling employees who have contributed suggestions not related to productivity. As a catalyst, the personnel manager provides orientation to all new personnel about the plan. He should also keep evaluation records on the plan (per Appendix F). He should expect that promotable persons may quickly surface in production committees. His knowledge of their contributions could be noted in their personnel folders. Because of his orientation and training, the personnel manager may be the best person to reinforce and "police" the policy governing the two other catalysts. By this we mean that training and discussion about "where we are" and "where we want to be" are fully appropriate. The plan is a form of organizational development. No firm will stay solely with the plan as originally established. It may be one of a series of steps leading to greater job satisfaction and higher levels of productivity. Thus, as the personnel manager evaluates the progress of the plan per our Appendix F, it would be appropriate for him to ask management to assess itself in view of what it has learned each year with the plan.

A special consideration for the personnel manager should be his concern for continuity. Changes will occur in personnel, even his job or that of the general manager's. Thus his role as a catalyst is to also guarantee that contingency training could produce replacements which will make the plan work when so-called key people are gone. This training starts with the identification of likely replacements for production and screening committees. Then frank discussions with this group over their knowledge and attitudes toward the plan might help to develop a cadre of people to preserve the plan for the long haul. These sessions could be a part of a regular program of leadership training. They could include hypothetical discussions such as "how would you handle this suggestion?" Or the sessions could be an excuse to get leadership training started.

As a matter of policy, the role of the personnel manager should be developed to handle these new situations with an aim toward continuing plan integrity.

The personnel manager will invariably see the training potential the scanlon plan has; that is, leadership will be socially acknowledged by one's peers through the vote for the production committee. Then, over time, some individuals will excel in their capacity to elicit suggestions, improve them, and provide negative feedback if necessary. This is clearly good experience for first-level supervision. Frequently industry promotes the best worker to first-line supervision as a reward for good work. Supervision often requires other skills for which the plan can provide some useful experience. He should also establish training programs for supervisors.

6.1.4 Departmental Supervisors in Fact Find Themselves in a New Role When the Plan Is Installed

Usually it is a role they did not ask for, and as with most innovations, it could produce some anxiety over the basis of supervision. For example, some authority is given to the production committee. The strength of peer review of suggestions is obvious. However, first-line supervisors are not necessarily peers. Thus some strain over acceptance of low-cost suggestions could occur. If it does, the problem was already there; that is, first-line supervision that is autocratic will dislike the scanlon plan. Conversely supervisors who believe in management by objective, working through others, and who do not find human-relations supervision something to snicker at will prefer the scanlon plan.

Some supervisors may need help in adjusting to this new role; offer them this book and counseling. Their situation is no different from that of middle and top management, because the task before them is that scanlon requires good managers to manage better and good supervisors to supervise better.

For example, here is a common error that supervisors sometimes commit. Instead of putting suggestions into the record, supervisors accept these suggestions outside of the plan. They undermine the production committee by personally accepting the low-cost suggestions for the department. This preserves their type of authority, enhances departmental functioning, and cheats the plan of proper evaluation. It also hides recognition for the suggestion maker. Discourage this from happening. If it does, analyze the supervisor, and try to understand his motivation. If he or she falls in the above category, work with this individual to improve his methods of supervision and get him or her to see the importance of not doing things this way. Most scanlon companies are continually looking for training programs for supervisors. In fact, this is one of the most important activities of the Scanlon Plan Associates.

We have discussed how four new roles emerge because of the scanlon plan. Actually, everyone in the firm gets an expanded role because of the involvement and accountability system. In particular, members of production and screening committees learn at an accelerated rate how the involvement system is integrally linked to productivity. Scanlon plan firms enjoy a very high rate of suggestions and a very high rate of accepted suggestions. This fact can never be minimized. Suggestions flowing from an organization-wide involvement system place a premium on cooperation and teamwork. Under ideal conditions, the level of trust in others becomes so high that *being just a worker or just a manager* in a scanlon plan firm is impossible. These four work roles are broader in scope and action in scanlon firms than the same work role in nonscanlon firms.

6.2 INVOLVING RESOURCE WORKERS

Many manufacturing firms have as many or more indirect or resource workers than direct-labor employees. In service-oriented or nonmanufacturing organizations, all the employees could be classified as resource workers. Why do we call them resource workers rather than indirect or staff employees? In reality they provide the resources to allow production to occur. Without them, very little gets done. You could say that they permit productive assets to be productive. We prefer resource worker to that of overhead, burden or staff.

Unfortunately these workers have not always played a direct role in scanlon plan involvement. Past effort has often been concentrated on direct-labor employees and their effort. Why? Partly because of tradition, but also because measurement is difficult in the resource-worker areas. Another reason is because many thought that these employees often think about increasing productivity as a natural part of their jobs, which may or may not be true, depending on the circumstances.

One consequence of this attitude or action has been the perceived decrease in productivity and involvement of some of these resource employees in the successful, or unsuccessful, operation of the plan. Another consequence is the awareness that the direct-labor employee develops in what the resource worker does to make the scanlon plan successful. The role of the controller's staff and perhaps the industrial engineers should be apparent at this point or will be by the time you complete this chapter.

In this area you should attempt to develop an environment in which all resource workers question what they are doing and how they contribute to the success of the scanlon plan. The company should attempt to develop an attitude that they are working for the plan. How can you do this? With a lot of hard work. Some suggestions that scanlon plan companies have tried include the following:

1. Monitor and report on suggestions or lack of them from resource workers. Why should a professional resource worker not get as much recognition for proposing the elimination or change of a poor form as a direct-labor employee who suggests elimination of an unnecessary production step?
2. Either in the company or plant newsletter or in the screening committee— both are frequently used—have a resource employee describe how he contributes to the success of the scanlon plan. Tape or keep these for later reuse. Or as stated recently by one controller:

> At a recent bonus employee feedback session we highlighted the sales department as a major bonus contributor by showing them a bonus break-even chart. It became very clear that when production volume exceeded $70,000 per day, assuming no major mix changes, we were in a bonus-producing-volume level. Frequently plant personnel believe that efficiency of labor and material usage is the major contribution. They now believe that salesmen make a major contribution to the opportunity to earn bonuses, which knowledge they didn't have before. I believe this kind of information adds to the education of all employees; and I am thinking seriously of showing how our purchasing department makes a contribution next month, research and development the following month, and so on. It will become evident, I believe, that all employees will see the interdependence required to produce bonuses.

3. Hold sessions with personnel in the respective resource departments to show them how important their activities are to the successful operation of the plan. They must also be convinced that they should work on increasing their own productivity for the sake of the scanlon plan and the company by questioning their own work and what they do for others. They must learn to ask how well others feel that they are doing in their work and listen to the response.

6.3   ORGANIZATIONAL AND DEPARTMENTAL GOAL SETTING

This is one of the most important aspects of the scanlon plan but, unfortunately, is one of the most neglected. Why is this so? Perhaps because goal setting is so complex. But all large, well-managed organizations practice it to some degree, because this is how they can increase accountability. The scanlon plan broadens and extends this activity to all organizational levels. Another problem is that increasing this involvement is tough to accomplish.

Unfortunately in some companies the scanlon plan calculation is used as a control tool, something for which it was never intended. This may actually result in less goal setting because of the belief that the scanlon plan covers any inefficiencies in one area with increased efficiencies in others. Thus management may hide behind it and not concentrate on further improvements if bonuses, and profits, are at a reasonable level. They, of course, are losing an opportunity to increase performance to even higher levels through cost-reduction goal setting.

Successful scanlon plan organizations accomplish this in a variety of ways. However, scanlon company employees and managers should have significantly different attitudes about such activities. Why? Because the participants share directly in the benefits of the efforts. They have something to gain by getting involved in such activities, and this fact is a strong selling point in trying to obtain such commitments; that is, all employees share in the extrinsic monetary savings, but all those who actively participate hopefully help satisfy their higher-order needs such as recognition and self-esteem of doing a good job.

Some of the programs used by scanlon organizations include the following:

1. With the purpose of setting goals, many scanlon organizations start on this activity by working in easily measured areas such as past-due or late orders, split-shipment percentages, shipping-error percentage, plant rejects, customer complaints, safety indexes, absenteeism (long- and short-term), turnover, and so on. For each one of the items selected, a goal is established, and performance is then measured against it. Depending on the particular measure, you should attempt to get the relevant personnel involved in how to improve performance. Start out small; some firms work through the screening and production committees in establishing these goals and working on improvements.

2. Some scanlon firms have sets goals for the suggestion system to attain. Often, these are just in the form of numbers of suggestions, and a common goal is to beat the previous period. For example, if five suggestions were made by a department in previous quarters, the goal to beat this period is five. Some departments get to the point at which it becomes hard to beat, so that you would not want to continue this program indefinitely. Perhaps rating suggestions for quality is more useful than encouraging a high number of suggestions.

3. The most creative approach used by scanlon companies is to open the cost-reduction activity to all departments. Every department must show, for example, how they are going to increase their productivity by 10 percent with the same input (i.e., they have to document how they will increase their output by 10 percent, or they will reduce other costs by 10 percent). This can be savings on materials, labor, capital, or energy. This whole activity gets somewhat complex, what with documentation desired of specific costs. If you think about the way the typical scanlon calculation is made,

this procedure may not be so tough as it sounds. For example, if sales are expected to increase by 10 percent in physical quantity without any change in selling price or major fluctuation in product mix, the labor allowed for any department would increase by 10 percent also. If they were able to hold the line with no increase in projected labor cost (i.e., assume a 10 percent increase in wages and a 10 percent decrease in hours by not replacing employees who left the firm), their productivity would increase by 10 percent. Behaviorally it is more desirable to concentrate on nonlabor expenses in the beginning even if they do not directly affect the bonus. You should be able to see how this procedure can be a natural educational lesson in how the scanlon plan is calculated and factors that influence it.

4. Highly desirable goals are those designed to beat the competition. Some companies have their screening-committee representatives—management and factory or other workers—analyze a sample of competitors' products for pricing and quality. In some complex product situations, professional R and D personnel or engineers are used to assist in this process. When it is possible and practical, this process for analyzing and trying to beat the competition makes considerable sense. It provides a common target and also educates employees about the economic facts of life.

5. As you develop in system capability, you should be able to make a fairly good projection of the bonus a month or two in advance and then analyze how well you are proceeding on a week-by-week basis. This somewhat forces the organization to discuss openly all the interdependent variables of marketing, shipping, purchasing, manufacturing, personnel, and so on. It also allows for considerable analysis of results after the fact. Consequently such programs are desirable if they are sufficiently accurate. No one can predict to the dime what the bonus will be, so that we strongly suggest you forecast based on ranges (e.g., 10% to 14%) rather than on exact percentage. Also, expect reactions such as the following one made by a scanlon controller:

> Isn't it interesting how production gets credit for those bonuses which are produced above accounting's projections and accounting gets the credit for all those bonuses below its projections. It never fails that when we exceed our expectations, production gets the credit; when we miss, accounting must have done something to screw up the books and manipulate the bonus.

Accountants must learn to live with such comments, since they are convenient fall guys. This, of course, is one of the problems of forecasting the bonus. But the long-run rewards more than offset the associated problems.

6. All the questionnaires we have provided in Appendixes A and D should provide useful additional goals. You should certainly not overlook these,

because they provide specific targets against which you can measure yourself, especially from a behavioral standpoint.
7. Successful scanlon companies also use all the other techniques found useful
   to modern managers, such as return on investment as a diagnostic tool, good
   capital-budgeting techniques, direct and relevant costing, and so should you.
   The best target to have is to be the best-managed company in your area.

Organizational and departmental goal setting is a complex process, and yet
also rewarding from the standpoint of involvement and productivity improvement. It takes continual encouragement and hard, dedicated work on the part
of the controller's staff and others. It must have the support of the highest organizational levels. Yes, you will find it very frustrating and discouraging at
times. But in the long run, goal setting is what makes the scanlon plan
successful.

6.4 MAINTENANCE OF SUGGESTIONS

Just as the formula may evolve over time from simple to complex, the involvement system becomes more sophisticated. Behaviorally you can expect these
kinds of changes with the involvement system:

1. Suggestions caused by irritants decline.
2. Productivity-related suggestions increase and then start to decline as ideas
   dry up.
3. The mix of suggestions ultimately reflects cost considerations and not
   quality and quantity, though you continue to receive suggestions in these
   areas.

Here are some experience data concerning what happens to the involvement
system over time. Figure 6.1 shows the trial year in terms of quantity and type
of suggestion made.
    The results of Figure 6.1 indicate that each suggestion falls into one of four
categories. The rating system permitted tallying multiple-category suggestions
in their primary category. The first category is for irritants; that is, it is for a
suggestion that may have improved working conditions but not necessarily the
quality or quantity of the product being manufactured. Other categories
reflected in Figure 6.1 are (1) quantity, the increase of number of units, (2)
quality, the increase of the product value so that it will obtain a higher price or
draw fewer complaints, and (3) cost reduction. It has been argued that workers
would focus mostly on cost reduction, such as methods to reduce waste, save
raw materials, and conserve resources allocated for overhead costs.

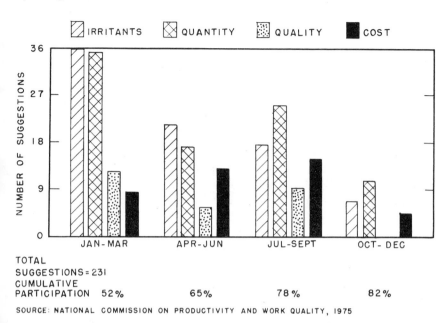

Figure 6.1   Types of suggestions and degree of participation over time (plant A).

The 91 different types of suggestions made during the first three months of 1971 involved the majority of the work force. By the end of the trial year, 82 percent had made at least one suggestion.

Figure 6.1 also indicates that in the first three months, irritations with work conditions dominated the suggestions. This is to be expected for two reasons: (1) suggestion making is a new activity, and common sources of ideas come from the irritants (the dissatisfiers that exist in the work environment), and (2)) time is required for the consultant, management, and the committee system to determine which suggestions can influence the bonus. As production committees can put some suggestions into immediate use, they are required to look at costs. An awareness of the true impact of a given suggestion occurs at this time, and priorities become established. This learning also helps to reduce the flow of suggestions, since only productivity-producing suggestions are sought. Production and screening committees become more critical over time.

This last characteristic of the suggestion system is borne out by Figure 6.1. As the irritants are taken care of, suggestions for quality, quantity, and cost are processed. Then ideas appear to dry up. Another factor explaining the rate of suggestion making is the ability of the organization to put good suggestions into effect. For example, when business conditions are poor, management is reluctant to make a capital investment on worthy suggestions. Also economies of scale are necessary to make suggestions profitable. Holding up a suggestion feeds back to the suggester the information that future attempts at suggestion making have a reduced probability of being accepted.

Now, let us look at the following two years of the involvement. Figure 6.2 shows how irritants drop out of the suggestion picture. You can see that the management and staff of this firm were successful in changing the character of suggestions made from a high percentage of irritants, which is common during the trial year, to productivity-related suggestions.

The "irritants" category in Figure 6.2 was changed to NPR (not productivity-related, referred to as NP in Figure 6.2). The only reason for this change was that careful analysis indicated that most NPR suggestions were related to safety rather than irritations with the work environment. However, "non-scanlon" suggestions were referred to other committees. The main story in Figure 6.2 was that quantity suggestions led in 1972 and 1973, continuing the trend from 1971. The amount of productivity-related suggestions ranged from 53 to 65 percent; that is, summing quantity, quality, and cost suggestions, productivity-related suggestions were the dominant type of suggestion. NPR suggestions were greater than quantity alone but not the sum of productivity-related suggestions.

Given the discussion above, just what can management do to feed the involvement system to keep suggestion-making behavior viable? The involvement system always requires an infusion of new ideas, constant care, and continued direction by management. Remember, however, it is the process of the involvement system that produces so many intangible benefits for the firm.

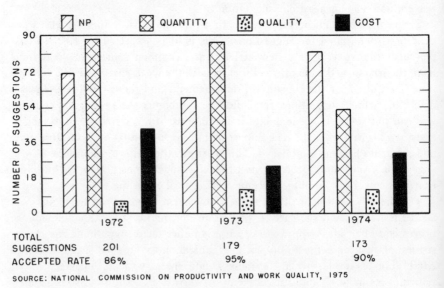

Figure 6.2   Types of suggestions (plant A).

Feeding the system becomes a way of life, a management style for those directing the plan.

Here are some additional concrete techniques which have worked successfully in maintaining the quality and quantity of suggestions:

1. Prepare to do some problem surfacing at the end of the trial year.
2. Rotate the controller through production-committee meetings.
3. Rotate high suggestion makers through production-committee meetings.
4. Increase formula knowledge by offering lunch seminars with the controller.
5. Consider releasing any information which can stimulate problem solving and suggestion making.
6. Encourage the suggesting of problems; others may have solutions.
7. Scrap any vestige of individual suggestion systems or extrinsic rewards for individual suggestions.
8. One company has a shortened suggestion form as a paycheck stub.
9. Carefully monitor the number of suggestions during each quarter, at least, and investigate with screening committee the reasons for declines.
10. Work with representatives from each department in getting them to help employees make and write suggestions.
11. Encourage everyone to write out all suggestions even if already implemented. This encourages employees who make small suggestions to think about more significant suggestions.
12. Encourage suggestions from indirect areas such as accounting and purchasing. These areas are typically almost excluded from the scanlon plan suggestion aspects when, in reality, they contribute very significantly to total firm productivity. Everyone can do his or her job better, and nothing is wrong with giving credit for it. Such activities build enthusiasm if larger percentages of employees get involved. You do, however, have to overcome the problem of some staff-area personnel feeling that it is their job to improve productivity.
13. Encourage suggestions that save items other than labor even if your calculation includes only labor. You must convince employees at all levels that the success of the scanlon plan depends on the success of the company. The more costs can be reduced in all areas, the better off the company and all employees will be in the long run.
14. Some companies post a chart showing the number of suggestions, and type and acceptance rate, for the last several years by month or quarter, as you see in Figures 6.1 and 6.2. At times they include the capital costs of the suggestions and expected benefits if determinable. They often encourage and report suggestions that may only directly influence labor productivity, such as material and energy savings. Remember that the scanlon plan is only as successful as the company. It does help to point out declining sug-

gestions. Another useful technique is to monitor which areas are submitting the most suggestions so that you can give recognition to this. Also, work on the other areas to see what the problems are. Small numbers of suggestions from one area or department may be indicative of inactive representatives, foremen, or departmental supervisors who discourage suggestions in a variety of ways. Leadership from one of the catalysts mentioned in Section 6.1 is probably missing.

The key to a good scanlon suggestion system is listening and then rapid follow-up. You would be amazed how few managers really listen. After a couple of times through such an experience of no one really listening, it takes a lot of work to get that employee to contribute again. This reaction is clearly illustrated by the following scanlon employee comment:

> When will it be understood that every individual employee has needs other than money?

A well-run suggestion system can help fulfill these other needs such as recognition and self-esteem.

6.5 FEEDBACK OF INFORMATION—SOME EXPERIENCE

This is a perennial scanlon plan problem but an educationally rewarding opportunity. It appears the management of almost every starting scanlon plan company wants to give employees all the information at its disposal. Some managements are at the opposite end of the continuum, and they want to give little information.

Our recommendation is to start slowly and worry about information overload. You can always add, but it may take a long time to repair the damage of giving sensitive information at the wrong time. One example might be giving the performance of one department that is not doing well to the screening committee. Until you develop a good open climate of problem solving rather than criticizing, use considerable care. Increase the information as employees request it or when you think they are ready for it. The risk of saying something at the wrong time is always a problem for scanlon plan companies. For example, one of the authors was at a company and was invited to one plant's screening-committee meeting. One committee member asked an inventory-related question which the plant manager could not answer. The question was deferred to the visitor. Unfortunately, the visitor had discussed the problem with the controller earlier in the day and accordingly attempted to answer the question in a general way. The self-image of the plant manager was reduced, and he attempted to have the visitor ejected from the company. Of course you will say that this manager will not be comfortable in a scanlon environment, which is true, but every organization is filled with such managers.

Now back to specifics. If we assume that the single- or split-ratio method is used, we suggest you use the form and content outlined in Section 4.7. This includes sales (less returns, allowances, and discounts), inventory adjustment, allowed labor, actual labor, and how distributed. Other information should include bonus reserve, percentage earned to date, and backlogs. If the allowed-labor method is used, normally start with only a few broad labor categories, but keep the formal form short and concise; most give only total allowed and actual labor cost.

We have seen Christmas tree forms in which as many as twenty adjustments have been made to either production value or actual labor for a variety of reasons. Why would a company want to provide this information? They think that they have to be open and aboveboard in all dissemination of information, but in reality by the time all the adjustments are explained, not even the controller believes what he is saying, and the distrust starts to build up. Keep the calculation fairly clean and straightforward.

In the screening committee you, of course, can and must openly discuss problem areas and attempt to find solutions. You must start working with individual departments by helping them isolate and solve problems. To bring all these out in the open at first just asks for trouble. Concentrate more on suggestions and improving coordination problems. Then work with individual departments on problems of that department only.

6.5.1 Feedback by Department

Should bonus contribution by department be disseminated (i.e., to each department only, or each department to other departments)? If your calculation is based on a ratio of sales value of production, you might be asking for trouble by doing so. You, of course, would have to estimate the effect, because the calculation is so broad. Some companies do make this estimate, however, with some success. You can take the opposite task of concentrating on improvement rather than measurement as an aid to improvement. Any other information such as standard performance for direct labor and budgets performance for indirect and resource departments should be disseminated, as is normally the case. The only problem is that these items probably are not tied directly to the bonus calculation, which may cause some difficulties.

If you have our so-called allowed-labor calculation installed, the bonus calculation is normally tied much closer to your financial-information system. In this situation it makes a lot of sense to feedback allowed labor and actual labor to each department so that they can see their own performance. In fact you should give the allowed times and dollars by product for direct labor before the item is produced, since after production little can be done to improve performance. Operation information, when available, is sometimes fed to individual employees, but great care must be exercised as to how this information is used. If you beat them over the head with it or if it is unrealistic, your plan is probably doomed to failure. Let them see how they can improve, and encourage them to ask for help from industrial engineers when needed.

Not to use this information in helping to improve operations would be a waste, even though some risk exists. For example, you can compute a productivity index for each department. These could be both performance and financial indexes for direct labor and financial for all others. The calculations might proceed as follows:

Performance Productivity Index

$$= \frac{time\ per\ product \times number\ of\ each\ produced}{actual\ time} \times 100$$

$$= \frac{allowed\ time}{actual\ time} \times 100$$

This could be plotted or put in table form over time; any one measure has limited usefulness, but trends are important.

Financial Productivity Index

$$= \frac{allowed\ time \times allowed\ rate \begin{vmatrix} per\ unit\ of\ time \\ for\ direct\ labor \\ or\ percentage\ of \\ direct\ labor,\ or \\ sales,\ for\ indi- \\ rect\ departments \end{vmatrix}}{actual\ cost} \times 100$$

$$= \frac{allowed\ labor\ dollars}{actual\ cost} \times 100$$

Another question is whether one department's performance should be disseminated to others. The real question is what can be gained by doing so? In many situations little is gained, and only finger pointing develops, since each department has to solve many of its own problems to increase productivity. If significant interdependencies are present, the answer may be different. Proceed with caution; watch out for comments such as, "Why not pay bonus by department?" Remember also that memories of past performance soon grow hazy.

6.5.2   Feedback over Time

After a time when employees are used to the plan and how it works, all the items below and any others you can think of can be tried. You must try to get individuals and groups to work continually on increasing their productivity. This is the organizational-development part of the plan that never ends for a scanlon or any other progressive and well-run company for that matter. But you must keep trying things, or the plan and any other OD effort will die. Before you do something with information feedback or involvement, try it out on a select group of employees to see what their reactions are to the information. You might want to use the screening committee. But do keep working on the information feedback and education aspects of the plan. Some of the additional techniques that you may want to try include the following:

1. Most successful scanlon companies post in most departments some sort of "fever" or performance chart large enough for employees to see without difficulty. This chart sometimes shows earned labor and actual labor with a colored space between to indicate bonus. Dollars are on the vertical axis. The purpose behind this is to remind employees on a continual basis that you do have a scanlon plan. Do not forget the resource workers. Post one for the whole firm, not by department.
2. Many scanlon companies compute the bonus weekly when possible, at least roughly, to increase the rapidity of feedback. The computer helps significantly with this process. This also may help isolate problem areas.
3. Many companies project a scanlon bonus. This is tied in with the production-scheduling system. This allows them to say, "If we get this much production through these various checkpoints, the bonus should be approximately this percentage." One company we know of has used ranges of bonus projections (e.g., bonus should be 10 to 14 percent) quite successfully. This decreases the accounting department's natural inclination to be conservative in their projections, which could over time decrease the trust placed in the accounting department. A word of caution is advisable here. We have seen several companies stung by putting out such forecasts on the basis of poor data. Learn the reliability of the system before giving it to employees. As stated by one very successful scanlon company vice-president, "We found that we could control all expenses within the range (e.g., 14 to 18 percent) and avoided the trauma that resulted from building false expectations for bonus." If a bonus is projected, comparing results with planned activity permits you to say fairly specifically why the projected bonus was not attained.
4. Many scanlon companies, over time, prepare other charts that are posted in relevant areas on things that influence productivity. These include items such as turnover, absenteeism, plant quality indexes such as rejects and

returns, safety records, and grievances. Pie charts have been useful to explain the economic facts of life. Some organizations, such as hospitals, would want to stress feedback on variables such as quality and utilization.

5. Some scanlon companies use signs such as "Work smarter, not harder," "We're all in the same boat, let's pull together," "Stop an error before it happens," for example. These are not really feedback mechanisms but can be useful in some situations. Take care in not overemphasizing such items, because they may not be action-oriented and are viewed by some employees as being somewhat paternalistic.

6. Last, but not least, is information on the competition and general economic conditions. Some organizations can isolate their markets and competitors fairly well. If you can, concentrating on beating them in sales prices, quality, and profits is desirable. It is more desirable to concentrate on how you can beat the competition than beating yourselves. And the scanlon plan has been said to be a natural economic education plan. So develop, if possible, information on your competitors. Evidence such as sales prices, quality, growth, and profits would be useful. Start out small and build up. The scanlon plan probably must prove itself on these grounds or ultimately fail. You must convince your employees of these facts. If you do not tell them what these facts are, they will certainly not be convinced that they are important.

The feedback process discussed above and in other sections in this chapter indicates that the effect of information can be very significant, both good and bad, on recipients. Start out slowly, working with information that individuals can relate to while thinking about the recipient's reactions to the information. Will they understand it? Should it be important to them? Will it likely increase or decrease their involvement? How can you help them relate to it and use it positively? The task is formidable, and the results can be productive and rewarding. If you stop, however, you will soon not have a scanlon plan. For example, an accountant recently made the following statement when asked what he was doing to work with one department, "I don't stop there anymore; they just give me a hard time about my figures." Of course he took the easy way out and lost the opportunity to do some real educating. The criticism was symptomatic of some problem, but he refused to find out what the problem was. Do not fall into such traps.

6.6 VIGILANCE OF THE FORMULA—ANALYSIS AND ADJUSTMENT PROCEDURES

As we discussed in Chapter 4, maintaining equitability can become a major problem. When conditions such as material prices, sales prices, and product mix change rapidly or materially, you will have problems. Such is not generally the case so why do measurement problems crop up in the typical scanlon plan calculation? Often because vigilance is not maintained over the calculation; that is, scanlon organizations often lose control of their calculation, and the plan can and has failed as a consequence. But this is not necessary, as you will see.

If you do not establish a mechanism for changing the calculation when it becomes necessary, you are just asking for trouble and loss of control. Since few employees can really completely understand the change, you must build trust in the calculation and especially in the accountants who work with the calculation and employees. You develop this trust by working closely with the various employee groups in their cost-reduction activities, by being open and willing to admit mistakes, and by getting employee representatives involved in the change process if possible.

On the other side, if you change the calculation for every minor fluctuation in the variables, you will give the impression that the calculation is being manipulated at the whims of management, and trust and reliance in the calculation will tend to erode. You must find a happy medium, or your plan will suffer. Remember also that the calculation is more of a hygienic variable; that is, the calculation by itself probably can hurt the plan's success more than help. Now on to some specific recommendations about vigilance of the formula. In addition, overall financial evaluation suggestions are discussed in Section 7.4.

First of all, whatever analysis you made in establishing your calculation in the first place, continue making it on at least a quarterly basis. For example, in Chapter 4 we discuss various diagnostic analyses for the single-ratio and allowed-labor calculations. These analyses should be continued, because they give you a good key as to whether the relationship between the variables has gotten out of kilter. Before setting up the plan, you also should have thought about possible future problems. Have any of these conditions happened? Planning for problems and their effect on the scanlon plan calculation is perhaps 80 percent of the way toward solving them. Unfortunately, our experience has been that scanlon organizations often do not make these analyses or problem isolations until it is too late and things are out of control. We wish we could remember how many accountants have said, "We know something is wrong, but we don't know what." Hopefully, this book will help you to avoid these conditions or at least to cope with them better. Some general adjustment procedures and considerations of the four common broad calculations are considered below. To discuss all the possible diagnostic and adjustment procedures would double the size of this book. These four are:

1. Single- and split- (labor) ratio calculations.
2. Multicost-ratio calculation and profit sharing.
3. Allowed-labor calculation.
4. Value-added calculations.

6.6.1   Single- and Split- (Labor) Ratio Calculations

$$\text{METHOD.} \quad \begin{array}{l} \textit{Base ratio (one ratio} \\ \textit{or several for different} \\ \textit{lines)} \end{array} = \frac{\textit{personal costs included}}{\textit{sales value of production}}$$

As we extensively discuss in Chapter 4, probably the two greatest problem areas caused by this method of calculation are (1) sales-price changes at different rates of change from labor (e.g., because of material-price changes or competition) and (2) product-mix changes.

Consequently, any time you have a significant change in average selling price (or billing rates for a hospital or other service organization), it is time to take a close look at the calculation. You may have to use a weighting system if the price change is not across-the-board. Then, assuming that only the selling price changed and an adjustment was deemed appropriate, a good approximation of the new base ratio should normally be obtained by (1) adjusting the revenue (or sales value of production) in the base period (up for increases in prices and down for decreases) by the percentage change in prices and (2) then computing what the base ratio would have been in the base period given the new prices.[7] The greatest problem with this procedure is that a specific base period's sales probably would have to have been used (e.g., one year's revenue). A good estimate normally is sufficient in many situations.

Wage increases could be handled in a similar way if you do not desire to have the plan itself absorb the increase. For example, say you increase wages approximately 10 percent on the average, but because of competitive conditions you are unable to increase selling prices to offset this increase; that is, you pay for all or part of the increase out of the productivity of the plan. In such a situation the bonus, of course, drops unless the base ratio is increased. The adjustment procedure would be similar to the one discussed above if you desired to increase the base ratio. This adjustment procedure for all the changes is highly unlikely or probably inadvisable for all the increase in most situations or the firm is likely soon to be in poor financial condition. In recent years selling prices and wages have often moved in tandem so that you have to worry only when the relative percentages are different.

If a technological change has occured requiring major capital expenditures, some adjustment may be necessary. The rationale of this whole area is extensively discussed in Chapter 4 and is not repeated here. The adjustment procedures, if desired, would consist of analyzing what the labor content would

---

[7] For example, assume you develop a base ratio of 20 percent sales value of production ($200,000 payroll costs ÷ 1,000,000). Later you decide to increase sales prices by 10 percent. The new base ratio is 18.18 percent ($200,000 ÷ [$1,000,000 × 1.10]). Now if sales quantity remains the same ($1,000,000 + $100,000), the allowed labor will remain the same ($1,100,000 × 18.18 percent = $200,000).

be with and without the capital expenditure and then adjusting the base ratio accordingly. Companies have often found that many capital expenditures do not save so much labor as they originally thought but rather provide added capacity. Alternatives other than adjusting the base ratio for capital expenditures are discussed in Chapter 4, especially Section 4.10.

If you perform your diagnostic analysis originally and on a continuing basis by product line, you should have a good idea of what is happening to product mix and whether it is helping or hurting the plan's bonus over time. As discussed in Chapter 4, the complex issue of product mix is partially resolved by establishing a calculation in which different allowed percentages are established by the different major product lines. But if we assume that you have started with and still have a single-ratio calculation, how do you adjust the base ratio? Essentially if you cannot figure out what the mix was in the base period, you have problems. But if we assume that you can and the following information is available, here is the rationale.

BASE PERIOD.

Labor content in line or product $X = 10$ percent.
Labor content in line or product $Y = 20$ percent.
Output consists of 50 percent of each line.

SOME FOLLOWING PERIOD.

Labor content in line X and Y is the same.
New line Z with a labor content $= 30$ percent.
Output now consists of $33\frac{1}{3}$ percent of each line.

The calculation may proceed along the following lines:

BASE PERIOD.

Line or product $X = 0.10 (0.50) = 0.05$
Line or product $Y = 0.20 (0.50) = \underline{0.10}$
                                    0.15
Or output now consists of 15 percent of sales value of production (plus something for other indirect labor costs).

NEW PERIOD AFTER SWITCHES.

Line or product X $= 0.10 (0.33\frac{1}{3}) = 0.033$
Line or product Y $= 0.20 (0.33\frac{1}{3}) = 0.067$
Line or product Z (new) $= 0.30 (0.33\frac{1}{3}) = \underline{0.100}$
                                         0.200
Or output now consists of 20 percent of sales value of production (new ratio).

In actual practice, the calculation is normally more complex because of multiple product lines and other changes, and trying to make such adjustments accurately and fairly does, at times, become difficult. In the above example we did not indicate whether the figures were for all labor costs or just direct labor. But the process is not impossible, as numerous scanlon companies have discovered. The key is to make the original diagnostic analysis carefully and follow up over time. Do your homework and plan for problems.

In determining the extent of adjustment, you must consider the financial health of the organization or segment. It does no good in the long run to be good to employees at the expense of the company itself. The employees must naturally be convinced of this fact at different times, since some of them periodically seem to forget.

6.6.2 Multicost-Ratio Calculation

METHOD. $$Base\ ratio = \frac{labor\ +\ other\ costs\ included}{sales\ value\ of\ production}$$

From the discussion in Chapter 4 you should have seen that this calculation has some major advantages from an adjustment standpoint. The broadest measure would, of course, be all costs (profit sharing). For practical purposes, if all major costs are included, such as material, labor, and perhaps some capital costs (let us say the ratio is 80 percent) or even profit sharing, you really do not have to worry much about adjustment procedures, because almost everything is already included; that is, product mix, selling-price changes, and various cost changes all are taken care of for practical purposes. The only real time you normally should seriously consider changing the ratio is when you add or delete items from the calculation. The problem with this calculation, as we discussed earlier, is not its flexibility in administration or adjusting to changing conditions but rather the inability of employees to relate to it. We have found that it takes a highly competent management to get it to work in the plan's favor.

6.6.3 Allowed-Labor Calculation

METHOD. $Base\ ratio = allowed\ activity \times allowed\ wage\ (or\ percentage)$

Much of Section 4.20 is devoted to this method. We think it offers significant advantages over some other calculations from a measurement standpoint, since it solves to a great extent the product-mix problems. Also material and other price changes, including selling prices, do not directly affect the calculation, although this may not always be desirable. As such it is flexible to meet changing conditions. But what changes must still be considered?

For the most part, the calculation itself will isolate problem areas if made in sufficient detail, as we recommend in Chapter 4. Innumerable subanalyses have been made using this calculation. The calculation also forces you to establish procedures on how to handle a variety of possible problem areas. For example, you must establish procedures to follow on new products (normally allow an estimate until experience is built up); capital expenditures (normally adjust the standard allowed downward after a six-month period for non-scanlon investments and longer for scanlon suggested capital expenditures—often a year, but some firms do not ever adjust); and wage changes (adjustments made in allowed dollars, depending on economic conditions at the time, how productivity and profits are progressing at the time and expected future, etc.). If economic conditions force a major reduction in selling prices, you may want to decrease allowed dollars. Additionally, if shifts occur from direct labor to indirect labor because of equipment or product-mix changes, you may want to adjust the relationship between allowed direct labor (or revenue) and the indirect labor (allowances). In reality, this method is just a split-ratio calculation greatly expanded.

When this calculation is installed, a committee is normally formed to make recommendations for changes (it may sometimes make minor adjustments itself). It is provided guidelines to follow in proposing or making changes. Engineered changes are sometimes automatically made. The committee normally meets at least twice a year, and on call, to analyze whether any major changes should be proposed for wage increases. The allowed rates are seldom increased for merit wage adjustments. Recommendations are presented sometimes to the screening committee for review and then to top management, depending on the formality of the organization. Normally the committee is composed of at least a representative from the controller's office, the plant manager's office (often an industrial engineer), an elected foreman, and an elected screening representative. Sometimes a personnel-oriented employee is added. You must, of course, use common sense in deciding on representation on such a committee.

Consequently, we might say that this method of calculation forces you to make decisions by isolating the problem areas. No, it does not make the decisions for you, but good managers want to be involved in such activities. Neither does it solve all your problems. In fact it causes problems just by isolating them; weak management does not like to be held accountable for decisions. And yes, the calculation itself may cause additional difficulties which are discussed in Section 4.20.

6.6.4 Value-Added Calculation

METHOD. *Production or revenue − outside purchases = value added × base ratio = allowed labor*

If after your diagnostic analysis you decided that value-added was for you, what problems are you likely to encounter? Probably not too many. Inflation is pretty well taken care of if all outside purchases are subtracted and if product mix reflects a partial adjustment. If problems do crop up, your continuing diagnostic analysis should isolate them, and your adjustments should be along the lines of those discussed above in Section 6.6.1. One major advantage of such a system is that the plan gets partial credit for savings of material quantities. It could, of course, be penalized for material and other price increases if selling prices are not adjusted accordingly.

No, we do not present solutions for all the possible problems you are likely to encounter in formula vigilance. But we do present some general guidelines and suggestions. We do not believe our role is to tell you what to do but rather to offer suggested alternatives. You have to live by your actions and get people involved in the adjustment process. Other suggestions are presented in Chapter 7.

Remember, the final decision for setting up and making changes in the calculation must rest with the management. This authority is not negotiable. Or as aptly put by one controller, "We are not running a popularity contest in this activity." At the same time, the controller's staff must be convinced of the equitability of the adjustments, or they will not be able to convince others. Participants will adjust to whatever system you design or adjustments you make. Do your homework, or regret it later.

6.7 CALCULATION EDUCATION

No matter how much you try, some employees will never understand the scanlon calculation. One problem is that some people refuse to look at financial data. But at the same time you must continually try to get them to comprehend, since the more they know, the better they will relate to the system. As we stated earlier, difficulty with understanding often goes up and down with the size of the bonus; the bigger the bonus, the more that they understand, and vice versa. Employees seem to be able to relate to and understand the allowed-labor calculation more than the single-ratio. This is due partly to the fact that the average employee can relate to physical measures (quantities) more easily than dollar measures.

Several things have been attempted to increase employee understanding of the calculation itself. These include:

1. Some companies have had groups of employees actually work through a calculation of their own. Groups have included the screening-committee members, foremen, and new employees in their orientation meetings.

Approaches have included providing them a blank form and allowing them to fill it in and also having them fill in the calculation form in detail.

2. Your scanlon plan booklet (see Appendix B) should have a sizable section on the calculation and factors that affect it.

3. New-employee-orientation meetings, if any, should include a section on the calculation and factors that influence it, even if they do not become eligible until some later date.

4. Some companies have found short questionnaires very useful in increasing knowledge. Sometimes they are discussed in a short memo, with the questions following along the writing. An easily scored, true-false scale is appropriate, and you can do this by department, as some companies have. Questions often include both how the calculation is made and variables that influence it. You, of course, have to feed back the results along with suggestions for improvement. A program such as this must be fairly streamlined but has proved to be quite successful.

5. Calculation education should, of course, occur in every screening- and production-committee meeting. We have to say that many controllers, or accountants, at these meetings take this role too lightly. Their education role in the scanlon plan is extremely important.

6. Most accounting people are too desk-bound. Others, such as personnel department employees, have little inclination to help in this education role. What can be learned by the controller or his assistants in a short stroll through the factory cannot be overestimated. This procedure should be a regularly assigned task for someone who is good in this educational role. If you have the wrong person doing it, more harm than good could develop.

6.8 MANAGERIAL SUCCESSION

Any serious discussion of operating the plan over time must deal with the obvious effects of turnover. Turnover at lower levels of any organization is dealt with by constant training and orientation. Generally, if turnover levels are not high, the natural attrition of personnel can be overcome by good supervision and on-the-job and formalized training. However, managerial succession is another kind of turnover, since the influence and effect of management change is so profound to the organization's climate.

If managerial succession brings managers who are not predisposed to the plan, the plan will certainly be in trouble. One selection criterion for upper-level management should be a management philosophy in harmony with the plan.

Corporate levels of management might wonder whether scanlonism is particular to the individuals who brought it to their organizations. This corporate level of management (for instance, at a headquarters with many branch locations) might speculate whether they are free to transfer branch-level management about. The answer is yes.

In Chapter 8 we offer some corporate experience that includes firms with this kind of history. Evidence suggests that the structure of the plan is strong enough to socialize a plant manager, controller, or personnel manager into the philosophy of the plan. Thus when management changes are made, due care is needed to select from the ranks of management those who are likely to adopt the plan's principles.

In our judgment, the experience of other corporations is strong enough to claim that managerial succession, as a likelihood, is not a reason to reject installing the plan.

6.9 YEAR END MEETING PREPARATION

Each organization has its own climate, history, and style. Therefore, our advice here is not on how to handle the year-end meeting. Instead, we offer you some thoughts on what to include in this meeting.

The purpose is to review the scanlon year. In keeping with that objective it is reasonable to:

1. Announce any bonus due from the reserve, or explain why deficits wiped out the reserve.
2. Recap the suggestion year by analyzing the kind of suggestions that made a difference (see Appendix F for a guideline on this).
3. Hold a screening-committee meeting, and let everyone observe.
4. Elect new members to the production committees.
5. Present special reports on plan-related topics that stem from evaluation of your own organizational development (see Chapter 7).

The last point is subtle and yet probably the most profound for the organization. Why? Taking stock of where the organization is and where it wants to be contributes to the structure of the plan, since productivity is only achievable through the process of cooperation and sound communication. Many OD strategies (discussed in Chapters 1 and 8) strive to open up problem solving, begin goal setting, and resolve conflict. Naturally enough, these are common outcomes of successful scanlon plans. However, each of these outcomes began as processes embedded in the plan itself. By evaluating where you want to be with the plan, you are enhancing understanding of these processes. The plan provides the structure or platform. In a sense it offers a means for the process to happen, unlike simulations produced for OD purposes. Therefore point 5 above focuses on your own OD objectives. What we stress is the evaluation of where you stand with any of the goals that emerged from plan activity.

6.10 SUMMING UP

This chapter deals with a considerable amount of "inside" information on how to keep the scanlon plan viable over the long run. The authors have consulted in this area and have evaluated the work of other consultants. This experience is collected and organized into the nine sections that make up this chapter.

The roles of the catalysts who impact the plan are carefully delineated. Hints to improve performance in these roles as well as pitfalls which impede performance are discussed. This chapter, which talks out the fulfillment of the formula by the human process, is as important as Chapter 4 is on the formula.

Especially important is our discussion on involving resource workers. Scanlon plan firms try to move away from too much emphasis on direct labor. We offer some tried and true methods to involve this part of the human resource.

Successful, tested examples of how to administer the plan over time are offered in this chapter (e.g., goal setting, maintenance of suggestions, and information feedback). Scanlon firms either discover these approaches to keep the plan alive, or outside consultants bring these ideas into the organization.

Finally, we deal with vigilance of the formula as well as calculation education. These topics combine naturally, and we offer you the insights and experiences of the many scanlon firms. Thus this chapter ranges from the role of catalysts who aid the plan, to concrete experiences with the plan over time, and back again to managerial succession and the year-end meeting. We try to anticipate for you what to expect over time. Then we list examples of the best experience dealing with plan viability. The rest is up to your own leadership and ingenuity.

EVALUATION STRATEGIES 7

By synthesizing from key areas throughout the book we show how to evaluate the scanlon plan year by year and phase by phase. Of necessity, we have organized the topic of evaluation around an idealized scanlon plan installation. Your own situation will dictate how to select from sections of this chapter.

7.1 PLAN FOR EVALUATION AT VARIOUS INTERVALS

Figure 7.1 illustrates five phases during the trial year. One of the first possibilities for evaluation, as indicated by arrow 1, is an annual organizational survey. Since there are many uses of this type of information, the attitudinal questionnaire listen in Appendix A.1 is much broader in scope than a questionnaire focusing solely on the plan. This is in keeping with the evolutionary development possible due to the plan; that is, organizational development can be assessed with this kind of questionnaire, especially if the results are displayed in the kind of graph we suggest in Figure 2.3. The questionnaire in Appendix A.1 is more comprehensive than you are probably willing to try, but consider it item by item. Then we suggest you use only those items that fit your needs. For example, let us say that you would like to measure attitudes about job satisfaction. Generally a comprehensive set of questions (see "Satisfaction," Sections 1 and 7 of Appendix A.1) will measure each facet of job satisfaction from pay to work itself. By assessing job satisfaction before the plan is installed, you may be able to infer if the plan increased some or all these facets when you repeat the survey in the following year.

We know of several organizations that use these surveys but have them done by an independent third party (a consultant or university professor). The results are best if they are confidentially collected with anonymity guaranteed.

134

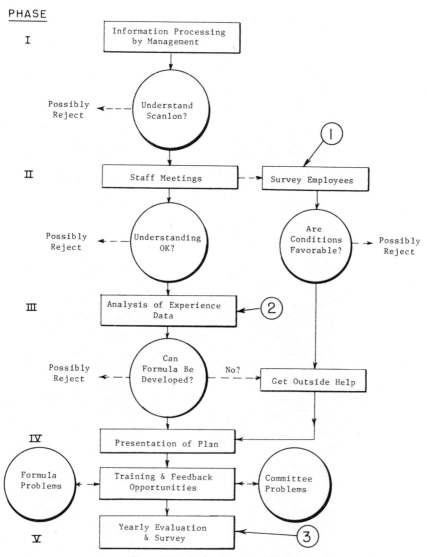

Figure 7.1 Evaluation timetable.

Then analysis of results is best if it is kept in summary form; that is, do not break the data down for very small departments or easily identifiable groups. Please note the beginning statement in Appendix A.1.

At arrow 2 in Figure 7.1 we indicate that analysis of accounting-experience data that led to formula construction also is continually undertaken for formula vigilance (see Section 6.6). In general, Chapter 4 addresses most of the issues of formula diagnostics and construction. As the accounting function develops its worksheets from the examples in that chapter, it is wise to critique each step so that you can adopt it to your kind of system. Remember, the formula must satisfy two criteria: (1) it must be understood so that the behavioral implications of the plan can work, and (2) it must capture with fidelity the desired productivity changes. The trade-offs between these two criteria are many, and that is why Chapter 4 deals with so many ramifications.

Evaluation of the understanding of the formula, achievable through formal questionnaire or even casually interviewing workers, interacts with the need to keep the formula accurate. Our best advice is not to be afraid of changing the formula as long as you are sure of the changes (again see discussion in Chapters 4 and 6). However, you will have more confidence about any changes if you monitor with an evaluation methodology.

At arrow 3 in Figure 7.1, you have your first bench mark for plan understanding. It is fully appropriate to select questions from the "Plan Evaluation Questionnaire" found in Appendix A.2. Most of these questions are useful for all employees, and others are designed for supervisors and managers or solely for employees. The year-end meeting is an excellent time to discuss the results of the questionnaire.

It is a good idea to keep separate your general questionnaire subtitled the "Before Scanlon Survey and Annual Survey" (Appendix A.1) from the year-end evaluation survey. The questionnaires for both could be overly long. And if you combine questions about morale with the plan questions, this could affect the answers. Thus by administering the two at different times of the year, the results will be more meaningful, since you can separate them out for each measurement period. Also since we are suggesting that you compare these results over time, it argues strongly to measure and assess those conditions and factors which "hang together." Morale and organizational climate are general conditions affected by many forces. These are best measured with the annual survey. The scanlon plan introduces factors which are conveniently measured when they are salient at the year-end meeting. So, using a specific questionnaire on the plan is aimed at those factors which can be evaluated and improved. Conversely, using a comprehensive questionnaire on employment conditions helps to evaluate if the plan is affecting the overall climate of the firm.

7.2 THE SURVEY—BEFORE AND AFTER

One strategy we have strongly argued for is the need for evaluation. The usefulness of data on the plan and the firm has been demonstrated time and again.

Therefore, evaluation measures should be consistent over time. After all, knowing what your evaluation information means implies that you have a basis of comparison. Thus if you wish to know if plan understanding increased, ask the questions about the plan the same way each time. If you wish to understand your work force's relative levels of job satisfaction, use the same questions each year to compare trends. People will not remember their answers and, hopefully, will attempt to gauge their feelings accurately. Do not compare your survey results with another branch. Make comparisons with competition, or, better, internal comparisons within your own firm, as suggested in Figure 2.3. Do not try to ask too many questions; keep the questionnaire short.

We have provided a "cafeteria-style" questionnaire in Appendix A. Therefore, you must think about which attributes you would like to measure. The entire questionnaire in Appendix A is longer than any organization should try. All the items in the questionnaires have been used by scanlon companies, however. At a minimum, your annual questionnaire should include facets of job satisfaction, perceptions of the reward system, and attitudes toward supervision. Your scanlon evaluation questionnaire should include, at least, formula understanding, involvement-system understanding, and expectations about the plan—all these appear as specific dimensions in this section and in Appendixes A.1 and A.2.

In keeping with the idea of consistency in a before-and-after evaluation, set up a schedule for data collection that fits into your business cycle. For example, if you decide to do an annual morale survey, why not choose a period that coincides with a slack period of business? The survey itself does not compete with high periods of productivity and possibly offers moments for reflection. Thus organizational climate may get an honest reading at that time, and repeated surveys offer a good basis of comparison year by year.

7.3 DATA ASSESSMENT—MANAGEMENT AND COMMITTEE INVOLVEMENT

As you address the issue of evaluation, you will want not only to design your research effort to fit your needs but also to lend itself to simple data analysis. The simpler, the better, in order to enhance understanding. Therefore almost all of the questions throughout Appendix A are scaled positively to give you a feeling of the magnitude of each dimension; that is, the higher the score, the more positive the result. However, it is best to percentage these responses for a given level of magnitude. For example:

Question: All in all, how satisifed are you with your supervisor?

Response:

Very dissatisfied	Dissatisfied	Undecided	Satisfied	Very satisfied

$$\begin{pmatrix} \text{Percentage agreeing at} \\ \text{``sat'' or better} \end{pmatrix}$$

Almost all the questions have a five-point scale attached to them to aid responding and quick data analysis (see Appendix A.3 on "Coding and Scoring Your Questionnaire"). Divide by total responding in department, zone, or company. Now, express that percentage as "those agreeing on (question) is 80 percent" for a given department, zone, or entire company. This simple percentage treatment is good for virtually all the items in Appendix A, and we give a simple reporting system for you to follow in Appendix A.3.

Aside from the five-point agree-disagree (Likert) scaled questions, you will see difference-scaled questions. Examples are Sections 6 and 7 of A.1 and Sections 7.1. and 7.2 of A.2. Here we are looking for differences between two dimensions such as "should be − actual" at one point in time, or we are planning to measure differences on one dimension over time in future surveys.

First, let us look at difference measures between two dimensions at one point in time. For instance:

Question: The pay I get from my job.

	Min						Max

a. How much is there now?   1 2 ③ 4 5 6 7

b. How much should there be? 1 2 3 4 ⑤ 6 7

Should be = 5

Actual   = 3

Difference 2

The interpretation of these data is that the item is perceived to be more important than actual behavior. Now what about the same item answered this way:

Question: The pay I get from my job.

	Min						Max

a. How much is there now?   1 2 3 ④ 5 6 7

b. How much should there be? 1 2 3 4 5 6 ⑦

Here the respondent is telling you that the magnitude of this particular feeling is very high, and yet actual practice is perceived to be average. If we are talking about pay, which many people believe is a motivator, the discrepancy between ideal and reality cannot be ignored. In sum, difference questions offer a unique way to assess the perceptions of the relationships between pay and performance, the plan and the bonus. Remember, coding and scoring difference questions are explained in Appendix A.3. The interpretation of difference scores as well as the interpretation of all the results from the questionnaire are separate from data-analysis considerations. For that reason, we suggest you involve scanlon committees in the interpretation of results. How? First of all glance at Figure 2.3. This shows the process. After the results of your year-end scanlon survey are computed, break them out into coherent tables so that committees can interpret them. They are listed here in the same order you will find them in Appendix A.1:

1. Satisfaction—global.
2. Supervision.
3. Cooperation and communication.
4. Suggestion making.
5. Performance.
6. Pay policy.
7. Job-satisfaction facets.
8. Participation.

Plan questions to assess understanding are in Appendix A.2.

1. Scanlon plan understanding.
2. Committees.
3. Production attitudes.
4. Expected scanlon plan success.
5. Participation.
6. Perceived scanlon plan success.
7. Operational expectations.
8. Knowledge test.

As you can see, allowing the committee structure to evaluate the results of these surveys is consistent with the plan philosophy and with the goals of organizational development (OD) cited in Chapter 1. Figure 1.1 outlines the strategy of OD, and feeding the committee system with the results of the surveys before releasing them, or filing them away, is a valuable check with reality. This is especially true with these kinds of data. The communication gap that can exist between management and the work force is caused by differing values, attitudes, and levels of understanding each other's world. Interpretation of survey results by the committee structure before any final report or memos are written aids in understanding the context surrounding the results. By that we mean management might want to believe that pay, supervision, trust, and so on, exist at the highest levels possible. The interpretation by the committees can help to attenuate these beliefs plus show how unusually low levels of satisfaction or trust may be caused by some external factor. In other words, data collection and analysis will be found to be straightforward. Data interpretation is more difficult but is best done with a broad base of evaluators, such as exists in the committee system. The final disposition of results is a decision for management. We favor a report on survey results which summarizes the survey. If it can be released via company newsletter or magazine, so much the better. Otherwise, distribution of results could be made via a memo to be displayed in each department. Of course, we suggest something in the format seen in Figure 2.3. This quickly presents the relative information in a form that most of us appreciate. Also because you used the committee system to interpret the results, you enhanced feedback and communication toward overall OD, as we depicted in Figure 2.2. Appendix A.3 also offers a report format.

7.4 FINANCIAL EVALUATION

Many individuals feel that the scanlon plan must prove itself in one of two ways: (1) by increasing the quality of work for employees or (2) by increasing productivity. Hopefully both can be the consequence, although we probably have stressed the latter. Implicit in the organizational-development approach, however, is the belief that a change in the way we manage people and get the work done is essential if long-run productivity improvement is to occur. This of course is certainly true under the scanlon plan.

But how do we determine that the scanlon plan has proved itself? Is the bonus enough, or was it just cause by increased volume? These, of course, are not easy questions to answer. Successful scanlon companies attempt all the traditional analyses and techniques, including variance analysis (e.g., labor, material, and volume), flexible budgeting, cost-volume-profit analysis, and return on investment, but they still have trouble proving the merits of the scanlon plan from a financial standpoint.

Part of the problem is the complexity of the principles underlying the plan from an OD standpoint. Given this, perhaps you should be satisfied if your long-term bonuses average about 10 percent (a common outcome); your product quality has increased; your return on investment has increased; you can compete more easily in your markets; and your selling prices are going up less (or even down) than your major costs other than labor without a decrease in profits. For ultimately, the market probably should determine how well you have done with your scanlon plan. This should be the best payoff for a plan and the country as a whole.

But scanlon companies have tried a multitide of analyses to help prove that the plan is improving productivity however defined. We strongly encourage these analyses. For example, you can divide constant dollar (i.e., corrected for selling-price changes) of sales by number of employees or workhours. Indexes are frequently developed to help with this. You can also do this to determine the financial productivity of labor (i.e., using only dollars). You can try to keep track of actual money saved by suggestions. You must continue your comparative analysis started in your diagnostic analysis. This latter analysis is particularly useful if you, at the same time, also look at the percentage changes over time of average sales prices, material, and labor costs. You can analyze the effect that product mix and capital expenditures have had on labor costs. Reasonably accurate estimates can be made in most of these areas without undue "digging" effort.

But in the end, you will still have great difficulty substantiating in perfectly accurate terms exactly what the plan has done for you. Part of this is because you will never know what the results would have been without the plan. But be happy for your successes and try harder to decrease the failures.

A final note is of some significance. Some divisionalized managers will be confronted with a real problem if they do not do their homework; that is, higher corporate managers often question the scanlon plan managers regarding whether the bonus is really being earned. This is particularly true if the bonus gets above, say, 15 percent. If you are in this situation, remember that they will ask these questions so be prepared with answers if possible. Some good, hard analyses can help persuade corporate managers of the merits of the plan, even though they may not prove them to everyone's complete satisfaction. Some corporate managements have tried to eliminate the effect that volume has on the bonus; so be prepared. This also means that developing the scanlon philosophy works best if it starts at the top.

7.5 OUTSIDE EVALUATION

Some scanlon firms do their own evaluation not to save money but because they believe the activity and process of evaluation are beneficial. However, it does take hours. There are some skills in data collection that consultants can bring to your organization that may not currently exist with your own staff. The strongest reason to consider outside evaluation is objectivity. An objective third party can collect data and protect anonymity in a way, perhaps, that is beyond the firm. For this reason this section offers some guidelines.

Outside evaluation must be perceived as fair and objective. So why not let the screening committee be a part of deciding who should get your contract. Outside evaluation is best if you can have the same team of evaluators each time. They get better at their task and will be more acceptable to the work force over time.

Per Figure 2.1 you may have turned to outside help at phase III of formula development. Can this same helper handle your surveys? If so, it is probably a plus. There are other approaches though. One scanlon firm we know has had an annual survey done for years as part of a university research project. The university researchers have been collecting job satisfaction from a large number of firms for many years to add to their data bank. Work out an arrangement with the university for each of you to get the data you both find useful. Then, this service should be low-cost as well as independent of the firm.

Outside evaluators who are willing to spend some time with your people and do interviewing are to be preferred. The evaluators should be encouraged to spend as much time with the workers and union leadership, if any, as with management. We should mention that under the leadership of Carl Frost, of Michigan State University, the role of an outside evaluator has shown itself to be quite useful. For years the Massachusetts Institute of Technology has supported research in this area as well. Many other universities have active research programs that focus on the quality of working life. By identifying university researchers with those interests, complementarity between your assessment of scanlonism and their research is guaranteed. Nevertheless, there are many models to follow. Our preference is that your evaluator be objective and knowledgeable and provide continuity to your assessment strategy.

7.6 SUMMING UP

This chapter deals with evaluation strategies. As such it is closely linked with figures and discussion in Chapters 1, 2, and 4. Appendixes A and F support the discussion of this chapter with complete questionnaires and sample feedback illustrations.

The purpose of evaluation is to be able to measure your progress, or lack of it, in order to set goals. This chapter strives to deal with key ideas associated with evaluation, namely, who should do it, how should it be done, when should it be done, and of course how to maintain consistency in your evaluation efforts.

We suggest two kinds of surveys at two different time periods. One deals with plan understanding. The other deals with your organizational climate. Plan understanding is specific, and organizational climate is more general. The two interact, but keeping them separate as evaluation strategies has merit.

Data analysis and its process are dealt with. Guidelines on interpreting data are reviewed. Outside evaluation is reviewed. Suggestions are offered to facilitate selection and continued use of third party evaluators.

SUMMING UP **8**

Experience of Others
and the Future

This chapter summarizes the key ingredients of the scanlon plan; provides other corporate experience with the plan; and, finally, deals with scanlonism, organizational development, and the future prospects for the plan.

8.1 THE PHILOSOPHY, THE FORMULA, AND THE INVOLVEMENT SYSTEM

Espousing participation and cooperation is merely rhetoric unless people really believe in their value and make active participation and full cooperation a way of working life. Idealism is not bad per se. But idealism requires an environment in which it has a chance to flourish and be reinforced. Clearly, participation and cooperation between management and the worker is only possible where trust exists. Trust according to the dictionary is the reliance on the integrity, strength, ability, and surety of a person. It is the confident expectation of something—hope. It is the obligation or responsibility imposed on one whom confidence or authority is placed. That is a tall order to fill if we are talking about the historical adversary relationship characterizing many managements and their workers. We say historical because, although conditions may have warranted a conflict model between management and the worker in the past, in today's economy the worker is too well-educated, and well off, to see his goals that differently from those of management's.

Nevertheless trust, as defined above, does not just grow out of a better-educated work force; it is shaped and reinforced by the efforts of enlightened management. This type of management is naturally drawn to the scanlon plan, because the plan offers a structure for the philosophy of cooperation to happen. That structure exchanges a bonus for productive work in the organization. In addition, an involvement system reinforces cooperation and participation by permitting everyone to increase efficiency through more intelligent work.

Now if you accept the fact that the American worker is of a higher quality and caliber than anywhere else in the world, it is important for management to tap the intelligence that lies fallow in the underdeveloped organization. The involvement system can achieve that purpose. It offers a structure for eliciting and processing productivity-related suggestions. It offers a social process for learning about how to contribute to organizational effectiveness. It provides social recognition to contributing, cooperating employees. Instead of the conflict model of management-worker relations of the past, a more harmonious model emerges out of the structure and process of the involvement system. Talk of trust is replaced by the scanlon philosophy, which is the practice of trust.

How some companies have fared with scanlon plans is dealt with next. You will see that one significant factor is the formula. There is no question that a true measure of productivity permits everyone to focus his attention on those variables which affect the bonus. There is no question, either, that being able to pay a bonus aids acceptance of the plan. Capturing the true ups and downs of business in the formula makes learning about productivity possible. True learning about efficient use of resources in the production of goods or services improves the flow of goods through a factory or paper work through an office. Ultimately, the formula allows employees to understand the difference between financial productivity and performance productivity. The opportunities for learning by way of the formula and its construction are boundless. Thus the formula is an integral part of the philosophy and the involvement system.

8.2   OTHER CORPORATE EXPERIENCE

Neither paying high bonuses nor the construction of a poor formula causes scanlon plan failure or success. There are usually many reasons. Yet poor formulas are associated with plan failures. Table 8.1 tabulates all known case studies of the plan. Admittedly, there is a paucity of good research in this field, but Table 8.1 cites thirty successes against fourteen failures of many plans in existence. These case studies are just the few that were analyzed and written up. Many plans began as a means for saving threatened companies. This table includes that kind of example. Nevertheless six out of fourteen failures reported poor formulas. The remaining eight provide no information whatsoever. It is plausible that they too had formula problems.

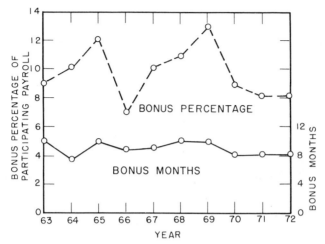

BONUS RANGE   0-20%
PERCENTAGE OF MONTHS A BONUS EARNED 75.8%
PERCENTAGE OF YEARS WITH A YEAR-END BONUS 67.5%

Figure 8.1   Ten years of bonus experience in seven firms.

Table 8.1 also gives the number of years each case study has had the plan as well as the range of bonuses. These range anywhere from 0 to 50 percent. Also, over half of the firms reported significant increases in cooperation. One factor associated with productivity-sharing plans is size of firm. It has been held that smaller firms at one location have a better chance to benefit from this type of plan. Firm size in Table 8.1 ranges from 75 to 6000. Undoubtedly smaller firms do make up the modal success category. But is 2000 a small firm? Atwood Manufacturing has more than 2000 employees. The key, as far as size is concerned, seems to be whether everyone feels he can influence productivity and see the results in the bonus. In our judgment, keeping the plan at the plant, branch, or functionally autonomous level is important.

An even better example of continuous corporate experience is seen in Figure 8.1. Seven firms belonging to the Scanlon Plan Associates[8] have permitted the pooling of their data to provide an excellent picture of healthy companies enjoying the benefits of productivity sharing. The average annual bonus for ten years is almost 10 percent, and the range is from 0 to 20 percent. These businesses managed to have bonuses in almost 76 percent of their working months and still were able to pay out year-end bonuses almost 68 percent of the time.

[8] The Scanlon Plan Associates is a not-for-profit association of firms who meet periodically to discuss common problems.

Table 8.1 Breakdown of Plan Studies by Key Characteristics

Company, Author, Year	Type of Industry	Employment	Years of Plan	Bonus Range	Coopera-tion	Outcome	Comments
1. Adamson/Scanlon/47	steel fabrication	125	10 plus	0–50%	very good	success	few bonuses complex formula, and management changes
2. American Optical Johnson/59	optical equipment	150	18 plus	0–11%	no change	failure	
3. Anderson Bro./Johnson/59	machine tools	150	6 plus	"quite good"	very good	success	
4. Atwood/Lesieur & Puckett/69	automotive hardware	2000	17	5–20%	very good	success	
5. Canfield/Sweeney/54	rubber specialties	300	3 plus	9.5 ave.	apparently good	success	
6. Dalton/Dreyer/52	steel fabrication	200	2 plus	0–3.6%	poor	failure	poor formula and management attitudes
7. DeSoto/Moore & Goodman/72	chemical coatings	180	2	0–12%	very good	success	
8. Embossing Co./Morris/54	wood games	75	2 plus	0–40%	very good	success	
9. Lapointe/Schultz & Crisara/52	broaches	1000	25	0–52%	very good	success	
10. Linwood/Gray/71	auto bodies	6000	3	0–?	poor	failure	large inequities in pay, rapid changes in product mix
11. Market Forge/Goodman/64	steel fabrication	300	3	"regular & good"	significant increase	partial success	
12. Michigan Wheel/Production/69	propellers	250	24	9–72%	very good	success	

13. Parker Pen/Lesieur & Puckett/69	writing instruments	1000	17 plus	6–20%	very good	success	
14. Pfaudler/Lesieur & Puckett/69	glassed steel equipment	750	17 plus	3–18%	very good	success	
15. Stromberg-Carlson/Tait/51	electronic products	—	—	"12% ave."	apparently good	success	
16. Towle/Humphries/52	silver flatware	500	3 plus	0–25%	very good	success	
17. Anonymous/Gilson & Lefcowitz/57	ceramics	80	1	0–6%	very poor	failure	formula poorly constructed, individual incentives better, changes in product mix
18. Anonymous/Helfgott/62	survey across 6 manufacturing firms	—	—	0–?	no change to good	4 successes	2 failures; no bonuses ever paid
19. Anonymous/Jehring/67	household fixtures	200	6	0–11%	apparently good	partial success	
20. Anonymous/Preston/51	manufacturing	1000	2	—	very good	success	
21. Anonymous/Ross/69	raw material processor	250	15	—	apparently good	success	
22. Anonymous/Ruh, et al/72	survey across 18 manufacturing firms	—	—	—	no change to very good	10 successes	8 failures; no reasons given
Total = 22 studies (44 firms)					30 successes	14 failures	

Source: National Commission on Productivity and Work Quality, 1975.

Figure 8.1 is not a fairy tale. These are real corporations with employees working smarter, not harder.

Table 8.2 shows how one plant of a Fortune 500 corporation computed its productivity from cost data. This plant is one of four of this large corporation which have successfully adopted the plan. Since it was the first of the four, this type of cost analysis was made to assess the impact of the plan before installing it elsewhere.

The figures are disguised, since absolute values are privileged information. However, the relationship of the figures is correct so that the percentage of increase in gallonage (productivity) is accurate. Thus if you scan line 6 and 14, you can see that labor cost went up 15 percent and gallonage 41 percent in 1973. The last year of operation before the scanlon plan was 1970, and 1971 was the trial year. Lines 5, 12, and 13 are of note, since no major changes in technology influenced these figures. For example, labor cost per gallon with bonus was 15 percent greater than without it (line 5). A reduction of 115, 646 hours is indicated (line 12). Thus the production per hour for 1973 shows a 41 percent increase over 1970. In 1972 the increase was 28 percent over 1970. At the time of publication, productivity is up even higher than 1973.

Given our discussion of financial and performance productivity, there are many factors which could have affected these gains. However, the management of this plant is convinced that tangible benefits of productivity are being measured in these figures.

Will these experiences of other firms be duplicated in your firm? No one can say for sure, but you now have more knowledge than any of these firms had before they adopted their plans.

8.3 SCANLONISM, ORGANIZATIONAL DEVELOPMENT, AND THE FUTURE

We have adapted Figure 8.2, the Involvement System, from Figure 1.1. You can now see why the involvement system is really an organizational-development system. Instead of creating a training exercise, as OD specialists often do, the plan asks for and gets similar results. However, the big difference is that through the structure of the involvement system we have a concrete task directly in our view—making and processing suggestions for a more productive company. A casual look at Appendix C (the minutes of either screening or production committees) shows how earnest these suggestions are. Remember, firms with individual suggestion systems (i.e., they pay cash for them) never have more than 26 percent[9] of their employees participating in their plans.

---

[9] J. Short and B. E. Moore, "Preliminary Findings of a Multi-Variate Analysis of Suggestion System's Impact on Productivity," Working Paper No. 75-27, University of Texas Press, Graduate School of Business, Austin, 1975.

Table 8.2 Annual Comparison with Base Year for Completed Years (1972 and 1973)

Line	1973	1972	1970	1970 with Payroll Adjusted to 1973 Rates	1970 with Payroll Adjusted to 1972 Rates
1. Scanlon payroll without bonus	$ 3,464,368	$ 3,380,320	$ 3,357,389	$ 4,158,252	$ 3,915,491
2. Scanlon payroll with bonus	3,974,134	3,694,662	3,357,384		
3. Gallons produced	19,456,870	17,872,806	15,965,951	15,965,951	15,965,951
4. Cost per gallon without bonus	37.9	40.1	44.7	55.4	51.1
5. Cost per gallon with bonus	43.5	44.1	44.7	55.5	51.0
6. *Percent increase payroll*	*(+15%)*	*(+10%)*			
7. Budgeted scanlon payroll without bonus	3,707,842	3,399,906			
8. Budgeted scanlon payroll with bonus	4,006,302	3,471,687			
9. Budgeted gallons produced	19,655,638	14,831,194			
10. Budgeted cost per gallon without bonus	40.3	48.7			
11. Budgeted cost per gallon with bonus	43.5	49.8			
12. Hours worked	676,515	684,845	792,161		
13. Gallons per hour	57.1	51.8	40.5		
14. *Percent increase productivity*	*(+41%)*	*(+28%)*			

Source: National Commission on Productivity and Work Quality, 1975.

149

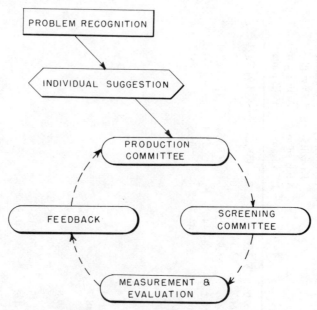

Figure 8.2   The involvement system.

Scanlon firms have a range of 45 up to 98 percent participating every year. That is participation and involvement.

As Figure 8.2 shows, the involvement system has its feedback phase, just as the formula has; that is, the bonus calculation is made and fed back monthly, along with explanations as to why a bonus was or was not made. Similarly the involvement system feeds back to the suggester the disposition of his or her suggestion. This channels learning, shapes productive behavior, and molds positive attitudes better than OD exercises.

One of the definitive statements of OD is found in the *Handbook of Industrial and Organizational Psychology*.[10] F. Friedlander and C. D. Brown review the field of OD extensively and have produced this rather comprehensive definition:

. . . OD is a method for facilitating change and development in people (e.g., styles, values, skills), in technology (e.g., greater simplicity, complexity), and in organizational processes and structures (e.g., relationships, roles). . . . The objectives of OD generally can be classified as those optimizing human and social improvement or as those optimizing task accomplishment or more likely as some (often confused) blend of the two.

---

[10] M. D. Dunnette (Ed.), Rand McNally, Chicago, 1976, p. 314.

Extending this definition, W. L. French and C. H. Bell, Jr., have characterized the OD process as an identifiable flow of interrelated events which is made up of interventions and responses to interventions.[11]

Just what are these interventions? And how do they facilitate change in people and in technology?

First of all, no one OD program has all types of interventions, but practitioners of OD have classified the various kinds of intervention activities which were cited in Section 1.1.

OD Activity	Scanlon Counterpart
1. Diagnostic activities: attitude and opinion measurement, including formal questionnaires or interviewing to ascertain the state of the organization	1. Phase II, especially in trial year
2. Problem identification: process consulting to help perception and understanding of individual, group, and organizational level issues	2. At all times in the involvement system
3. Goal setting and methods achievement: planning, utilizing information from problem solving, and to compare the real versus the ideal	3. Management's direction, especially through the screening committee and through the influence of the formula
4. Communication improvement: survey feedback activities, education and training activities to improve coordination	4. All committees improve this plus annual questionnaire will help
5. Conflict identification and resolution: third-party peacemaking, confrontation counseling to improve cooperation	5. Peer review of suggestions in production committees is a form of open problem solving

[11] W. L. French and C. H. Bell, Jr., *Organizational Development: Behavioral Science Interventions for Organization Improvement,* Prentice-Hall, Englewood Cliffs, N. J., 1973.

6. Task forces: team-building intergroup activities to enhance cooperation

6. Group suggestion making is a very common outcome of the plan.

7. Job design: technostructural activities to improve technical or structural aspects of work

7. One of the most common outcomes of scanlon plans is acceptance of technical change

8. Measurement and evaluation: assessment activities to produce information on "where we are"

8. Annual survey, financial analysis, and annual scanlon meeting

---

Given these very consistant definitions of OD objectives and intervention activities, the outcome of OD is to create

> . . .an open problem solving climate, supplementing the authority of role and status with the authority of knowledge and competence, locating decision making and problem solving as close to information sources as possible, building trust and collaboration, developing a reward system which recognizes the organizational mission and the growth of people, helping managers to manage according to relevant objectives rather than past practices, and increasing self-control and self-direction for people within the organization (Friedlander and Brown, p. 316).

It should be clear the the best-known definitive definitions of OD are congruent with the philosophy of scanlonism. One distinct difference is that scanlonism predates OD, at least as a philosophy. Also, each principal component of the OD framework finds its counterpart in the plan. For example, the facilitation of change and the development of the human resource is one of the principal outcomes of successful scanlon installations. Optimizing the use of technology in an organization for maximum productivity is the key to successful scanlonism. The blend of human resource with technology marks successful scanlon firms.

We have pointed out that OD interventions are sometimes artificial or simulated (many are not). The scanlon plan, as delineated in this book, offers structures and processes connected to work but consistent with the value assumptions of OD, namely, faith in the continued personal development of each person in the organization and the attainment of individual goals through corporate goals—the process of identity. Therefore, the necessary administration of the plan can easily lead to any of the OD interventions listed in Chapter 1 and in the expanded list above. For example, Figure 8.2 diagrams a process that is on-going. When you consider that as many as 96 percent of a firm's employees may be making suggestions, the involvement system is a clear example of an OD intervention activity. It is instructional to glance at Figure 1.1 at the beginning of the book. Problem recognition and diagnosis lead to a series of interventions under the plan. These interventions are represented by the process of the involvement system. Thus, Figure 8.2 is very similar to Figure 1.1. Instead of one of the above-mentioned interventions occurring, any or all could occur.

The involvement system, in concert with plan philosophy and the formula, operates to reduce hierarchy and barriers to communication within corporations. Undoubtedly, social cohesion is slightly increased as a function of the plan. To convey these ideas, Figure 8.3 depicts the perceived influence under scanlon. The higher the levels of hierarchy, the less perceived influence or control members of an organization perceive. But under scanlonism, the approach is to change organizational influence because, all organizational levels perceive that their influence increases, not as when a union is installed with a real or perceived loss of management prerogative.

You can see that, ideally, everyone gains under scanlonism, because the whole curve should shift upward with everyone from the administrator down to the lowest skilled employee gaining in perceived influence.

8.4 SCANLON WORKING PRINCIPLES

The best summary for this book is to end with a list of scanlon principles. These were developed by Joe Scanlon, nurtured by and added to by many cor-

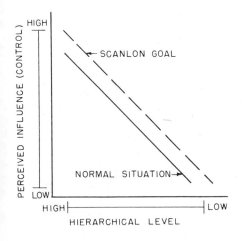

Figure 8.3 Perceived influence under scanlon.

porations, then carefully honed by Carl Frost, of Michigan State University. We have added to this list and have made some modifications. Therefore we take responsibility for the list that follows.

The scanlon plan is an innovative system for total organizational development. The scanlon plan is a means to increase productivity and profitability, provided the following principles are fully understood and implemented:

1. Each plan must be designed individually to fit the specific location and operation.
2. Competitive wage and fringe programs should be operative prior to any consideration of a scanlon plan.
3. The plan should not be used as a "salvage operation" but in successful and competently managed companies.
4. A scanlon plan should not be installed along with any other type of incentive program.
5. A scanlon plan should include all employees at a given facility (from janitor, least skilled, to plant manager).
6. Scanlon plan bonuses should be paid to all employees on a pro rata basis.
7. Where there is a union involved, it should be understood by all employees that the company does not intend to negotiate any elements of a scanlon plan (you must, of course, work with the union to gain its acceptance and endorsement).
8. Scanlon plan years should be kept out of the phase with the facility labor contract termination date.
9. Scanlon plan consideration for a facility should be communicated in an education program that enlists the great majority of employees' support to request its implementation.
10. When a scanlon plan is being installed to replace an existing incentive plan, special provision should be made to ensure productivity minimums where red-circle rates are required. Provision should be made for the most practical and rapid termination of such red-circle rates.
11. Installation of any new scanlon plan should be subject to a significant majority affirmative vote of all production, maintenance, and staff employees.
12. Where appropriate, scanlon plans should make provision for a minimum one-year trial period. Continuation may be then subject to an additional favorable employee vote. Thereafter, plan cancellation would be subject to a 90-day notice by either party. This event would be a clear indication of a drastic change of management (merger or sale of company) or a clear rejection of participative management.
13. The basic computation of the scanlon plan bonus should be kept as simple

as possible and particularly adapted to the needs of management and employees in that particular location toward productivity and profitability.

14. The scanlon bonus ratio must be monitored regularly and carefully to ensure the equity of all parties. The effect of mix changes, labor increases, price increases, and so on, may dictate an immediate change in the formula—with the necessary education program of all employees.

15. Discussions of labor-contract and fringe-benefit provisions should be avoided at all screening and production committee meetings.

16. Success of a scanlon plan largely depends on the dedication, enthusiasm, and competence of the plant manager. His insistence on the quality of suggestions and the openness of communications helps guarantee continuing success of the plan.

17. The role of the catalysts in developing, disseminating, and educating on the operating facts of life are very important in assuring trust in the relationships and confidence in management's ability to manage.

18. When a plant manager is transferred from a non-scanlon plant, it is imperative that he fully understand and be committed to the principles and concepts of the scanlon plan. To assist in his education, it is recommended that he spend an appropriate "internship" in a scanlon plant prior to his assignment.

19. All suggestions and minutes of the screening-committee meetings should be posted and distributed to provide maximum employee recognition and reinforcement.

20. Quality of production should be increased as a route to total organization productivity.

21. A certain percentage of the bonus should be reserved for deficit months to help protect the company and to increase long-run thinking by employees.

22. Screening committee is a consultative or advising body and not a decision-making one—management manages, the committee advises.

23. Problems isolated before the installation often become minor afterward.

24. Encourage skepticism about the plan, especially the formula.

25. Rapid follow-up on the disposition of suggestions encourages more suggestions.

26. Develop a task force to consider and implement the plan to ensure that tasks are performed.

27. Foremen and first-line supervisors must be involved in the plan, or they can undermine it.

28. Productivity-sharing calculation must be established at a level which ensures a company profit.

29. Bonus earnings should be separated from normal earnings.

30. All changes in the calculations must be decided on competitive conditions in existence at the time changes are considered.

31. Do not overemphasize factory workers at the expense of resource workers.
32. Productivity-increase goal setting should be the responsibility of every department.

You are now ready to begin a new kind of future under scanlonism. Your firm's experience will be unique, but the path is now well-lighted by the information you have processed because of this book.

A.1

BEFORE SCANLON SURVEY AND ANNUAL SURVEY

Dear employee: Your responses are handled confidentially and summarized by department or for the entire firm. No individual responses are ever used. Please be candid and do not sign questionnaire.

Department or Area_____

Position _____   Date _____

1 Satisfaction

1.1 All in all, how satisfied are you with your supervisor? (Check one).

_____	_____	_____	_____	_____
Very dis- satisfied	Dissatis- fied	Undecided	Satisfied	Very satis- fied

1.2 All in all, how satisfied are you with your job? (Check one).

_____	_____	_____	_____	_____
Very dis- satisfied	Dissatis- fied	Undecided	Satisfied	Very satis- fied

1.3   All in all, how satisfied are you with this company? (Check one).

_____	_____	_____	_____	_____
Very dis-satisfied	Dissatis-fied	Undecided	Satisfied	Very satis-fied

1.4   How do you feel about your future with this company? (Check one).

_____	_____	_____	_____	_____
Very dis-satisfied	Dissatis-fied	Undecided	Satisfied	Very satis-fied

1.5   How satisfied would you say you are with your pay? (Chech one).

_____	_____	_____	_____	_____
Very dis-satisfied	Dissatis-fied	Undecided	Satisfied	Very satis-fied

2   About Your Immediate Supervisor

2.1   How much influence does your immediate supervisor have over your salary and advancement in this organization? (Check one).

_____ 1.   No influence
_____ 2.   A little
_____ 3.   Some
_____ 4.   Quite a bit
_____ 5.   A great deal of influence

2.2   To what extent do you have confidence and trust in your supervisor? (Check one).

_____ 1.   To no extent; I don't trust him at all
_____ 2.   To a very little extent
_____ 3.   To some extent
_____ 4.   To a considerable extent
_____ 5.   To a very great extent

2.3 How well does your supervisor know the technical side of his job? (Check one).

    ——— 1.   He does not know the technical parts of his job at all well.
    ——— 2.   Some well, and others not so well.
    ——— 3.   Fairly well.
    ——— 4.   Very well.
    ——— 5.   He knows the technical parts of his job extremely well.

2.4 How well does your supervisor do the administrative side of his job—by this we mean planning and scheduling the work, indicating clearly when work is to be finished, assigning the right job to the right man, and following up on the work that is done, and so on? (Check one).

    ——— 1.   He does not handle the administrative parts of his job at all well.
    ——— 2.   Some well, and others not so well.
    ——— 3.   Fairly well.
    ——— 4.   Very well.
    ——— 5.   He handles the administrative parts of his job extremely well.

2.5 How well does your supervisor do the human-relations side of his job— getting people to work well together, getting individuals to do the best they can, give recognition for good work done, letting people know where they stand, and so on? (Check one).

    ——— 1.   He does not handle the human-relations parts of job at all well.
    ——— 2.   Some well, and others not so well.
    ——— 3.   Fairly well.
    ——— 4.   Very well.
    ——— 5.   He handles the human-relations parts of his job extremely well.

3 Cooperation and Communication

How would you rate cooperation between departments? (Circle one).

	Low		Average		High
3.1 Cooperation	1	2	3	4	5

3.2   How would you rate communication between departments? (Circle one).

	Low		Average		High
Communication	1	2	3	4	5

4   Attitudes toward Suggestion Making

4.1   Are people around here willing to accept suggestions you make?

_____ 1.   Never willing to accept my ideas.
_____ 2.   Seldom willing.
_____ 3.   Sometimes willing.
_____ 4.   Willing.
_____ 5.   Very willing to accept my ideas.

4.2   Are people around here willing to accept suggestions others make?

_____ 1.   Never willing to accept suggestions others make.
_____ 2.   Seldom willing.
_____ 3.   Sometimes willing.
_____ 4.   Willing.
_____ 5.   Very willing to accept suggestions others make.

4.3   Does your supervisor ask your opinion when a problem comes up that involves your work?

_____ 1.   He never asks my opinion.
_____ 2.   Seldom asks.
_____ 3.   Sometimes asks.
_____ 4.   Often.
_____ 5.   He always asks my opinion.

4.4   How often do you offer suggestions about improving the operations of your job, work area, or department?

_____ 1.   I never make any suggestions.
_____ 2.   Seldom make any suggestions.
_____ 3.   Sometimes make suggestions.
_____ 4.   Often make suggestions.
_____ 5.   I very often make suggestions.

5 Performance

We would like you to consider your job performance. How would you rate yourself on the following dimensions? (Circle one).

		Low		Average		High
5.1	Quantity of work	1	2	3	4	5
5.2	Quality of work	1	2	3	4	5
5.3	Effort put into job	1	2	3	4	5

6 Pay

6.1 What determines how much you get paid around here? Please indicate how important these *are* for determining the pay for someone in your position. Circle the number on the scale that represents your feeling of its importance. Low numbers represent unimportant characteristics; high numbers represent characteristics that _____ (company) uses in deciding on your pay.

		Very unimportant						Very important
1.	Length of service	1	2	3	4	5	6	7
2.	Amount of job responsibility	1	2	3	4	5	6	7
3.	Quality of work	1	2	3	4	5	6	7
4.	Quantity of work	1	2	3	4	5	6	7
5.	Cost of living	1	2	3	4	5	6	7
6.	Loyalty to company	1	2	3	4	5	6	7
7.	Ability to do the job	1	2	3	4	5	6	7
8.	Age	1	2	3	4	5	6	7

6.2 In the above question you indicated what factors are important in determining your pay. In this question we want to know what factors you think *should be* used in determining the pay for someone in your position. Circle the number on the scale which best indicates how important that factor should be.

		Very unimportant					Very important	
1.	Length of service	1	2	3	4	5	6	7
2.	Amount of job responsibility	1	2	3	4	5	6	7
3.	Quality of work	1	2	3	4	5	6	7
4.	Quantity of work	1	2	3	4	5	6	7
5.	Cost of living	1	2	3	4	5	6	7
6.	Loyalty to company	1	2	3	4	5	6	7
7.	Ability to do the job	1	2	3	4	5	6	7
8.	Age	1	2	3	4	5	6	7

7 About Your Work

Here are some things connected with your job. For each of them you will be asked to give two ratings.

1. How much is there now connected with your job?
2. How much do you think should be connected with your job?

In the following questions, circle the number on the scale that represents the amount of the characteristic being rated. Low numbers represent low amounts, and high numbers represent high amounts. If you think there is "very little" or "none" of the characteristic presently associated with your job, you would circle numeral 1. If you think there is a "great deal but not a maximum amount," you would circle numeral 6. For each scale, circle only one number.

7.1 The pay I get from my job.

		Min					Max	
1.	How much is there now?	1	2	3	4	5	6	7
2.	How much should there be?	1	2	3	4	5	6	7

7.2 The opportunity for participating in the setting of goals, methods, and procedures.

		Min					Max	
1.	How much is there now?	1	2	3	4	5	6	7
2.	How much should there be?	1	2	3	4	5	6	7

7.3   The interest from the work itself.

		Min					Max
1. How much is there now?	1	2	3	4	5	6	7
2. How much should there be?	1	2	3	4	5	6	7

7.4   The feeling of satisfactory relationships with my supervisors.

		Min					Max
1. How much is there now?	1	2	3	4	5	6	7
2. How much should there be?	1	2	3	4	5	6	7

7.5   The feeling of worthwhile accomplishment in my job.

		Min					Max
1. How much is there now?	1	2	3	4	5	6	7
2. How much should there be?	1	2	3	4	5	6	7

7.6   The feeling of satisfactory relationships with my co-workers.

		Min					Max
1. How much is there now?	1	2	3	4	5	6	7
2. How much should there be?	1	2	3	4	5	6	7

7.7   The feeling of being informed in my job.

		Min					Max
1. How much is there now?	1	2	3	4	5	6	7
2. How much should there be?	1	2	3	4	5	6	7

7.8   The feeling of pride I have in the company.

		Min					Max
1. How much is there now?	1	2	3	4	5	6	7
2. How much should there be?	1	2	3	4	5	6	7

7.9   The feeling of security in my job.

	Min					Max	
1. How much is there now?	1	2	3	4	5	6	7
2. How much should there be?	1	2	3	4	5	6	7

8   Attitudes toward Participation

8.1   When decisions are being made, to what extent are the persons affected asked for their ideas?

_____	_____	_____	_____	_____
To a very little extent	To a little extent	To some extent	To a great extent	To a very great extent

8.2   To what extent are the persons who make decisions aware of problems at lower levels in the company?

_____	_____	_____	_____	_____
To a very little extent	To a little extent	To some extent	To a great extent	To a very great extent

8.3   Usually everyone in a company has a great deal of practical know-how. To what extent is this know-how widely shared in this company so that those who make decisions can use it?

_____	_____	_____	_____	_____
To a very little extent	To a little extent	To some extent	To a great extent	To a very great extent

8.4   How important is the opportunity to participate in decisions concerning job, work area, or department?

_____ 1.   Unimportant.
_____ 2.   Slightly unimportant.
_____ 3.   Slightly important.
_____ 4.   Important.
_____ 5.   It is very important to me.

A.2

PLAN-EVALUATION QUESTIONNAIRE

Department or Area_____

Position _____   Date _____

This questionnaire pertains to your attitudes toward various aspects of the scanlon plan and the company. The purpose is to improve the communications within the plant and to improve the operation of the scanlon plan. Read each statement carefully.

1 Scanlon Plan

1.1   How well do you feel you understand how the scanlon plan bonus is calculated and distributed at this point?

I do not understand it at all	Slightly	Somewhat	Well	I understand it very well

1.2   How well do you feel you understand how the committee system works at this plant?

I do not understand it at all	Slightly	Somewhat	Well	I understand it very well

1.3   Compare your understanding of the scanlon plan with your profit-
       sharing plan. Would you say your understanding of the scanlon plan is

Much less	Somewhat less	About the same	Somewhat better	Much better

       than your understanding of the profit sharing plan?

1.4   There are a number of things you can do that might influence whether
       you receive a bonus. How important do you think the following factors
       are:

       1.   Suggestions submitted to production committee.

                     1   2   3   4   5
                   Very   Average   Very
               unimportant   important

       2.   Quality of work.

                     1   2   3   4   5
                   Very   Average   Very
               unimportant   important

       3.   Quantity of work.

                     1   2   3   '4   5
                   Very   Average   Very
               unimportant   important

2 Committees

       There are a variety of activities that your departmental committee could
       perform. We would like you to describe your committee in terms of the
       following activities.

2.1   My committee processed suggestions quickly and efficiently.

Describes not at all well	Slightly	Somewhat	Well	Describes very well

2.2 My committee members did everything they could to get the higher-cost suggestions accepted by screening committee.

Describes not at all well	Slightly	Somewhat	Well	Describes very well

2.3 My committee members put a lot of time and effort into their job.

Describes not at all well	Slightly	Somewhat	Well	Describes very well

2.4 My committee kept us very well informed about how the scanlon plan was operating (when we got bonuses, how much, and why).

Describes not at all well	Slightly	Somewhat	Well	Describes very well

2.5 My committee encouraged us to come up with new suggestions and to rework others to make them better.

Describes not at all well	Slightly	Somewhat	Well	Describes very well

3 Production Attitudes

3.1 The company should install new equipment whenever possible in order to increase productivity.

Strongly disagree	Disagree	Undecided	Agree	Strongly agree

3.2   The scanlon plan encourages an individual to use his experience and knowledge on the job.

| ———— | ———— | ———— | ———— | ———— |
| Strongly disagree | Disagree | Undecided | Agree | Strongly agree |

3.3   The scanlon plan encourages the whole plant to work as a team.

| ———— | ———— | ———— | ———— | ———— |
| Strongly disagree | Disagree | Undecided | Agree | Strongly agree |

3.4   The scanlon plan representatives really do represent the employees who elected them.

| ———— | ———— | ———— | ———— | ———— |
| Strongly disagree | Disagree | Undecided | Agree | Strongly agree |

3.5   The installation of new equipment will not reduce job security.

| ———— | ———— | ———— | ———— | ———— |
| Strongly disagree | Disagree | Undecided | Agree | Strongly agree |

3.6   Management should allow employees more control over themselves such as setting their own production rates for the department.

| ———— | ———— | ———— | ———— | ———— |
| Strongly disagree | Disagree | Undecided | Agree | Strongly agree |

3.7   I have a great deal of control over what happens on my job.

| ———— | ———— | ———— | ———— | ———— |
| Strongly disagree | Disagree | Undecided | Agree | Strongly agree |

3.8   The bonus-period calculations are reliable.

Strongly disagree	Disagree	Undecided	Agree	Strongly agree

3.9   Defective materials are not permitted to continue in production once they are detected.

Strongly disagree	Disagree	Undecided	Agree	Strongly agree

3.10   The accountants try to be impartial in putting together the figures; they do not lean in favor of management or the employees.

Strongly disagree	Disagree	Undecided	Agree	Strongly agree

3.11   The scanlon plan statement is not too complicated for me to understand.

Strongly disagree	Disagree	Undecided	Agree	Strongly agree

3.12   The accounting reports we receive give us the information we need.

Strongly disagree	Disagree	Undecided	Agree	Strongly agree

3.13   Most of the employees in my department really care what the accounting reports say.

Strongly disagree	Disagree	Undecided	Agree	Strongly agree

3.14   My group receives enough information from the accounting department about performance to know where we stand.

Strongly disagree	Disagree	Undecided	Agree	Strongly agree

3.15   We should be given more accounting information on such things as material losses.

Strongly disagree	Disagree	Undecided	Agree	Strongly agree

3.16   Problems in areas other than labor should be brought into the open and discussed in the committee meetings.

Strongly disagree	Disagree	Undecided	Agree	Strongly agree

3.17   Management should develop a method of including material in the bonus.

Strongly disagree	Disagree	Undecided	Agree	Strongly agree

3.18   Suggestions for reducing material costs are encouraged by management.

Strongly disagree	Disagree	Undecided	Agree	Strongly agree

3.19   I see places where material savings would be possible.

Strongly disagree	Disagree	Undecided	Agree	Strongly agree

4 Expected Level of Scanlon Plan Success

4.1 I feel the scanlon plan will do much for me on my job.

| _____ | _____ | _____ | _____ | _____ |
| Strongly disagree | Disagree | Undecided | Agree | Strongly agree |

4.2 I feel the scanlon plan will be good for the company.

| _____ | _____ | _____ | _____ | _____ |
| Strongly disagree | Disagree | Undecided | Agree | Strongly agree |

4.3 I think the scanlon plan will change many things in this company.

| _____ | _____ | _____ | _____ | _____ |
| Strongly disagree | Disagree | Undecided | Agree | Strongly agree |

4.4 I feel the scanlon plan will make it easier to ask questions about company policy.

| _____ | _____ | _____ | _____ | _____ |
| Strongly disagree | Disagree | Undecided | Agree | Strongly agree |

4.5 I feel the scanlon plan will make it easier for my suggestions to be heard.

| _____ | _____ | _____ | _____ | _____ |
| Strongly disagree | Disagree | Undecided | Agree | Strongly agree |

4.6 I feel the scanlon plan will make it easier for the employees to work as a team.

| _____ | _____ | _____ | _____ | _____ |
| Strongly disagree | Disagree | Undecided | Agree | Strongly agree |

4.7   I feel the scanlon plan makes it easier for me to get my fair share.

Strongly disagree	Disagree	Undecided	Agree	Strongly agree

5   Participation in Decision Making

5.1   To what extent are you able to decide how you do your job?

Very little extent	Little extent	Some extent	Great extent	Very great extent

5.2   In general, how much say or influence do you have on what goes on in your work group?

Very little extent	Little extent	Some extent	Great extent	Very great extent

5.3   In general, how much influence do you have on decisions which affect your job?

Very little influence	Little influence	A moderate amount of influence	Much influence	Very much influence

5.4   In general, how much say or influence do you have on how you perform your job?

Very little influence	Little influence	A moderate amount of influence	Much influence	Very much influence

5.5   My superiors are receptive and listen to my ideas and suggestions.

Never	Seldom	Occasionally	Often	Always

6   Perceived Level of Scanlon Plan Success

6.1   I feel the scanlon plan does much for me on my job.

| Strongly disagree | Disagree | Undecided | Agree | Strongly agree |

6.2   I feel the scanlon plan is good for the company.

| Strongly disagree | Disagree | Undecided | Agree | Strongly agree |

6.3   I think the scanlon plan has changed many things in this company.

| Strongly disagree | Disagree | Undecided | Agree | Strongly agree |

6.4   I feel the scanlon plan makes it easier to ask questions about company policy.

| Strongly disagree | Disagree | Undecided | Agree | Strongly agree |

6.5   I feel the scanlon plan makes it easier for my suggestions to be heard.

| Strongly disagree | Disagree | Undecided | Agree | Strongly agree |

6.6   I feel the scanlon plan makes it easier for the employees to work as a team.

| Strongly disagree | Disagree | Undecided | Agree | Strongly agree |

7 Expectations

7.1 There are a number of things you can do that *might influence* whether you receive a bonus. How important do you think the following factors are?

		Very Unimportant				Average			Very important	
1.	Suggestions submitted to production committee	1	2	3	4	5	6	7	8	9
2.	Quantity of work	1	2	3	4	5	6	7	8	9
3.	Quality of work	1	2	3	4	5	6	7	8	9
4.	Amount of effort	1	2	3	4	5	6	7	8	9
5.	Other factors you feel are important (specify)_____	1	2	3	4	5	6	7	8	9

7.2 In the question above you rated the importance of those factors which might influence whether you receive a bonus. Now, the question changes somewhat. What are the chances that *you will be able to:*

		Chances are very low				Average			Chances are very high	
1.	Make suggestions	1	2	3	4	5	6	7	8	9
2.	Increase quantity	1	2	3	4	5	6	7	8	9
3.	Increase quality	1	2	3	4	5	6	7	8	9
4.	Increase amount of effort	1	2	3	4	5	6	7	8	9
5.	Other factors you feel are important (specify)_____	1	2	3	4	5	6	7	8	9

7.3 Often when people think about the scanlon plan, they think only of the bonus. There are many other outcomes of the plan that are possible. Consider the list below, using the same kind of scale we have used in the past. What are the chances these factors will increase:

		Low		Average		High
1.	Participation	1	2	3	4	5
2.	Communication	1	2	3	4	5

3.	Control over work	1	2	3	4	5
4.	Cooperation	1	2	3	4	5

8 Knowledge

This part of the questionnaire is concerned with your knowledge of the scanlon plan's computation. To complete this part, read each statement and then decide which answer—TRUE, FALSE, or DON'T KNOW—best fits your knowledge right now.

TRUE	The statement is true
FALSE	The statement is false.
DON'T KNOW	You are uncertain or you do not have any knowledge about the statement.

Read each statement carefully. You will find some statements are true and some are false. If you do not know whether a statement is true or false or have no knowledge about the statement, circle the DON'T KNOW answer (do not guess), since one of the main goals of the survey is to find things which need improvement.

T   F   DK   All plant personnel live in ⎯⎯⎯⎯⎯⎯ .
                                            (your city)

If you feel the statement is TRUE, you would circle T. If FALSE, circle F. If you are uncertain or DON'T KNOW, circle DK. Be sure to mark every statement.

Plant Mean*

8.1   T   F   DK   If you now produce more, you will receive the full increase in your next weekly paycheck. F^a

8.2   T   F   DK   After one month, a new employee automatically receives his 100 percent share of the scanlon plan bonus.   F

8.3   T   F   DK   Overtime increases an individual employee's pay but reduces everyone's scanlon plan bonus.   T

8.4   T   F   DK   Production standards are changed only at the beginning of the year.   F

* Use same questionnaire for summarizing your data and compute plant mean. See Appendix A.3 for details.

[a] These items are scored. Please delete answers before using.

8.5   T   F   DK   Improper maintenance of machines reduces the scanlon plan bonus.   T

8.6   T   F   DK   The total gross bonus earned is paid each period.   F

8.7   T   F   DK   Employee absenteeism affects the scanlon plan bonus.   T

8.8   T   F   DK   The standards for indirect labor allowances, such as for shipping and janitorial, are changed at the beginning of each year.   F

8.9   T   F   DK   If one employee turns in more production than he actually completed, the scanlon plan bonus for the period will be affected.   T

8.10   T   F   DK   Clerical costs at the plant have no effect on the scanlon plan bonus.   F

8.11   T   F   DK   Variations in the thickness of material have no effect on the scanlon plan bonus.   F

8.12   T   F   DK   The number of laborsaving suggestions has been decreasing the last year.   T

8.13   T   F   DK   Merit pay increases are paid out of the scanlon plan bonus.   T

8.14   T   F   DK   Machine downtime does not affect the scanlon plan bonus.   F

8.15   T   F   DK   The amount of production at the plant affects the scanlon plan bonus.   T

8.16   T   F   DK   The scanlon plan bonus could be increasing at the same time as the company's profit is decreasing.   T

8.17   T   F   DK   When defective output is returned from our plants, the plant's scanlon plan bonus is not affected.   T

8.18   T   F   DK   Labor savings are paid as material moves through departments.   F

8.19   T   F   DK   When a new employee begins work, his lack of job knowledge and experience affects the scanlon plan bonus.   T

8.20   T   F   DK   Errors made in counting the inventory at the end of any period affect the scanlon plan bonus.   T

8.21   T   F   DK   If you now work harder and produce more, the company gets the full benefit.   F

8.22   T   F   DK   Laborsaving suggestions are a small percentage of the total scanlon plan bonus.   F

Plant Average

CODING AND SCORING YOUR QUESTIONNAIRE

Appendixes A.1 and A.2 can be coded either by hand or set up for computer assistance (i.e., keypunching). Since expertise and type of computational facility varies, it would be fruitless to describe in detail how to code format and report out your data. Nevertheless, you should know that only three arithmetic operations are necessary to get a handle on your own data.

This section provides the necessary guidelines to enable you to produce a clean, meaningful report. We present just the basics. Remember Chapter 7 offers emphasis and a finer level of discussion concerning this process.

The most common way to report your final analysis is to use the actual questionnaire as a summary questionnaire. In this way, total data are reported out in the same way they were collected. Each respondent can compare his or her own recollection of their response with that of the organization. Thus, the summarizing questionnaire is an aid to memory and facilitates the feedback process.

EXAMPLE OF SUMMARY QUESTIONNAIRE

Based on 150 questionnaires collected in October, 1977, the percents in the brackets show our response to each question.

1 Scanlon Plan

1.1 How well do you feel you understand how the scanlon plan bonus is calculated and distributed at this plant? (Number answering question: 150.)

(25%)	(30%)	(45%)	(—)	(—)
I do not understand it at all	Slightly	Somewhat	Well	I understand it very well

1.2 How well do you feel you understand how the committee system works at this plant? (Number answering question: 149.)

(—)	(—)	(45%)	(30%)	(25%)
I do not understand it at all	Slightly	Somewhat	Well	I understand it very well

Now, for the three ways you would normally analyze your survey data.

1. As you saw in the summary questionnaire, simple percentages can be computed for most of the questions. It is important, however, to note that the total responding to each question is the base you would use for computing the percentage. This base should not vary by much. All of us can miss a question and skip one by mistake. But if you notice that the base varies greatly, scan the question very carefully. People are avoiding it and are, in effect, answering it by not placing "true" response in the space. Once in a while, however, the question may be ambiguous and this alone can cause the base to vary (i.e., nonresponse).

2. The next arithmetic operation is for computing a mean for all your questions except the difference measures. Clearly, the mean can be graphed as we suggest in Figure 2.3 and can be compared from year to year. Total the returns for each category, and multiply by the weight of each item. Then the grand total of the products should be divided by the number of returns to ascertain the average weight. For example:

	Weight	Questionnaire returns	Weight times returns
*Very satisfied	5	60	300
*Satisfied	4	50	200
*Undecided	3	15	45
*Dissatisfied	2	15	30
*Very dissatisfied	1	10	10
		150	585

585 divided by 150 = 3.9 (average weight)

* These descriptors vary, depending on the scale used.

The average weight is 3.9, a score more than midway between 3 (unde-
cided) and 4 (satisfied). The score may be compared with scores of other surveys of a like nature or with standards secured from a trade association.

This mean can be graphed for comparisons over time, as we have indicated, to show change.

3. The last arithmetic operation is nothing more than a variation of number 2
    above. However, it is for the difference scores discussed in Chapter 7. For
    example:

	Should be	Now	Subtraction	Score	×	Should be weight	Score
*Min	1	1					
	2	2	=	2	×	3	= 6
	3	3					
	4	4	=	2	×	4	= 8
	5	5					
	6	6	=	0	×	5	= 0
*Max	7	7					
							14

14 divided by 3 = 4.6 (average weight)

* This is simplified to three responders.

By subtracting "actual" or "now" from "should be," you obtain the
perceived difference. This difference times the weight, which is the magnitude of a given attribute, gives you the score. The higher the score, the
greater the perceived difference. Ideally, the firm would like the score to be
zero. This would mean an identity of individual needs and the organization's ability to provide them. It is very important to divide the total
responding into the scores in order to make the average weight score a meaningful statistic. This mean, however, has a range of values of 0, which is
ideal, to 42 ($7 - 1 = 6 \times 7 = 42$). Thus, the highest possible difference score
would be the greatest difference times the highest value on the scale.

These mean scores can be graphed in a fashion similar to Figure 2.3:

Attribute	Mean Score
	0 5 10. . .15. 42

Pay
Participation
Interest
Supervisors
Accomplishment
Coworkers
Being informed
Company pride
Security

Finally, questions 6.1 and 6.2 of Appendix A.1 and questions 7.1 and 7.2 of Appendix A.2 are just variations of the difference measures already described. The distinction is that one set of questions is presented at a time, but you still subtract one parallel item of each set from the other. For example:

Question 6.2 minus 6.1 of Appendix A.1

Difference score = should be − perceived organizational importance

Question 7.1 minus 7.2 of Appendix A.2

Difference score = should be − perceived chances

The scores from these sets of difference measures can be graphed as shown in the above example. They will help in shedding light on the perceptions of employees about the organization's reward system and the functioning of the scanlon plan.

APPENDIX

MEMO OF UNDERSTANDING

Definition

What is the scanlon plan? The scanlon plan is a program whereby all the employees of the (name of plant) have an opportunity to participate in managing the plant. Employees can participate in managing the plant by making suggestions as to when, where, what, why, and how their job or other jobs should be performed.

Objective

Objective of the scanlon plan. The objective of the scanlon plan is working together as a team in order to be more productive and efficient, to reduce waste, to reduce costs, and to produce a monthly bonus for all employees who have (number of days) or more service.

Origination of Plan

Who started the scanlon plan? The scanlon plan is based on principles developed by the late Joseph N. Scanlon. Mr. Scanlon was a former union official and was associated later with the Massachusetts Institute of Technology. His concept was that the employee and the employer have much in common. Also, he felt that every employee has a contribution to make concerning ways to make improvements on the job. He believed that any improvements that could be made on the job would help to improve the company's business in the market place and in turn would provide increased job security.

XYZ's History

When and how did the scanlon plan get started in (name of plant)? The scanlon plan in the (name) plant resulted from an agreement between the employees and the (name of company).* It became effective on (date) for a trial period of fifteen (15) months. At the conclusion of the trial period, the employees will have the opportunity to vote on whether they want the plan to remain permanently in effect.

Why do we have a bonus plan? In addition to being a plan whereby all employees work together to better manage the plant and secure their jobs, the plan also pays a cash bonus when labor saving improvements are made. This cash bonus is a true incentive for everyone to participate in making the plant more efficient. An efficient company will be able to maintain a competitive position in its markets. This means being able to produce our product in large quantities at the highest-quality levels for the lowest prices. The greatest productivity gains are made by working smarter.

The scanlon concept of participative management provides the framework for all employees to get their productivity-increasing ideas into use and then pays a bonus for the resulting increased productivity. The bonus is not a giveaway program. It is paid when it is earned by bettering the normal performance of labor costs. But if performance is only average or below, then no bonus can be paid.

Participation

How do employees participate in the scanlon plan? A committee structure (production and screening committees) has been established to process employee suggestions. Suggestions are submitted to the production committee first, and each person has the opportunity to make a written suggestion to any member of his or her elected production committee. The purpose of a suggestion should be to improve:

How Improvements Are Made

1. Methods:
   Eliminate unnecessary operations
   Simplify your own job
   Simplify other jobs
   Suggest new methods
   Simplify present methods

* If unionized, state that the scanlon plan is set forth in a memo of understanding between union and the corporation.

2. Machinery and equipment:
   Improve machine output
   Improve design or construction
   Reduce machine setup time
   Reduce machine downtime
   Reduce maintenance costs
3. Paper work:
   Eliminate duplicate work
   Simplify reports
   Eliminate unnecessary reports
   Simplify, combine, or eliminate unnecessary forms
   Reduce or simplify filing
   Reduce phone, postage, shipping, or other costs

Production Committee

What is a production committee?   The plant is divided into (number) production committees representing designated areas and shifts within the plant (see Figure B.1). These committees can be structured in any way which would best serve the people whom they represent and can be changed to meet changing needs. Each group has its own production committee made up of a management representative and two (2) elected employee representatives. The production committees solicit monthly suggestions from the employees whom they represent. Periodically the committees meet and discuss what should be done with each of the suggestions. There are five dispositions which can be made to a suggestion at this level.

Disposition of Suggestions in Production Committee

1. Accept the suggestion and put it into use.
2. Reject the suggestion.
3. Accept the suggestion and put it under investigation. Suggestions are normally put under investigation when there are not enough facts to make a decision, and when it is necessary to find out whether the savings involved would offset the cost of putting the suggestion into effect.
4. Accept the suggestion and refer it to the screening committee. These are suggestions which a production committee feels should be placed into effect but cost over a specified amount to implement.
5. Rejected—difference of opinion. These are suggestions in which there are differences of opinion among two or more committee members as to whether or not a suggestion would be put into effect. These suggestions are then referred to the screening committee.

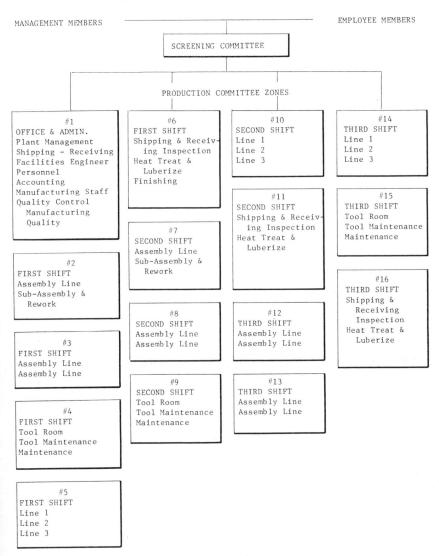

MANAGEMENT MEMBERS —————————————— EMPLOYEE MEMBERS

SCREENING COMMITTEE

PRODUCTION COMMITTEE ZONES

#1
OFFICE & ADMIN.
Plant Management
Shipping - Receiving
Facilities Engineer
Personnel
Accounting
Manufacturing Staff
Quality Control
  Manufacturing
  Quality

#2
FIRST SHIFT
Assembly Line
Sub-Assembly &
  Rework

#3
FIRST SHIFT
Assembly Line
Assembly Line

#4
FIRST SHIFT
Tool Room
Tool Maintenance
Maintenance

#5
FIRST SHIFT
Line 1
Line 2
Line 3

#6
FIRST SHIFT
Shipping & Receiv-
  ing Inspection
Heat Treat &
  Luberize
Finishing

#7
SECOND SHIFT
Assembly Line
Sub-Assembly &
  Rework

#8
SECOND SHIFT
Assembly Line
Assembly Line

#9
SECOND SHIFT
Tool Room
Tool Maintenance
Maintenance

#10
SECOND SHIFT
Line 1
Line 2
Line 3

#11
SECOND SHIFT
Shipping & Receiv-
  ing Inspection
Heat Treat &
  Luberize

#12
THIRD SHIFT
Assembly Line
Assembly Line

#13
THIRD SHIFT
Assembly Line
Assembly Line

#14
THIRD SHIFT
Line 1
Line 2
Line 3

#15
THIRD SHIFT
Tool Room
Tool Maintenance
Maintenance

#16
THIRD SHIFT
Shipping &
  Receiving
  Inspection
Heat Treat &
  Luberize

Figure B.1   Committee structure.

A production committee may spend up to (amount) dollars on any one suggestion and up to (amount) in one month.

The production committees may request and will receive whatever assistance is necessary from the other departments in the plant in order to process and implement suggestions.

Screening Committee

What is the screening committee? The screening committee consists of (number) of the elected employee members from the production committees and (number) management employees, consisting of the plant manager and other appointed management representatives. The committee meets monthly prior to announcing the bonus results.

One purpose of the screening committee is to assist the production committees in reviewing the calculations of the monthly scanlon bonus and to discuss any improvements which could be made to earn a bonus. The committee also discusses the reasons why a bonus is not earned, if that should occur, and any other business which the production committees ask them to discuss.

Another purpose of the screening committee is to review and evaluate productivity suggestions coming from the production committees. All suggestions get a review or final hearing here. Since many productivity ideas involve other departments or capital expenditures, the screening committee strives to process input from all perspectives before management decides on how to adopt suggestions.

Bonus Calculation

How the bonus is calculated. The increases in productivity and the reductions in other costs resulting from working smarter under the scanlon plan will generate a monthly bonus expressed as a percentage of each individual's gross monthly income. This bonus is paid monthly for the bonus earned the previous month. It is paid in a separate check, usually about the fifteenth of the month.

The bonus is calculated from a base ratio which is the ratio of total payroll costs plus vacation and holiday accruals to the sales value of production. The base ratio is established to represent the normal or expected total payroll cost to produce one dollar's worth of sales, which is expressed as a percent of the sales value of production. In the example shown in Table B.1 the base ratio is 8.15 percent. This means that in that period, the normal total labor cost would be 8.15 percent of the sales value of production or 8.15 cents for each dollar of product or service produced at sales value. Once the base ratio is established, it is adjusted only to allow for significant changes in the factors which affect its calculation.

In the example, the total sales value of production is $8,572,500, and so the allowed or expected total labor is 8.15 percent of this, or $698,659. However, the actual total labor cost is only $615,389. The difference of $83,270 then becomes the scanlon bonus pool.

For each one dollar in the bonus pool, 75 percent is paid to the people participating in the plan, and 25 percent is retained by the company. The people

Table B.1   Bonus-Calculation Example

	Sales value of production	$8,572,500
	Allowed payroll at 8.15%	698,659
	Actual payroll	615,389
Bonus	Bonus pool	$ 83,270
Example	Less reserve for deficit months—25%	20,818[a]
	Balance	$ 62,452
	Company share—25%	15,613
	Employees' share—75%	$ 46,839
	Participating payroll	$ 590,773
	Bonus percentage ($46,839 ÷ $590,773)	7.93%

Note: The participating payroll is less than the actual payroll, because no bonus is paid to employees on the job less than 30 days or for nonworking pay such as jury duty, vacation, and holidays. In addition to this bonus payment, the employees have a 75 percent stake in the reserve.

This is an example of how an individual pay record would look with bonus:

Name	Total Hours Worked	Overtime Hours	Hourly Rate
John Doe	190	30	$4.75

Total Pay	Bonus %	Bonus	Total
$973.75	7.93%	$77.22	$1,050.97

Individual Example

The amount of bonus pay may vary from one month to another month, because it is based on the gross earnings for a month, even though the percent of bonus earned may be the same for both months.

The bonus is calculated on the basis of actual hours worked during a month and includes shift premium, overtime premium, and any other pay adjustments. Since bonus is paid on the basis of work participation, any wage or salary received for absence from work (jury duty, holidays, vacation) is not considered in the computation of bonus pay.

[a] If you look at Section 4.10, you will see that we recommend you give the company its share before computing the reserve for deficit months.

Table B.2 Deficit-Month Example

Value of productivity	$7,500,000
Allowed payroll at 8.15%	611,250
Actual payroll	615,225
Bonus pool	(−3,975)
Reserve for deficit months	(−3,975)

In this example, the actual payroll was greater than the allowed payroll, which results in a deficit bonus pool. This is charged against the bonus reserve account and reduces the amount left in the reserve at the end of the scanlon year.

MONTH	ADD THIS MONTH	TOTAL RESERVE
MARCH	$11,360	$11,360
APRIL	15,225	26,585
MAY (DEFICIT MONTH)	(-3,975)	22,610
JUNE	7,985	30,595
JULY	13,450	44,045
AUGUST	10,175	54,220

COMPANY SHARE - 25%	$13,555
EMPLOYEES' SHARE - 75%	40,665
TOTAL	$54,220

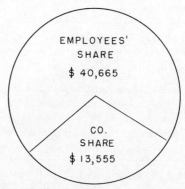

Figure B.2 Reserve-account example.

get 75 percent of this bonus because they have increased productivity by working more intelligently, and the company gets 25 percent of this bonus because it supplied the capital needed to take advantage of the laborsaving ideas. Prior to making the monthly bonus payment 25 percent of all bonus (both the employees' and the company's share) is set aside in the form of a reserve for any deficit months. A deficit month is a month when payroll cost exceeds allowed payroll (see Table B.2).

The Reserve

The scanlon year ends on (date), and all money remaining in the reserve account at that time is distributed. Seventy-five percent is distributed to the employees, and 25 percent is distributed to the company in what is referred to as a thirteenth monthly scanlon bonus check. In the event a scanlon year ends with a deficit balance in the reserve account, the entire deficit is absorbed by the company and is not charged against any future bonus. The reserve-account example shows how this works and illustrates the effect of a deficit month (see Table B.2 and Figure B.2).

You have had a brief introduction to the scanlon plan in this memo of understanding. The scanlon plan will work only if we want to make it work. In this program everyone is a partner, and it requires people who are willing to put forth effort as well as ideas. It offers all employees an opportunity to submit their suggestions and to work to make them succeed. So let us do our part as individuals and make the program work!

EMPLOYEE'S SUGGESTION

(Please Print or Write Plainly)

HOW TO MAKE YOUR SUGGESTION

1. Using a plan similar to the one below, write your suggestion in the simplest manner you can:
   a. (What) My suggestion is
   b. (Why) I believe it should be done because
   c. (How) It is done as follows
   d. (How) My suggestion can be accomplished by
2. You may, if you choose, include sketches, samples, or models. Note: If sketch is required which cannot be placed on the front of this sheet without cramping, use a separate sheet of the same size.
3. Your supervisor will be glad to assist you in any way he can.
4. Turn in your suggestion to your department committee representative.

Date_____

Suggestion #[a] _____

Department_____

Zone #_____

Submitted by: _____(print name)_____

1. _____ Labor-saving

2. _____ Product Improvement

3. _____ Working Conditions

4. _____ Materials Saving

5. _____ Miscellaneous

[a] Number consecutively by department; see screening-committee minutes for example.

I SUGGEST THAT _____

_____

_____

_____

_____

_____

Use back of sheet if necessary to finish your suggestion.

_____

PRODUCTION COMMITTEE ACTION: _____

_____

_____

FINAL DISPOSITION: _____

_____

_____

EXAMPLE OF SCREENING-COMMITTEE MINUTES

ABC, Inc., XYZ Plant
Scanlon Screening-Committee Meeting Minutes
May 15, 1972

Posting the bonus calculation showed that we had earned a 9.79 percent bonus for the month of April. This is greater than the anticipated figure, indicating that we are operating at a higher level of efficiency this year. We now have a reserve balance of $6,873 which we want to preserve, if at all possible, since this is where our Christmas bonus money will come from.

Everyone was reminded of the importance of getting the production minutes in promptly and holding committee meetings on a regular schedule. By doing this, suggestions can be handled in a way that we can derive the greatest benefit from them. Since we are all extremely busy, Jane Doe will send a reminder a few days before the minutes need to be turned in.

Information needed to prepare the checks has been submitted to the administrative center. Hopefully, we will have them by next Monday.

Mr. Smith reminded us that ZWR business was excellent, but we must keep an eye on inventory. A. Y. told us that the construction business has been especially good; in fact, a record may be set during the month of May. This sounds encouraging, particularly when we look back to this period of time last year when business was way off.

Office	Review of Screening-Committee Minutes

1-27   2-22-72[a]
J. Jones

Let's do away with color card back orders, or if we can't, let's mark a 5B on cancelled picker's tickets after a month.
Disposition: Accepted—under investigation. (Ron Roberts is going to check on this to see what can be done).

Filling

3-25   6-3-71
M. Waterson

Suggest we use Signode banding on epoxy cans.
Disposition: Back from HOLD. This has now been referred to the RST Plant, as it is anticipated that they will be packaging this material in the future.

3-31   7-6-71
T. Sawyer

Need maintenance to make more quart and gallon gauges.
Disposition: Accepted—in process.

3-46   1-15-72
G. Hernandez

We need remote switches for all the portable pumps.
Disposition: Accepted—in process.

3-50   2-1-72
H. Finn

Better lighting around rack area is needed.
Disposition: Accepted—under investigation.

3-56   2-26-72
M. House

Repair dividers for accumulation table and build some new ones.
Disposition: Accepted—in process.

3-61   3-3-72
R. Austin
G. Hernandez

Put a pay telephone somewhere in the plant.
Disposition: Rejected—reasons stated.
(G. Monahan will write a memo on this).

Mixing and Grinding

4-54 and 4-58
G. Hightower
S. Underwood

Suggestion 4-54 is to pipes 81-151 and 35-176, 35-175 overhead in 2-inch lines. Suggestion 4-58 says we need two oil lines run to MB3 76-156 and 76-158 and one thinner line 35-113. A report on both of these suggestions will be ready before the next screening meeting.
Disposition: Accepted—awaiting report.

[a] The legend for these symbols is: 1 = department or zone; 27 = suggestion number; 2-22-72 = date. By numbering this way you can recap total suggestions by department at the end of each scanlon year and then start numbering over again.

4-55 1-17-72	Meters won't cut off after being set for x number of
M. Smith	gallons needed.
	Disposition: Accepted—in use.
4-60 2-25-72	Move sand mill away from tanks 7 and 8.
J. Downs	Disposition: Accepted—under investigation. Plan is to move the sand mills back to see if this will solve the problem.
4-65 4-10-72	Coil coating comedown should be a closer match.
P. Patrick	Disposition: Reopened. Accepted—under investigation. Need to see if there is some new thinking on this problem.

Shipping, Receiving, and Warehouse

5-45 9-26-71	To remove reflectors from ceiling lights in warehouse.
J. Gomez	Disposition: Rejected—Tests showed reflectors do give more light than the painted ceiling.
5-49 2-15-72	All P.O.'s for resin department be marked to show that is where they should be delivered.
D. O'Brien	Disposition: Accepted—under investigation.
5-51 5-2-72	Mark some light pallets for fill floor use.
F. Jones	Disposition: Accepted—in use.

Resin

6-4 2-5-71	Reopened. Repair and reinstallation of new ammonia addition system for the cooling tanks. This suggestion was in use but has been reopened because the equipment was out of order.
R. Cole	Disposition: Accepted—in use.
6-19 6-28-71	Put air-operated hoists in operation.
R. Saunders	Disposition: Accepted—in process.
6-29 11-30-71	Clean R-9 reactor over weekend with a cuastic solution.
R. Cole	Disposition: Accepted—in process.
	Placed in HOLD until September.
6-35 3-3-72	Install metal preformed grating under electrical connections.
Q. Jones	Disposition: Accepted—in use.

EXAMPLE OF PRODUCTION-COMMITTEE
MINUTES

ABC, Inc., XYZ Plant
Scanlon Production-Committee Minutes—May 2, 1972
Department—Office

Suggestion No. and Date	Old Business
1-27 2-22-72 J. Jones	Let's do away with color card back orders, but if we can't, here is a suggestion which would help. After back-ordering a certain color card such as No. 5 for one month, mark as a 5B on picker's ticket which is canceled. Parent will advise. Disposition: Accepted—under investigation.
1-33 3-30-72 B. Watts	On the no-charge orders that have to be typed, ask each department to secure and keep on hand blank picker tickets, and, on an order being created, that department secure a picker ticket number from sales and type their own. Time elapses from the orders not having all information on it, and being brought down to the accounting department, picked up, etc. It could be typed on spot and delivered to proper mail slot, thus eliminating several steps. Disposition: Accepted—under investigation.

New Business

1-34   4-18-72
C. Price
T. King

Establish as standard procedure flash point on all products. This would include establishing flash point on all current formulas as well as future formulas. This could be incorporated as part of the product specification sheet.

Savings: Sales would have a record of all flash points to include on air shipments, eliminating many phone calls by shipping.
Materials with flash point below 81°F require a more expensive drum; this could save money in drum purchases.

Disposition: Accepted—under investigation.

Old Business

3-15   3-25-71
S. Houston

Need operator's maintenance manual for each machine.
Disposition: Accepted—in use.

3-25   6-3-71
M. Waterson

Suggest we use Signode banding on epoxy cans instead of plastic snaps. This could speed up operation of packaging these products.
Disposition: Returned from HOLD.

3-31   7-6-71
T. Sawyer

Need to get maintenance to make us more quart and gallon gauges where the filler will not have to spend good time hunting them.
Disposition: Accepted—in process.

3-46   8-26-71
B. Hays

Have some new tables built for hand fills, etc.
Disposition: Rejected

3-46   1-15-72
G. Hernandez

We need remote switches for all the portable pumps.
Disposition: Accepted—in process.

3-50   2-1-72
H. Finn

Better lighting around rack area. all lighting on fill floor is under investigation.
Disposition: Accepted—under investigation.

3-56   2-26-72
M. House

Repair dividers for accumulation tables and build some new ones as needed.
Disposition: Reopened—accepted—in process.
(The divider which was made was not satisfactory).

3-61	3-3-72	Put a pay telephone somewhere in the plant.
R. Austin		Disposition: Accepted—under investigation.
G. Hernandez		

3-66   4-9-72   The dead conveyor in quart line be motorized so that
M. Hall   boxes will go in case seal without turning sideways.
Disposition: Accepted—in use.

3-70   4-21-72   We need another lift for depalletizer area. The one
T. Jones   we are now using is assigned to maintenance. They
come and get it as the need arises; it is also used on
second and third floors when they have one breakdown.
Disposition: Rejected.

New Business
_____

3-72   5-1-72   We need one more dumpster for the XYZ side of fill
M. Sheet   floor.
Disposition: Accepted—under investigation.

EVALUATING YOUR COMPANY'S ECONOMIC FACTS OF LIFE AND SOPHISTICATION OF ACCOUNTING SYSTEMS

Appendix outline:

1. Reasons for using appendix.
2. Overall financial strategy.
3. Involvement in and awareness of financial operations.
4. Productivity assessment.
5. Knowledge of competition.
6. Perceived trust in reliability of accounting data and trust in employees.
7. Use and understanding of accounting information.
8. Evaluating accounting system's sophistication.

D.1 REASONS FOR USING APPENDIX

In this appendix we present a series of areas that should be of concern for all well-managed companies, not just scanlon or prospective scanlon companies. They are primarily concerned with the economic facts of life of your company. These areas are not intended to be all-inclusive (hundreds more would be possible) but rather to get you to think about your current financial organizational-development status and where improvement would be possible and desirable. Perhaps you can even think of other areas of interest to your particular company.

We strongly suggest that individuals or groups of managers at all levels be provided the questions to respond to and then hold meetings to discuss the results. For they can assist you in establishing economic goals of the plan and then be used later in the evaluation procedures. The orientation of the questions is the same as those presented in Chapter 2, which were more general in orientation. The ones presented here should assist in pinning down problem areas. Some of the questions may not be applicable, depending on your particular type of business. Try to answer and discuss them with different groups, adding or deleting as you think appropriate. The scale is from 1 to 7 and should compare your current perceived situation. Compare it with what you think your situation should be.

D.2 OVERALL FINANCIAL STRATEGY

All firms should have an overall financial strategy independent of type of business, even if difficult. The basic reasons for such goals include something to shoot for, analyze why you did not attain them, assist in avoiding past mistakes, and isolation of problem areas.

1. Operational financial goals such as a certain target return on investment, sales levels, and net income are developed on an annual basis by segment.

	Min				Max		
Current development of operational financial goals	1	2	3	4	5	6	7
Development should be	1	2	3	4	5	6	7

2. Attainability, awareness, and acceptance status of overall financial goals.

	Min				Max		
Current status	1	2	3	4	5	6	7
Status should be	1	2	3	4	5	6	7

3. Detailed variance analysis done at least quarterly regarding why goal(s) are or are not being attained or exceeded.

	Min				Max		
Currently done	1	2	3	4	5	6	7
Analysis should be	1	2	3	4	5	6	7

For the above questions, the total possible score is 18 (should be—actual). Subtract your current status to isolate problem or possible improvement areas.

D.3 INVOLVEMENT IN AND AWARENESS OF FINANCIAL OPERATIONS

Most companies try to involve managers in the financial operations of the company. For example, you probably have managers at various levels participate in the budget process; unions and certain employees get involved in the standard-setting activities at the lower levels, and so on. This is normal business practice today and very desirable from a behavioral standpoint. For it was learned some time ago that employees are more likely to accept as goals those things which they were involved in setting in the first place.

But the scanlon plan ideally pushes this involvement to new organizational levels. This section attempts to get at the current and desired involvement and awareness of financial operations of your company.

1. Managers and supervisors at all levels are involved in setting standards and budgets for their particular area of influence.

	Min						Max
Current involvement	1	2	3	4	5	6	7
Involvement should be	1	2	3	4	5	6	7

2. When standards or budgets are changed for any reason, managers are given good reasons for the changes, and they generally accept the reasons as sound.

	Min						Max
Reasons are currently given, and they are normally accepted	1	2	3	4	5	6	7
Improvement should be made in explaining reasons, and acceptance should be better	1	2	3	4	5	6	7

3. Key employees other than managers are brought into the standard-setting procedure.

	Min						Max
Involvement currently	1	2	3	4	5	6	7
Involvement should be	1	2	3	4	5	6	7

4. Employees are kept informed of objectives and standards as they influence them.

	Min						Max
Current informing status	1	2	3	4	5	6	7
Informing should be	1	2	3	4	5	6	7

5. Employees at all levels know what is expected of them, and they generally accept the norms.

	Min						Max
Current knowledge of what is expected	1	2	3	4	5	6	7
Knowledge should be	1	2	3	4	5	6	7

6. Employees understand each other's jobs and contribution; that is, direct-labor employees understand the contribution of administrative personnel (in scanlon plans, all indirect personnel are often referred to as resource employees), and so on.

	Min						Max
Current understanding	1	2	3	4	5	6	7
Understanding should be	1	2	3	4	5	6	7

7. Employees are aware of (1) how successful the company has been and is currently and (2) problem areas (e.g., sales production, financing).

	Min						Max
Current awareness	1	2	3	4	5	6	7
Awareness should be	1	2	3	4	5	6	7

8. In order to increase their contribution, employees at all levels seek performance standards.

	Min						Max
Current desire for information	1	2	3	4	5	6	7
Desire should be	1	2	3	4	5	6	7

The above items should be scored in the normal way to assess your current position. The point is that measurement in scanlon plan types of companies becomes very important. Employees at all levels want to understand each other's contribution to the success of the plan; they want to know what is expected of them; and they want to know how they can increase their contribution. To do this, they must become more personally involved in the measurement process. This is how improvements are made and understanding increased.

D.4 PRODUCTIVITY ASSESSMENT

As we have discussed throughout this book, productivity measurement is important to the scanlon plan, since it is the payoff of the involvement process.

1. You know from measurements how your current labor productivity is trending.

	Min						Max
Current knowledge	1	2	3	4	5	6	7
Knowledge should be	1	2	3	4	5	6	7

2. You know from present measurements where your current labor and capital productivity problems lie.

	Min						Max
Current knowledge	1	2	3	4	5	6	7
Knowledge should be	1	2	3	4	5	6	7

3. What is current level of overall productivity (labor, capital, energy, etc.)— measured or perceived?

	Min						Max
Current status	1	2	3	4	5	6	7
Status should be	1	2	3	4	5	6	7

4. In normal recent times, your labor productivity is trending.

	Min						Max
Current trend	1	2	3	4	5	6	7
Trend should be	1	2	3	4	5	6	7

5. Regarding capital, does it seem that you have to invest more and more with less return?

	Min						Max
Current status	1	2	3	4	5	6	7
Investment return should be	1	2	3	4	5	6	7

6. Are accurate measurements available of turnover (voluntary and forced) and absenteeism, and attempts made to control them?

	Min						Max
Current state of measurement	1	2	3	4	5	6	7
Measurement should be	1	2	3	4	5	6	7

7. Are attempts made to measure the productivity of indirect areas (resource workers' activities)?

	Min						Max
Current measurements	1	2	3	4	5	6	7
Desired measurements should be	1	2	3	4	5	6	7

Generally, companies really don't know how productive their various resources are. Do you? Can you really say that the performance productivity (e.g., output-per-hour) of your employees is increasing? If your company is a manufacturing firm, you probably do have direct labor standards. You may believe that they are decreasing. Is the increase in direct labor productivity being offset by declining indirect labor productivity? Sure your net income may be increasing; but is it because you are raising prices, because employees are working harder or smarter, or because of capital expenditures? Many companies really don't know, and if you do, you are probably unusual. Do you try to assess the productivity of all segments of your company including such areas as accounting, personnel, and so on? Some scanlon companies do because they believe that is how improvements are made.

But on the other side, neither your company nor scanlon companies should become so obsessed with measurement that it deters from the primary goal of the plan, that is, increasing productivity. Remember also that measurement is expensive, and you must develop your productivity-measurement system in an evolutionary not revolutionary way. When the actual or perceived costs of some measure exceed the actual or perceived benefits of the measurement, the value of the measure certainly should be questioned, even if dollar amounts are difficult to determine.

D.5 KNOWLEDGE OF COMPETITION

As we said earlier, we hope that scanlon types of companies become the most competitive in their respective industries. This will be the ultimate payoff of the scanlon plan philosophy. But in order to do it, you should assess how progress is being made over time. Or in other words you should size up the competition. For some companies this is already a carefully developed "art" and should become so for a scanlon plan company. To beat the competition in price, quality, and service would be important goals for all scanlon plan types of companies.

1. Are you knowledgeable of competition's pricing, quality, and service when compared with your practices in different product lines?

	Min					Max	
Current knowledge	1	2	3	4	5	6	7
Knowledge should be	1	2	3	4	5	6	7

2. Is this information disseminated to employees at all levels?

	Min					Max	
Current dissemination	1	2	3	4	5	6	7
Dissemination should be	1	2	3	4	5	6	7

3. Are employees concerned about and interested in beating the competition on prices, quality, and service?

	Min					Max	
Current concern and interest	1	2	3	4	5	6	7
Concern and interest should be	1	2	3	4	5	6	7

Score in normal way. Although this type of information is at times difficult to obtain, it is an area of concern for most scanlon plan types of companies over time. You should, of course, try to consider the cost of obtaining the information.

The effect of beating the competition on a variety of fronts can be operationalized. Consider the example of a scanlon plan company whose employees were complaining that a close-by, non-scanlon company's profit-sharing bonus system was paying a 15 percent bonus and their system was paying around 6 percent. The goal became—we are going to beat the 15 percent being paid by the non-scanlon company. In about the three months of effort, the 15 percent was made, and then the employees went on to earn even higher bonuses. They received a great deal of satisfaction in beating the other company, and because of the close proximity, everyone knew about it.

D.6 PERCEIVED TRUST IN RELIABILITY OF ACCOUNTING DATA AND TRUST IN EMPLOYEES

You should see that there are two sides to this picture. First, do managers think that the accounting reports are reliable, and, second, do the accountants and other managers trust employees? Unless trust on both sides is maintained at a fairly high level, the scanlon plan will be of limited success or actually fail. The following questions delve into this complex area. You should remember that perceived trust is probably more important than the actual facts. If managers and employees do not believe that the accounting data are reliable, does it really matter whether in fact they are reliable? But also if they are not reliable, managers will start looking on them with skepticism.

1. The accountants try to be impartial in putting together the figures.

	Min					Max	
Current impartiality	1	2	3	4	5	6	7
Impartiality should be	1	2	3	4	5	6	7

2. The accountants are concerned when errors are made in reporting.

	Min					Max	
Current concern	1	2	3	4	5	6	7
Concern should be	1	2	3	4	5	6	7

3. Accounting reports are generally accurate.

	Min					Max	
Current accuracy	1	2	3	4	5	6	7
Accuracy should be	1	2	3	4	5	6	7

4. Most employees (managers) really do not care what the accounting reports show.

	Min					Max	
Current care	1	2	3	4	5	6	7
Care should be	1	2	3	4	5	6	7

5. Employees generally put in a fair day's work for a fair day's pay.

	Min					Max	
Current work-pay status	1	2	3	4	5	6	7
Work-pay should be	1	2	3	4	5	6	7

6. Employees could contribute more to increased productivity if they wanted to.

	Min	Max
Current contribution to productivity	1 2 3 4 5 6 7	
Contribution should be	1 2 3 4 5 6 7	

7. Employees generally encourage installation of new equipment and methods to increase productivity.

	Min	Max
Current encouragement	1 2 3 4 5 6 7	
Encouragement should be	1 2 3 4 5 6 7	

Score the above perceptions in the normal way. If your company is like many, the questions should give you much food for thought.

D.7 USE AND UNDERSTANDING OF ACCOUNTING INFORMATION

These are very broad areas of concern for both scanlon and non-scanlon companies. In recent years more perceptive accounting staffs have become concerned about these areas. They often involve themselves by determining who receives the various, and often numerous, reports and what they use them for. They also may assist in increasing understanding by working with managers or holding short educational programs.

In scanlon companies these activities expand to new levels because of the significantly increased levels of communications and involvement in financial matters at all organizational levels. Some accountants are good at these activities, and some are poor. With the increased level of measurement and hopefully productivity improvement under the scanlon plan, at least one and hopefully more accountants in your organization will become very proficient in this area. Because if they do not, our experience has been that no one else may do it. And do not underestimate the difficulty and frustration of the task. The following questions delve into the use and understanding of the accounting process.

1. Managers currently using accounting information on a regular basis to make decisions.

	Min						Max
Current use	1	2	3	4	5	6	7
Use should be	1	2	3	4	5	6	7

2. Accounting information is timely enough to assist in making decisions.

	Min						Max
Current timeliness	1	2	3	4	5	6	7
Timeliness should be	1	2	3	4	5	6	7

3. Managers generally understand the reports they receive.

	Min						Max
Current understanding	1	2	3	4	5	6	7
Understanding should be	1	2	3	4	5	6	7

4. The accountants work with managers on a regular basis to eliminate unnecessary reports, assist with interpreting, and so on.

	Min						Max
Current effort	1	2	3	4	5	6	7
Effort should be	1	2	3	4	5	6	7

5. The accountants are aware that managers want information but do not know what, and work with them to develop systems that provide the desired information.

	Min						Max
Current effort	1	2	3	4	5	6	7
Effort should be	1	2	3	4	5	6	7

6. The accountants are aware of the cost of collecting data and try to decrease unnecessary data collection.

	Min						Max
Current concern	1	2	3	4	5	6	7
Concern should be	1	2	3	4	5	6	7

You can score in the normal way. These and perhaps other questions should give you food for thought and goal setting. Our concern is not to give you a complete and detailed list of all financially oriented variables with which you should concern yourself. Rather it is to get you to think in somewhat general but quantitative terms about how far your organization has developed from a financial orientation.

D.8   EVALUATING YOUR ACCOUNTING SYSTEM'S SOPHISTICATION

Data requirements for scanlon plan formulas vary from extremely simple to quite complex. Calculations vary from essentially considering only direct labor to practically profit sharing. Thus data requirements vary accordingly. This section presents a list of questions concerning system sophistication that will be used when covering the different calculations presently in use by scanlon companies. You are asked to evaluate your current system in terms of stages of development, minimum to maximum, as you evaluate your system for each of the items listed. Circle where you think you currently stand. Not all of them may be applicable, depending on your type of firm—indicate in the not applicable (N/A) column where provided—and may be applicable to production types of systems only.

Stage of Development

	Min						Max	
1. Sales, production, and other expense forecasts (budgets) are prepared before the start of a new year with involvement at multiple levels.	1	2	3	4	5	6	7	N/A

	Min						Max	
2. Actual results are compared with budgeted on a monthly basis by segment or line.	1	2	3	4	5	6	7	N/A

	Min						Max	
3. Actual results are compared with previous year results.	1	2	3	4	5	6	7	N/A

Stage of Development

Min						Max		N/A

4. Comprehensive analysis is made to determine why or why not actual results did or did not attain or exceed goals.

Min						Max		N/A

1 2 3 4 5 6 7   N/A

5. Various techniques are used to evaluate performance and trends (ratio analysis, return on investment diagnostic analysis, etc.).

Min   Max

1 2 3 4 5 6 7   N/A

6. Comprehensive "flexible" cost forecasts and budgets are prepared (some companies refer to "flexible" budgets as variable budgets).

Min   Max

1 2 3 4 5 6 7   N/A

7. A standard cost system is maintained.

Min   Max

1 2 3 4 5 6 7   N/A

8. The standards are engineered (i.e., industrial engineers are used).

Min   Max

1 2 3 4 5 6 7   N/A

9. You isolate out all common variances (labor rate and efficiency, material price and usage, volume).

Min   Max

1 2 3 4 5 6 7   N/A

Stage of Development
Min   Max

10. Perpetual inventory records are   1 2 3 4 5 6 7   N/A
    maintained for at least finished
    goods.

Min   Max

11. Inventory-control records are   1 2 3 4 5 6 7   N/A
    reliable.

Min   Max

12. Production-scheduling system is   1 2 3 4 5 6 7   N/A
    accurate and reliable.

Min   Max

13. Financial statements can be pre-   1 2 3 4 5 6 7   N/A
    pared by the end of the first week
    after the end of the month. Manu-
    facturing performance reports are
    prepared weekly.

Min   Max

14. Production records accurately   1 2 3 4 5 6 7   N/A
    reflect actual labor time and material
    usage at all major points.

Min   Max

15. The data base is accurate (do you   1 2 3 4 5 6 7 N/A
    perceive that you can isolate
    problems as they are occurring).

Min   Max

16. Production standards are estab-   1 2 3 4 5 6 7   N/A
    lished by operation (or service).

	Stage of Development	
	Min	Max

17. Statistics are maintained for   1   2   3   4   5   6   7   N/A
absenteeism and turnover.

	Min	Max

18. Standards, specific or performance   1   2   3   4   5   6   7   N/A
indicators, are established in areas
other than direct labor and material.

	Min	Max

19. Action is taken immediately after   1   2   3   4   5   6   7   N/A
some problem area is noted by the
accounting report.

	Min	Max

20. Accounting records provide a per-   1   2   3   4   5   6   7   N/A
ception of control (i.e., do you feel
that the accounting system provides
information before it is too late to
do anything about it?).

If you and your staff scored 5 or more on all the applicable questions, you can probably install practically any method you desire to measure the equitable payoff. If not you may have some difficulty installing certain of the systems. We cannot overemphasize the importance of a good cost-data base.

You may also wonder why no mention was made of computers. Depending on your company's size and complexity, you probably could not have answered the above statements positively without some computer assistance, either time sharing or on-site. In fact few companies can be found today without some computer assistance.

A final point should also be made. Installing a scanlon plan should not require any elaborate new information systems or data collection that would not already be available in a well-managed company. A well-managed, growing firm desires the above system sophistication and more to assist decision making and problem solving. A weak one does not know or care what it is missing.

GENERAL STEPS FOR CONVERTING BONUS
CALCULATION FROM SINGLE-RATIO-OF-
PRODUCTION METHOD TO
ALLOWED-LABOR METHOD

If a company establishes a bonus based on direct labor allowed in the beginning, the steps to follow can be quite simple and might proceed as follows:

1. Establish an allowed, direct-labor time for each product produced, probably built up by department, based on either engineered standards or the actual time it took to produce the item (average of the last two or three times to even out errors in reporting if the information is available).
2. Multiply this allowed time, for all products at various checkpoints of departments, by the average wage rate in existence at the time the plan is established. This is the average wage rate during the base period (four- to six-month period previous to installation). The total of this multiplication should be fairly close to the total direct-labor cost (actual) during the base period.
3. Divide the total direct labor (total of above steps) into each of the indirect items to be included in the calculation (e.g., indirect labor, selling, and administrative fringes). This produces the allowed percentages in each of the indirect accounts. Rather than being a percentage of direct labor, the allowed amounts in the indirect categories can be budgeted amounts or some combination of the two.

During the early periods of the plan, this calculation yields almost an identical result as the ratio of sales value of production method, since it is essentially working with the same figures but in a more detailed way. The problem comes in converting the old ratio method to a more detailed and precise measure of productivity if past bonuses were earned or if you want to provide the same bonus-earning possibilities. Probably the only way that this can be accomplished is by working from the bottom of the calculation (i.e., bonus and total actual cost) upward, since one really does not know who contributed to past bonus earnings. Use a "normal" year period in making this calculation revision.

An example should help explain how this can be done. We work you through the example in Table 4.7. At the bottom of column 3 (actual labor costs) of the table, you can see that the total actual labor cost for the period was $36,160 and that the gross bonus earned was $3,450 (or about 9.54 percent of total actual labor costs in the example). Now let us assume, as in the example, that the actual G and A expenses for the base period are $4,000. The allowed dollars in the base period are $4,000 × 1.0954 or $4,382.

You would do this same procedure for each of the indirect items to be included in the calculation. You then add the bonus percentage to the actual direct labor for the base period to yield the allowed direct labor. When the total allowed in each of the indirect payroll categories is divided by the total direct labor allowed, or sales if appropriate, you will have the percentages that will be used in the future for each of the indirect labor categories.

Continuing the previous G and A example, when the $4,382 is divided by the allowed labor ($18,000), the result is an allowed percentage of 24.34 percent (4,382/18,000), which would be the percentage used in following periods to determine the allowed G and A expense. When actual G and A expense is subtracted, you have the bonus contribution.

A key point is that you will have to be fairly sure that the individual direct-labor amounts allowed (time and wages) at the time the change is made are fairly close to the actual direct-labor cost in total. You can easily adjust the "direct labor wages" allowed to ensure that this will be the case. Naturally you should test this system over time (at least six months) to determine its equity compared with the old system and to become comfortable with it.

The purpose of feedback is, of course, error correction. Timely, well-managed, and understandable feedback permits learning to be oriented toward the correct goals and behaviors of the plan.

Consistent with the various strategies offered throughout the book (especially in Chapter 6), we have suggested that you develop your own feedback mechanisms, focusing on the principal elements of the plan.

One of these elements is the bonus formula. Aside from understanding the particular bonus calculation, employees will benefit if bonus feedback can be offered before the monthly calculation is computed and reported. Table F.1 shows how the accounting function could provide this type of feedback. Depending on the checkpoints of your information system, this type of table could be computed daily—which gives the maximum learning effect. If reported weekly, it would still have a beneficial effect on productive performance.

Suggestions made within the involvement system are another element of the plan that lend themselves to analysis and feedback. The personnel function could do this analysis, but it is entirely appropriate for members of production committees to do it as well. At least two general types of breakdowns are possible for feedback. The first is seen in Figures 6.1 and 6.2. The best way to proceed is to form a committee to evaluate suggestions made in a given time period. Establish criteria for judging whether a suggestion influences productivity and then how it influences it (i.e., quality, quantity, or cost reduction). Let all judges evaluate the same set of suggestions by themselves to see how well independent judgments agree. Then tabulate the results and report them out—perhaps in the manner of Figures 6.1 and 6.2.

**Appendix F.1 Sample Feedback Table for
Providing Information Prior to Bonus Calculations**

Participation Plan Bonus
----, 19--

	Month Total	Daily Average
Shipments		
Inventory change	_____	_____
Total production		
Labor earned		
Total payroll	_____	_____
Bonus earned		
Participating payroll		
% Bonus earned		
% Bonus paid		
Reserve balance		

The other general type of breakdown that is vital to the feedback process is participation. Table F.2 can be quickly tabulated from the screening committee minutes, because all suggestions are collated there. Many firms report this kind of table at the year-end scanlon meeting. One goal of this system is to involve, and one important measure of involvement is the number of employees making suggestions. It is not the only measure of involvement and, therefore, should not be overemphasized. It is, however, a handy indicator of the importance of suggestion making.

As a part of your feedback you may want to communicate with a pie chart showing the relationship of costs and profit to the bonus. This kind of diagram, seen in Figure F.3, effectively presents these percentages. Some scanlon firms include this fixed example in their scanlon plan booklet. Then, when it is time to present the monthly bonus report, they create the pie chart with the variable figures of the given month.

Another type of chart, seen in Figure F.4, is a month by month charting of labor earnings and actual payroll. Trends can be seen at a glance and just about everyone is accustomed to this kind of feedback graph. It could be posted in the cafeteria or other conspicuous place.

Appendix F.2   XYZ Scanlon Plan—Annual Suggestion Data

Year	Number of Suggestions	Number of Participating Employees	Average Number of Suggestions per Employee
1955	301	392	0.77
1956	476	412	1.16
1957	455	395	1.15
1958	419	453	0.92
1959	399	386	1.03
1960	340	375	0.91
1961	295	389	0.76
1962	92	437	0.21
1963	86	201	0.43
1964	300	250	1.20
1965	499	480	1.04
1966	513	470	1.09
1967	454	520	0.87
1968	596	529	1.13
1969	490	523	0.94
1970	491	563	0.87
1971	410	687	0.60.
1972	671	725	0.93
1973	695	750	0.92
1974	460	510	0.90
1975	350	415	0.84
1976	265	325	0.81

Appendix F.3   Where do XYZ dollars go?

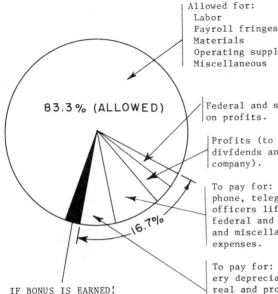

Allowed for:
Labor
Payroll fringes
Materials
Operating supplies
Miscellaneous

83.3% (ALLOWED)

Federal and state taxes
on profits.

Profits (to pay shareholder
dividends and to reinvest in
company).

To pay for: Law and audit, telephone, telegraph, directors fees,
officers life insurance, donations,
federal and state taxes, variable
and miscellaneous administrative
expenses.

16.7%

To pay for: Plan, office and machinery depreciation, general insurance,
real and property taxes, traveling,
advertising, samples, salaried insur-
rance expense, discounts allowed.

IF BONUS IS EARNED!

Allowed - Actual = Bonus of 3.3%

70% is returned to company to help
    pay for the above expenses and
    provide for growth.
25% is paid at the end of each
    month in security bonus.
 5% is added to a reserve and paid
    out at the end of the year in
    security bonus.

HOW DO WE MAKE A BONUS?

Beat the 83.3% allowed expense!
Produce $100,000 worth of pro-
duction for $80,000 and share
$3,300 in bonus.

Appendix F.4   Sample scanlon productivity.

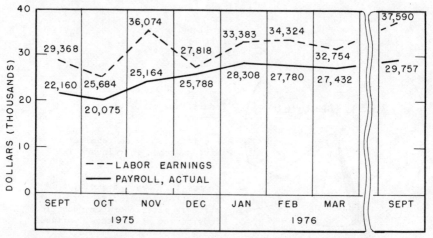

PAYROLL EXCEEDS PRODUCTION - RESULTS IN NEGATIVE BONUS

PRODUCTION EXCEEDS PAYROLL - RESULTS IN POSITIVE BONUS

SCANLON BIBLIOGRAPHY

Alberth, E. R. "The Scanlon Plan Applied to an Oil Refinery: Pros and Cons." Unpublished master's thesis. Cambridge: Massachusetts Institude of Technology, 1960.

Barry, A. "New Look at the Productivity Bonus," *Personnel Magazine,* **31,** 20–23 (November, 1965).

Beardsley, D. W. "A Look at the Scanlon Plan." Unpublished master's thesis. Cambridge: Massachusetts Institute of Technology, 1962.

Bullock, R. J., and Ross, T. L. *The Meaning and Measurement of Organizational Productivity.* East Lansing: Scanlon Plan Associates, Michigan State University, 1976.

Burnett, G. S. "A Study of Casual Relationships Between Organizational Variables and Personal Influence Variables During the Implementation of Scanlon Plan." Unpublished doctoral dissertation. East Lansing: Michigan State University, 1973.

Chamberlain, J. "'Everyman a Capitalist.' A Manufacturer Named Adamson Solves a Major U.S. Problem: Labor," *Life* 93–94 (December 23, 1946).

Describes the origin and development of an early scanlon plan that included a productivity measurement. Examines the thinking of the Adamson Company president and of Joseph Scanlon as they mutually pioneered the development of an employee participation plan, which in the first year of its operation resulted in a 54% increase in productivity and a 500% increase in profits for the Adamson Company.

Chaney, F. B. "Employee Participation in Manufacturing Job Design," *Human Factors,* **11,** 101–106 (1969).

Chase, S. *Roads to Agreement: Successful Methods in the Science of Human Relations.* New York: Harper & Bros., 1951. Pp. 139–143.

Chung, K. H. "Incentive Theory and Research," *Personnel Administration,* **35,** 31–41 (January, 1972).

Colletti, J. A. *Profit Sharing and Employee Attitudes: A Case Study of the Deferred Profit-Sharing Program at Motorola, Inc.* Madison: The University of Wisconsin, Center for the Study of Productivity Motivation, 1968.

Cougar, J. D. "A Challenge for ASPA," *The Personnel Administrator,* **6,** 16–18 (November–December, 1961).

This essay, awarded second place in the ninth annual ASPA essay contest, suggests that industrial engineers and social scientists cooperate in an endeavor to develop a financial incentive plan that will motivate employees toward increased productivity. The author cites the scanlon plan as evidence of a successful plan and urges the industrial relations profession to initiate cooperative study of financial incentives.

Cozan, L. W. "Job Enlargement and Employee Satisfaction," *Personnel Journal,* **38,** 95–96 (July–August, 1959).
Cites several examples indicating that job enlargement increases employee satisfaction. McCormick & Company's multiple-management system and the scanlon plan are described as plans that take the form of employee participation in management decisions and greater responsibility and control over the work environment.

Cross, B. "The Scanlon Plan," *The Queen's Commerceman* (Commerce Club of Queens University), **8,** 25–30 (Winter, 1952).
The author briefly reviews the development of the plan, how it works, and the experience of some of the companies that have adopted it.

Crystal, G. S. "Motivating for the Future: The Long-Term Incentive Plan," *Financial Executive,* **39,** 48–50 (October, 1971).

Daigneault, H. J. "Sharing the Profits of Increased Productivity," *Spotlighting the Labor-Management Scene,* Personnel Series No. 147, New York: American Management Association 1952.
The author, former president of the United Steelworkers' LaPointe local, tells how the scanlon plan was introduced at the LaPointe Machine Tool Co. in 1947 and how it worked.

Dale, E. "Increasing Productivity Through Labor-Management Cooperation," *Industrial and Labor Relations Review,* **3,** 33–34 (October, 1949).

Davenport, R. W. "Enterprise for Everyman. A Case History of How the Scanlon Plan, as Applied by Union and Management at LaPointe Machine Tool, Has Raised Productivity, Profits, and Pay," *Fortune,* Vol XLI, No. 1, 50–58 (January, 1950).

Dearden, J. "How to Make Incentive Plans Work," *Harvard Business Review,* **45,** (July–August, 1972).

De Nitish, R. "How Useful is the Scanlon Plan?" *Industrial Relations* (India), **18,** 194–211 (September–October, 1966).
Briefly examines the limitations of the conventional wage incentive plans in use in industry; turns to the new approach offered by the scanlon plan, describes and assesses the plan.

Derber, M., Chalmers, W. E., and Edelman, M. T. "Union Participation in Plant Decision Making," *Industrial and Labor Relations Review,* **15,** 83–101 (October, 1961).

Dowd, E. M. "Incentive Compensation and Increased Productivity," *Management Record,* National Industrial Conference Board, **17,** 230–243 (June, 1955).

Dowd, E. M. "The Scanlon Plan," *Management Record* (National Industrial Conference Board), **17,** 236–239 (June, 1955).

Doyle, R. J. "A New Look at the Scanlon Plan," *Management Accounting,* **48,** (September, 1970).

Doyle, R. J. "The PAL Plan as a Method of Management," Wolverine Shoe and Tanning Corporation, 1964.
Excellent article on the scanlon plan as a means of motivating our human resources.

Dreyer, H. E. "The Scanlon Plan: An Analysis and a Case Study." Unpublished doctoral dissertation. Cambridge: Massachusetts Institute of Technology, 1952.

Farley, J. C. "What Does the Scanlon Plan Have to Offer to Management and the Union?" Unpublished master's thesis. Cambridge: Massachusetts Institute of Technology, 1950.

French, W. L., and Bell, C. H., Jr. *Organizational Development: Behavioral Science Interventions for Organization Improvement.* Englewood Cliffs: Prentice-Hall, 1973.

Friedlander, F. and Brown, C. D., in Dunnette, M. D. (Eds.). *Handbook of Industrial and Organizational Psychology.* Chicago: Rand McNally, 1976, P. 314.

Frost, C. F., Wakely, J. H., and Ruh, R. A. *The Scanlon Plan for Organization Development: Identity, Participation, and Equity.* East Lansing: Michigan State University Press, 1974.
  Provides some thirty years of consulting and research experience with the scanlon plan and organizational development. An excellent source for the goals and the philosophy of the plan.

Gehman, R. "Workers' Ideas Pay Everybody," *Nation's Business,* **41,** 60–65 (August, 1953).
  Discusses the scanlon plan. About 70 small- and medium-sized plants reported using and experimenting with the plan.

"Getting at the Root of a Labor Crisis: ICI's Wage-Productivity Plan," *Business Week,* 56 (October, 1970).

Gilson, T. O., and Lefcowitz, M. J. "A Plant-Wide Productivity Bonus in a Small Factory. Study of an Unsuccessful Case," *Industrial and Labor Relations Review,* **10,** 284–296 (January, 1957).
  Describes the factors involved in the failure of a group-incentive plan of the scanlon variety in a small New Jersey ceramic plant. Questions the applicability of incentive plans without willful acceptance by both management and union.

Golden, C., and Parker, V. (Eds.). *Causes of Industrial Peace Under Collective Bargaining.* New York: Harper, 1955.

Goodman, P. S. "The Scanlon Plan: A Need for Conceptual and Empirical Models," *Symposium, Eighty-First Annual Convention American Psychological Association,* (1973).

Goodman, P. S., and Moore, B. E. "Factors Affecting Acquisition of Beliefs About a New Reward System." *Human Relations,* **29**(6), 571–588 (1976).

Goodman, R. K., Wakely, J. H., and Ruh, R. A. "What Employees Think of the Scanlon Plan," *Personnel,* **49,** 22–29 (September–October, 1972).

Gray, D. H. "Toward a Theory of the Interior of the Business Firm: The Dynamics of the Employment Relationship," Unpublished Ph.D. dissertation. Cambridge: Massachusetts Institute of Technology, 1958.

Gray, R. B. "The Scanlon Plan—A Case Study," *British Journal of Industrial Relations,* **9,** 291–313 (November, 1971).
  Compares the expectations derived from the underlying philosophy of the plan with the actual working of it in a British car plant, 1963–1966.

Hamilton, J. L. "Expansions Build Their Business," *Industry,* **23,** 11–14 (July, 1958).
  Describes growth of the Andrew Wilson Company in Lawrence, Massachusetts, the largest manufacturer of steel shelving and lockers in the New England area. Several paragraphs are on the operation of the scanlon plan in the company.

Harvard University. *Pfaudler-Permutit.* Cambridge: Graduate School of Business Administration, Harvard University, 1961.
  A case prepared by Roy Penchansky, Research Associate, under the direction of Professor E. Robert Livernash as the basis for class discussion on the installation of the scanlon plan.

Helfgott, R. B. *Group Wage Incentives: Experience with the Scanlon Plan.* (Industrial Relations Memorandum No. 141). New York: Industrial Relations Counselors, 1962.
  Critical article based on six case studies of experiences with the scanlon plan. Proposes several conditions necessary for success of the plan. Discusses features of the plan, analysis of company experience, problems, pitfalls, and conclusions.

Howell, W. J., Jr. "A New Look at Profit Sharing, Pension, and Productivity Plans," *Business Management*, **32–33**, 26–42 (December, 1967).

Humphries, J. J. "Production Committees in the Scanlon Plan," Unpublished manuscript. Cambridge: Massachusetts Institute of Technology, 1952.

Industrial Relations Research Association. *Proceedings of the Fourth Annual Meeting, Boston, December 28–29, 1951.* Part VII: Union Management Cooperation. "Introductory Remarks" by Clinton S. Golden; "Some Experiences with a Union-Management Cooperation Plan" by Robert C. Tait; "Local Union Experience with a Cooperation Plan" by Frederick G. Lesieur; Discussion by W. R. Dymond and William Gomberg.

Jarret, P. "Productivity Rewarded," *Industrial Society,* **50**, 4–6 (April, 1968).
Reports the experience of two British firms with incentive schemes based on the scanlon plan.

Jehring, J. J. "A Contrast Between Two Approaches to Total Systems Incentives," *California Management Review,* **10**, 7–14 (Winter, 1967).
Compares a scanlon-type production-sharing plan and a profit-sharing plan both used by the same manufacturing company.

Jehring, J. J. "Profit Sharing, Motivation, and Productivity," *Personnel Administration,* **33**, 17–21 (March–April, 1970).

"Joe Scanlon's Plan is Still Working," *Technology Review,* **6**, 24–34 (December, 1963).

Johnson, R. B. "The Scanlon Plan: Criteria for Success in Non-Union Plants." Unpublished master's thesis. Cambridge: Massachusetts Institute of Technology, 1959.

Koletsky, H. S. "Some Considerations for Installation of a Scanlon Plan in a Non-Union Company." Unpublished master's thesis. Cambridge: Massachusetts Institute of Technology, 1962.

Krulee, G. K. "The Scanlon Plan: Cooperation Through Participation," *Journal of Business,* The University of Chicago, **28**, 100–113 (April, 1955).
An excellent article on the employee participation aspect of the scanlon plan. Drawing on his own experience, the author analyzes the scanlon plan for union-management cooperation and concludes that its major virtue is that it attempts to help the organization profit from its own experiences, combining the requirements of productive efficiency with the need for individual worker satisfaction.

Laurier, M. J. "Participative Incentive Programs: Some Problems of Application in the Large Industrial Organization." Unpublished master's thesis. Cambridge: Massachusetts Institute of Technology, 1961.

Lee, J. M. "The Common Problems Found in the Introduction of New Ideas or Concepts into an Established Industry." Unpublished manuscript. Cambridge: Massachusetts Institute of Technology, 1951.

Lesieur, F. G. "Local Union Experiences with a Cooperation Plan," *Proceedings of the Fourth Annual Meeting of the Industrial Relations Research Association,* 174–181 (1952).

Lesieur, F. G. (Ed.). *The Scanlon Plan: A Frontier in Labor-Management Cooperation.* Cambridge: Technology Press, Massachusetts Institute of Technology and New York: Wiley, 1958. Joint Publishers.
One of the earliest books on the subject covering all phases of scanlon plan from philosophy to single ratio formula. Assembles articles on the scanlon plan designed for an overall picture of principles and practices. Includes material written by men in industry who are actively working with the plan.

Lesieur, F. G. "Worker Participation to Increase Production," *Management Record* (National Industrial Conference Board), **21**, 38–41 (February, 1959).

Summary of round table discussion held at the 389th meeting of the N.I.C.B. at Cleveland, Ohio. Cites the contribution that employees can make to their own and to company objectives if "restraining" influences in their environment are removed.

Lesieur, F. G., and Puckett, E. S. "The Scanlon Plan Has Proved Itself," *Harvard Business Review,* **47,** 109–118 (September–October, 1969).
Two of the country's experts on the plan examine its record in industry and evaluate its performance. Three are analyzed.

Lesieur, F. G., and Puckett, E. S. "The Scanlon Plan—Past, Present, and Future," Industrial Relations Research Association, *Proceedings of the Twenty-First Annual Winter Meeting, Chicago, Illinois, December 29–30, 1968,* 71–80 (1969).

Lincoln, J. F. *Incentive Management.* Cleveland: The Lincoln Electric Company, 1951.

Lubinsky, L., and Mitchell, J. "A Scanlon Plan for Schools," *Phi Delta Kappan,* 271–272 (December, 1972).

Management Record. "The Rucker Share of Production Plan," National Industrial Conference Board, **17,** 239 (June, 1955).

Martin, A. I. "Union Management Cooperation: The Scanlon Plan." Unpublished manuscript. Cambridge: Massachusetts Institute of Technology, 1952.

Martucci, N. L. A. "Productivity and Incentive Pay," *Management Record* (National Industrial Conference Board), Vol XIX, No. 10, 346–349 (October, 1957).
Description and analysis of Pfaudler Company's (Rochester, New York) experience under scanlon plan. Emphasis is on productivity gains as measured through the labor-cost ratio.

McGregor, D. *The Human Side of Enterprise.* New York: McGraw-Hill Book Company, Inc., 1960. Pp. 110–123.
A classic in human relations.

McKersie, R. B. "Wage Payment Methods of the Future," *British Journal of Industrial Relations,* **1,** 191–212 (June, 1963).
Focuses upon the important trends affecting the choice of wage payments methods and discusses the methods most useful. Particular attention is given to the scanlon plan.

Metzger, B. L. *Profit Sharing in Perspective, Second Edition.* Evanston, Illinois: Profit Sharing Research Foundation, 1966.

Metzger, B. L., and Colletti, J. A. *Does Profit Sharing Pay?* Evanston, Illinois: Profit Sharing Research Foundation, 1971.
A comparative study of the financial performance by retailers with and without profit-sharing programs.

Mihlon, L. F. "'Copartnership' Revived: Labor-Management's Hope for Harmony?" *Factory,* **120,** 82–87 (July, 1962).
Discusses the workings of the scanlon plan and the Rucker plan. Considers the possibility of using the two plans in conjunction with each other.

Moore, B. E., and Goodman, P. S. "Organizational Learning: The Relation of Antecedent Variables to Job Expectancies," *Proceedings, Eightieth Annual Convention,* American Psychological Association, 1972.

Moore, B. E., and Goodman, P. S. "Factors Affecting the Impact of a Company-Wide Incentive Program on Productivity." Final report submitted to the National Commission on Productivity, 1973.

Morris, L. R. "A Case Study of the Scanlon Plan for Labor-Management Cooperation." Unpublished master's thesis. Cambridge: Massachusetts Institute of Technology, 1954.

Morrison, J. "Organizational Climate, Individual Background, and Values and Job Goals in a

Sample of Scanlon Plan Plants." Doctoral dissertation. East Lansing: Michigan State University, 1970.

Murray, D. X. (Ed.). *Successful Profit Sharing Plans—Theory and Practice.* Chicago: Council of Profit Sharing Industries, 1968.

"New Tool: 'Reinforcement' for Good Work," *Business Week,* 76–77, (December, 1971).

Northrup, H. R., and Young, H. A. "The Causes of Industrial Peace Revisited," *Industrial and Labor Relations Review,* 31–47 (October, 1968).

Nunn, H. L. *Partners in Production: A New Role for Management and Labor.* Englewood Cliffs, New Jersey: Prentice-Hall, 1961. Describes the share-of-production plan, how it works, how it compares with the generally accepted plans of compensation, and how it differs from the Rucker and scanlon plans, yet pre-dates both.

O'Rourke, W. "An Evaluation of the Scanlon Plan in the Light of Catholic Social Principle." Abstract of doctoral dissertation. Washington, D.C.: Catholic University of America, 1956.

Pohlman, D. R. "Employee Incentive Plans," *Office Executive* **34,** 25–27 (December, 1959). Discusses the pros and cons of six types of plant-wide incentives including the scanlon plan and the Rucker share-of-production plan.

Preston, J. J. "An Application of the Effect of the Scanlon Upon Wage Structure." Unpublished manuscript. Cambridge: Massachusetts Institute of Technology, 1951.

"Profit Improvements Through Better Motivated People," *Production,* 160–164 (August, 1969). History of successful experiences with the scanlon plan at Michigan Wheel Company, a metal working company in Grand Rapids, Michigan.

Ross, R. L., and Jones, G. M. "An Approach to Increased Productivity: The Scanlon Plan," *Financial Executive,* **40,** 23–29 (February, 1972). Discusses the elements of the plan in general, then reports results of a case study investigating some of the criticisms directed at the plan, stressing financial variables.

Ross, T. L. "The Accountant's Role in Participative Decision-Making." Unpublished dissertation. East Lansing: Michigan State University, 1969.

Ross, T. L., et al. "Measurement Under the Scanlon Plan and Other Productivity Incentive Plans." Unpublished manuscript. Bowling Green, Ohio: Bowling Green State University, 1975.

Rucker, A. W. *Progress in Productivity and Pay.* Cambridge, Massachusetts: The Eddy-Rucker-Nickels Co., 1952.

Ruh, R. A. "Wage Incentive Systems and the Scanlon Plan." Paper presented to the Furniture Manufacturer's Association, Grand Rapids, Michigan, November 17, 1970.

Ruh, R. A., Johnson, R. H., and Scrontino, M. P. "The Scanlon Plan, Participation in Decision Making and Job Attitudes," *Journal of Industrial and Organizational Psychology,* **1,** 36–45 (1973).

Ruh, R. A., Wakeley, J. H., and Morrison, J. C. "Education, Ego Need Gratification, and Attitudes Toward the Job." Unpublished manuscript. East Lansing: Michigan State University, 1972.

Ruh, R. A., Wallace, R. L., and Frost, C. F. "Management Attitudes and Scanlon Plan," *Industrial Relations,* **12,** 282–288 (1973).

Rush, H. "Organizational Development: A Reconnaissance," The Conference Board, Research Report No. 605, 1973.

Scanlon, J. N. "Adamson and His Profit-Sharing Plan." *Production,* Series No. 172. New York: American Management Association, 1947. Pp. 10–12.

Scanlon, J. N. "Profit Sharing Under Collective Bargaining: Three Case Studies," *Industrial and Labor Relations Review,* **2,** 58–75 (October, 1948).
Also appears in Publications Series 2, No. 23, Department of Economics and Social Sciences, Massachusetts Institute of Technology. Contrasts a successful profit-sharing plan against two failures. Indicates causes of each result.

Scanlon, J. N., "Divy Your Gross and Double Your Profits," *Kiplinger Magazine,* **2,** (December, 1948).
About Joseph Scanlon and his plan at the LaPointe Machine Tool Company. Written shortly after installation of the plan. Hits only the high points of the plan.

Scanlon, J. N. "Remarks on the Scanlon Plan," *Proceedings of the Conference on Productivity, June 4, 1949,* 10–14 (1949). Sponsored by the University of Wisconsin Industrial Relations Center, Milwaukee Extension Division.
Article holds that great potential for productivity increases lies in workers.

Scanlon Plan Conference Report. "Cooperative Effort Plus Bonus Incentive," *Factory,* **120,** (July, 1962).
A good introduction for people new to scanlon and Rucker plans.

Scott, R. C. *Incentives in Manufacturing, Individual and Plant-Wide.* Volumes 1, 2, and 3. Cambridge Massachusetts: The Eddy-Rucker-Nickels Co., 1965, 1967, 1968.
Presents a critical review of individual and plant-wide programs in current use—an important series for anyone contemplating installation of a production-value-sharing program.

Scott, R. C. *Three Case Histories of the Rucker Plan.* Cambridge, Massachusetts: The Eddy-Rucker-Nickels Co., 1970.

Seltzer, B. "Paying Men to Pull Together," *American Business,* **23,** 20 (May, 1953).
Brief description of the scanlon plan at the H. D. Canfield Co., Bridgeport, Connecticut.

Short, J., and Moore, B. E. "Preliminary Findings of a Multi-Variate Analysis of Suggestion System's Impact on Productivity." Working paper No. 75-27. Austin: The University of Texas, Graduate School of Business, 1975.

Shultz, G. P., and Crisara, R. P. *Causes of Industrial Peace Under Collective Bargaining: The LaPointe Machine Tool Company and the United Steelworkers of America.* Case Study No. 10, Washington, D.C.: National Planning Association, November, 1952.
A thorough scanlon case study of LaPointe Machine. Analytically assesses results of operations under the scanlon plan in terms of both management and union objectives.

Siegal, A. L., and Ruh, R. A. "Job Involvement, Participation in Decision Making, Personal Background, and Job Behavior," *Organizational Behavior and Human Performance,* **9,** (2), 318–327 (April, 1973).

Smith, E. A., and Gude, G. "Reevaluation of the Scanlon Plan as a Motivational Technique." *Personnel Journal,* **50,** 916–919, 923 (December, 1971).

Strauss, G., and Rosenstein, E. "Workers Participation: A Critical View," *Industrial Relations,* **9,** 197–214 (February, 1970).
One of the strengths of the scanlon plan is that it provides a direct and dramatic incentive for higher production. Through its suggestion system and departmental production committee, it stresses participation in solving shop-level production problems.

Strauss, G., and Sayles, L. R. "The Scanlon Plan: Some Organizational Problems," *Human Organization,* **16,** 15–22 (Fall, 1957).
The main areas of difficulty that may reduce the effectiveness of scanlon plan are reviewed. Authors indicate likely stresses placed on top management, union leadership, middle management, rank and file union members, and foremen.

Sweeney, J. W. "Aggregate Employee Productivity Under the Scanlon Plan." Unpublished doctoral dissertation. Cambridge: Massachusetts Institute of Technology, 1954.

Tait, R. C. "Some Experiences With a Union-Management Cooperation Plan." *Proceedings of the Fourth Annual Meeting,* Industrial Relations Research Association, 167–173 (1951).

The National Commission on Productivity and Work Quality. *A Plant-Wide Productivity Plan in Action: Three Years of Experience With the Scanlon Plan.* Washington, D.C., May, 1975. (Prepared by Brian E. Moore).
This case study of De Soto Corp., Garland, Tx, is a unique and contemporary analysis of one firm's early experience with the plan. Productivity data and a review of plan literature are also included.

"The Promise of Financial Sharing and Copartnership," *International Management, 18,* 27–29 (April, 1963).
Notes the new Kaiser Steel Company (U.S.A.) share-the-wealth and copartnership scheme and the Mexican share-the-profits plan ordered by the government. Describes the scanlon plan and the Rucker plan. Analyzes the attitude to copartnership and financial sharing in Paris, Tokyo, Milan, and London, and application in these countries.

"The Scanlon Plan," *Time, 66,* 87–88, 90 (September 26, 1955).
Briefly presents biographical facts about Joseph Scanlon, a sketch of the organization and development of the scanlon plan, and some of the operating principles of the plan.

"The Scanlon Plan Spreads Teamwork Profits," *Industrial Bulletin* (New York State Department of Labor), *32,* 3–6 (April, 1953).
Description of the scanlon plan being used by the Stromberg-Carlson Company in Rochester, New York.

Thierry, H. "The Scanlon Plan: A Field Experimental Approach," *Symposium, Eighty-First Annual Convention,* American Psychological Association (1973).

Torbert, F. "Making Incentives Work," *Harvard Business Review, 37,* 81–92 (September–October, 1959).
Very good summary of advantages of group incentives over individual incentives. The scanlon plan and the Rucker and Nunn-Bush plans are discussed, and "conditions of success" are analyzed.

Wallace, R. L. "A Comparative Study of Attitude Scores of Managers Toward Employees and Toward Selected Leadership Policies in Groups of Firms Which Have Either Discontinued or Retained Cost Reduction Sharing Plans." Unpublished doctoral dissertation. East Lansing: Michigan State University, 1971.

Weltzer, B. "Paying Men to Pull Together," *American Business, 23,* 20 (May, 1953).

White, J. K., and Ruh, R. A. "Effects of Personal Values on the Relationship Between Participation and Job Attitudes," *Administrative Science Quarterly, 18,* 506–514 (1973).

White, J. K., Ruh, R. A., and Morrison, J. C. "Participation in Decision Making, Values, and Attitudes Toward the Job." Unpublished manuscript. East Lansing: Michigan State University, 1972.

Whyte, W. F. et al. *Money and Motivation: An Analysis of Incentives in Industry.* New York: Harper & Bros., 1955. Chapter 14, "The Scanlon Plan," pp. 166–188.

Young, W. M. "Application of a Scanlon Type Incentive Program to the Operations of a Heavy Machinery Dealership." Unpublished master's thesis. Cambridge: Massachusetts Institute of Technology, 1961.

Zollitsch, H. G., and Langsner, A. "Group and Plant-Wide Incentive Supplementary Compensation Plans," *Wage and Salary Administration.* 2nd ed. Cincinnati: South-Western Publishing Company, 1970.

INDEX

Allowed labor calculation, 81-87
  adjustments to, 128-129

Bonus calculation, adjustments to, 76-78,
  125-130
  breakeven position, 58
  check list, 30-31
  data feedback, 98-99
  deficit example, 188
  desired criteria, 22
  diagnostics, 46, 51-59
  distribution, 70-72
  division of bonus pool, 68-69
  education, 130-131
  interplant transfers, 58
  inventory adjustments, 63-64
  items to include and exclude, 59-63
  loss position, 58
  normalizing, 65-66
  projections, 115
  related to other elements, 46
  reserve, 69-70
  short-run emphasis, 71-72
  success ingredients, 47-51
  testing, 59
  types and examples, allowed labor, 82-87,
    212-213
    general comparison, 88-89
    multicost, 78-80
    single ratio, 66-71, 187
    split ratio, 74-75
    value added, 80-81
  understanding, 46
  vacations and holidays, 67, 70, 187
  verses quality, 21
  volume effects, 12

Check lists, formula determination, 30-31
  installation, 27-30
Committees, see Production (departmental)
  committee; Screening committee
Compensation practices, 100-101
Competition, knowledge of, 124
Consultants, evaluation of plan, 141-142
  installation of plan, 21
Controller's role, 109-110
Cooperation as basic element, 2-5

Departmental supervisors, 111
Dissemination of data, 120-125

Evaluation, 132-133, 134-142
  behavioral, 135-136
  evidence, 144-148
  financial, 140-141
  survey, 136-140

Feedback, 120-125
  departmental, 121
Financial policy, 102
Foremen, 111
Full employment, 106

Goal setting, organizational and departmental, 113-116

Hospitals, calculations, 91-95
  quality considerations, 95-96

Incentives, other, 130-131
Indirect labor, see Resource workers
Industrial relations and scanlonism, 104,
  107

Installation, checklist of conditions, 17-20
   committee formation, *see* Production (de-
      partmental) committee; Screening
      committees
   steps, list of, 15, 27-31, 36
   task force, 32
   timing, 35-36
   voting acceptance, 37
Inventory, 63-64

Managerial succession, turnover, 131-132
Memo of understanding, 40, 182-189
Multicost calculation, 78-80
   adjustment, 128

Organizational development, defined, 5
   evaluated versus scanlonism, 2-5, 148-153
Overtime, 99

Participating payroll, 70-72, 98-99
Personnel manager's role, 110-111
Plant manager's role, 109
Production (departmental) committee,
      duties, 26, 38-39, 184
   example of minutes, 195-197
   formation, 37-38, 184
   representatives' role, 39
   tenure, 38, 105
Productivity, defined, 9-10
   financial, 12
   performance, 11
      payments for, 13
   importance of, 9
Profit sharing, problems, 60
   relationship to scanlonism, 60-61, 101-
      102

Reserve, bonus, 69-70
Resource workers, defined, 112
   involvement, 112-113

Scanlon plan, basic elements, 1-2

capitalism compared, 3
history, 2
job security, 35
organizational development, 2-5, 148-153
reasons for, 16
what it is not, 8-9
Scanlon Plan Associates, 11, 36, 63, 111
Screening committee, agenda, 42
   duties and roles, 26, 39
   formation, 37-40
   minutes, example of, 193-194
   size, 38, 185
   tenure, 105
Service industry calculations, 90-96
Single ratio of labor calculation, adjustments
      to, 126-128
   critique, 73-74
   determination, 24
   reasons for using, 22-24, 51-52
Split ratio calculation, 73-74, 76-77
Suggestions, actions to take, 41
   encouragement, 42
   goals for, 114
   maintaining, 116-120
   procedures, 41-43
   sample form, 190-191
Survey, before installation, 157-164
   feedback, 136-140, 178-179
   plan evaluation, 165-177
   reasons for using, 21-22, 35
   scoring, 20, 178-181

Turnover and absenteeism, 114
   managerial, 131-132

Vacation and holiday pay, 67, 70
Value-added calculation, 80-81
   adjustments to, 129-130
Volume and bonus, 12-13

Wages, 98-99
   compensation practices, 100-101